CREATING LITERATURE
OUT OF LIFE

"Hermes in Repose" (by Lysippus), the masterpiece of art that inspired and transfigured Mann's representation of Tadzio in *Death in Venice*. An artist's rendering.

DORIS ALEXANDER

CREATING LITERATURE OUT OF LIFE

THE MAKING OF FOUR MASTERPIECES

Death in Venice
Treasure Island
The Rubáiyát of Omar Khayyám
War and Peace

The Pennsylvania State University Press
University Park, Pennsylvania

Also by Doris Alexander:

The Tempering of Eugene O'Neill
Creating Characters with Charles Dickens
Eugene O'Neill's Creative Struggle: The Decisive Decade, 1924–1933

Library of Congress Cataloging-in-Publication Data

Alexander, Doris.
    Creating literature out of life : the making of four masterpieces /
Doris Alexander.
        p.   cm.
    Includes bibliographical references and index.
    ISBN 0-271-01549-7
    1. Literature, Comparative—History and criticism.   2. Creation
(Literary, artistic, etc.)   3. Literature—Psychological aspects.
I. Title.
PN871.A44   1996
809—dc20   95–43556
                                                                      CIP

It is the policy of The Pennsylvania State University Press to use acid-free paper for
the first printing of all clothbound books. Publications on uncoated stock satisfy the
minimum requirements of American National Standard for Information Sciences—
Permanence of Paper for Printed Library Materials, ANSI Z39.48–1992.

Contents

Acknowledgments

Many thanks to those who have read the manuscript for this book critically along the way. I am particularly grateful to Professor Joann Ryan Morse of Barnard College and Professor Edward Margolies of the City University of New York for encouragement and suggestions from the beginning, and to Professor Wendell Harris of Penn State University for the acute comments that guided my final revisions. I profited enormously from a very stimulating correspondence with Professor Norman Fruman of the University of Minnesota (author of *Coleridge: The Damaged Archangel*) on the *Rime of the Ancient Mariner* apropos of my ideas on the one-great-book writer.

I have had staunch and ingenious assistance in my research from Professor George Wellwarth of the State University of New York at Binghamton, who cheerfully looked into sources for me from which I am geographically cut off. To the London Library, 14 St. James's Square, I give thanks for the steady lifeline of books through the mails that have brought the resources of a notable research library to my door over many years.

Above all, my thanks to all those of Penn State Press who have given life to my last two books and now to this one. More than gratitude to Philip Winsor, Senior Editor, for inspiration and reinforcement, and to Sanford Thatcher, Director. Thanks for expert copyediting to Peggy Hoover, and much admiration for my illustrator and designer, Steve Kress.

Introduction:
Impetus and Aliment for Creating

No easy answer can be made to the great riddle—the unsolved mystery—of how an author comes to write a great work of fiction or poetry, a work capable of altering the lives of notable people all over the world and endowed with a continuous history of doing so. What brings such a work to birth in a writer's mind? What shapes its singular emotional tone? By what means can we begin to gather the evidence for a genuine science of creativity? Somewhere in each particular great work, in the particular mind that brought it into being, is hidden the series of clues to how the seemingly unique miracle of a masterpiece of literature came about.

This study examines four very dissimilar masterpieces and their authors in search of evidence that will point to answers to some of the myriad unknowns in the great mystery of creativity. The hunt crosses conventional boundaries of nation, period, and genre to look into the why and how of Thomas Mann's creation of *Death in Venice*, Robert Louis Stevenson's *Treasure Island*, Edward FitzGerald's *Rubáiyát of Omar Khayyám*, and Lev Tolstoy's *War and Peace*—a novella by a German, a novel by a Scot, a long poem by an Irishman, and a gigantic epic by a Russian. Their very differences make them particularly useful as stages in penetrating both the singular and the usual in the acts of creativity that gave them life.

Although the psychology of the author, his intellectual assumptions, and his personal memories all enter into the search, the approach has nothing in common with what is understood as psychoanalytic criticism, biographical criticism, or traditional source studies. It does not take up psychological hypotheses of Freud, Jung, Stekel, or Lacan and treat them as universal principles of behavior that will explain the meaning of a work and the force that directed the author to write it. Above all, it does not see literature as stemming from disease and its works as either simple wish fulfillment on the part of the author or a release of his tensions ("abreaction") achieved by his retelling of what has happened to him or what he would have liked to have happened.

This study does not—as some biographers do—try to fill blanks in an author's biography with what appears in one of his stories, nor does it assume that fiction can be understood as a retelling of biography. Certainly, an author's philosophical ideas along with information he has found in books are pertinent to understanding his work, but in this study identifying these sources is taken not as an end in itself but as an initial step to provide the data necessary for finding out what he has done with them—how he has transformed and transfigured them in the writing.

Although the analysis does not take off from any particular a priori theory, it does rest on the shoulders of my two initial probes into the mystery of creativity: *Eugene O'Neill's Creative Struggle* and *Creating Characters with Charles Dickens*. Both O'Neill and Dickens were im-pelled—I discovered—to write a particular work by an urgent life problem. They were able to resolve the problem through the resolution they found for the problems of their characters in their story.

The author might be partly conscious or entirely unconscious of the real impetus to writing, but in any case his impelling problem worked in harmony or counterpoint with his conscious theme to shape his story. For each work a unique nexus of interconnected memories came alive in the author's mind and served simultaneously as the materials for solving the author's impelling problem and for setting up and resolving the problem in the fiction. Out of this nexus of memories—personal and intellectual—came the poetic imagery of the work, its emotional tone, its characters, its plot, even the historical setting, or in some cases the time sequence in which the action took place. Each work acted to change the author's attitudes, beliefs, and often the very structure of his life, for all along the way he was creating his own consciousness, achieving a wider understanding of himself and his world.

The present study strives to extend the inquiry and arrive at a larger body of evidence by analyzing four additional authors in the creation of a major work. The authors chosen—Mann, Stevenson, FitzGerald, and Tolstoy—throw much more light on the initial impetus to create a work, for they point to an answer to the fundamental question of why one writer moves through a lifetime producing one significant work after another, each unique in meaning and emotional effect, while another writer remains sterile virtually all his days, only to come awake during one miraculous year and create a masterpiece never again to be even remotely approached by him. These four authors also provide evidence to answer such questions as what constitutes *originality* in a work, and what are the unknowns in creativity hidden behind that very loose word "imagination."

This analysis can be read as a fresh kind of biography that starts where biography usually stops short, at the door to an author's writing room, for it shows him fighting his most intimate and important life battles in his work. In fact, major experiences in an author's life can be passed over altogether in conventional biography because their significance to the writer remains invisible to his biographer and he discards them as tangential. In the present analysis such an experience can reveal its actual importance by the outstanding role it plays in shaping an aspect of his work. So the ambiguous love affair between Tolstoy's sister Marya Nikolayevna and his early friend and mentor Ivan Sergeyevich Turgenev is ignored in Tolstoy biographies, passed over without a word, as irrelevant. Luckily it can be learned of through passages here and there in Turgenev's letters and by taking account of isolated references in Tolstoy's diaries. Its emotional impact on Tolstoy becomes apparent by the way he worked it out in his creation of the life story of a principal character in *War and Peace,* the Princess Marya Bolkonsky. Similarly, biographers of Edward FitzGerald pay small attention to his strange past-tense love affair with Elizabeth Charlesworth. In the present study it takes on great importance because it was one of the indispensable elements in the complex of causes that brought FitzGerald, for one brief year of his life, to write great poetry.

The present study can also be read for illumination of the four works analyzed. To this end, it strives—as far as possible—to marshal all the significant evidence on the work, quoting from the author's explicit comments in his letters, diaries, and notes and trying to reconstruct the memory system feeding into it from that evidence plus the evidence in the finished work itself. That means that the research for this analysis demanded a thorough study not only of the author but also of all the people in his life or people known to him through his reading. No one can succeed in searching out *all* the significant memories in another person's mind, but he can make it an ideal to try for. Thus it became essential to gather as much data about Gustav Mahler as about Thomas Mann for the study of *Death in Venice*, and about Alexander Pushkin, Alexander Herzen, Mikhail Bakunin, and a host of Decembrists as about Tolstoy for the study of *War and Peace*.

The criterion for supposing a particular memory system was actually feeding into a work lay in the extent to which a meaningful parallel could be shown between the memory and the work. Thus all along the way I was carrying out seemingly contradictory directives. On the one hand, I had to demonstrate a convincing enough parallel to indicate that the memory system actually was nourishing the fiction. On the other, I had to show clearly as many differences as I could between the memories and the fiction, for in the differences lay the evidence of how the author transformed those materials in the course of creation.

Of course, the primary purpose of this analysis is to delineate the creative process in action—to give a blow-by-blow report of what took place in these four authors as they created these four works. The analysis goes far beyond my first two probes, for it investigates more comprehensively the complex blending of memories out of which the real power of fiction emerges. The heart of this study is the evidence itself. Characters in it are shown to take their shape from all kinds of blends—from putting the personality of one real person into the life story of another, from combining two or three real personalities with two or three real-life stories, from combining a real person with an inert object rich in associations (for example, in one case, a blend of a real boy with a piece of sculpture, and in another a blend of a man with a death's head).

Also there may be nothing literal about the use of a real story in fiction. It may be used as a reservoir of images entirely removed from the real-life sequence, so that what was a fatal ending in the life of an original for a character can become an initial trauma in the fiction. Curious blends may be made of widely different geographical locations, and quite a mosaic of events from many lives can join together for the story of a protagonist in fiction.

Readers who are familiar with the four works analyzed will have an advantage, but readers who are not should be able to follow the discussion easily, for I have tried to present all the facts they need to know. Documentation and additional evidence are presented in the notes at the end, keyed to page number and phrase. In the case of *War and Peace*, where a multitude of Russian names may cause confusion, a Who's Who of people and characters appearing in Chapter 4 is in an appendix at the end of the book.

Although chronologically he comes last, the study begins with Thomas Mann because he had such extraordinary insight into his own creative process that I could quote him directly on several aspects of what he was doing in *Death in Venice*. Besides, *Death in Venice* is actually an investigation of the nature of art by Mann, and so is particularly relevant in all ways to this investigation of the mystery of creativity. *War and Peace* is placed last because its complexities pick up and substantiate points made about the creative process in analyzing the first three authors.

The findings of this analysis should be useful to the many persons trying to cope with the current crisis of the liberal arts and the humanities. An answer to what makes an author write literature may point the way to answer the question "Why read literature?" The meaning of a work to its creator—even if that author is by no means conscious of it during much or all of the writing—may give the answer to what it can mean for a reader.

1

The Birth of
Death in Venice

Death in Venice began for Thomas Mann on July 31, 1910, when his
younger sister, Carla—only twenty-nine years old—killed herself. It
was more than a bereavement. It shattered his ideals, broke the family
unity, called his very existence as an artist into question. When alone,
he found himself weeping "almost continually," and he kept repeating
to himself, "One of us!" All four young Manns had opted for art as a
way of life. First the eldest, Heinrich, became a writer. Then Thomas
followed. Carla became an actress. Even the older sister, Julia, despite
her bourgeois marriage, shared their dedication. Thomas Mann had
believed in their "brother-and-sisterly bond," their commitment to art
as somehow "superior to the realities of life." Carla's death shattered
that confidence. She had not thought, could not have realized, "what a
blow it would be to our lives when she smashed her own life." It became
desperately important for Thomas Mann "to come to some terms with
poor Carla's action."

For Carla the precipitating cause had been pain in love. As an actress,
she had never achieved the success of her two brothers. She could not
get beyond small parts in provincial theaters. At twenty-nine she hoped
for rebirth into a new life through love and marriage to a young Alsatian
manufacturer. It was really a return to an image of love and safety out

of the past. Her betrothed repeated the dignity and stability of her father, Senator Mann, distinguished scion of a great merchant family of Lübeck, whose death some twenty years earlier when she stood at the brink of adolescence had been as devastating for her and her sister and brothers as her own was to be. Despite the opposition of her betrothed's family to his marrying an actress, she saw her salvation in this marriage and blindly pushed ahead on it. But the years of her struggle as an actress had damaged more than her reputation. She had succumbed briefly to the seduction of a young doctor, and, refusing to give her up, he had succeeded in blackmailing her into a repetition. Then, to wreck her marriage altogether, he had sent an anonymous letter to her fiancé disclosing his liaison with her. Directly after an appalling interview with her betrothed, who had rushed to her in Polling where she was visiting her mother, Carla had taken poison, leaving a note for him in French— the language of her hoped-for new life—"Je t'aime. Une fois je t'ai trompé, mais je t'aime."

Carla had been a fragile child, very near death from convulsions and later from inflammation of the lungs. As a beloved child, infinitely more beloved because of the hold of death upon her, she had come to associate being loved with dying. Then her father's death had taken love from her into itself and buried it in the grave, so that death, the grave, became a lure and a pull within her. In the intensities of love in that family, the pull of death from the beloved father's disappearance into it must have taken a powerful hold. Seventeen years after Carla killed herself for loss of love, her older sister, Julia, would do so too.

In her girlhood, Carla had acknowledged that pull of death by keeping a death's head, a human skull, on her dresser and giving it a "scurrilous name." Some kind of subliminal association had linked for her lust and annihilation, lasciviousness and death, so that the dresser death's head with the scurrilous name represented an ambiguous flirtation with both. Death attracted her so powerfully that she kept with her for years before she used it enough potassium cyanide—as her brother Thomas knew she had boasted—to kill "a whole regiment." When her agony came, she swallowed enough, he said, "for a company."

All the details of her dying were etched indelibly on his mind. She had hurried past her mother with a smile, locked herself in her room, and after a few minutes she had been heard at the wash stand, gargling. Afterward they realized that she had been trying to cool her throat, corroded by the poison. When they broke in, she was lying on the sofa, her hands and face spotted a blackish-blue with congested blood from suffocation through instant paralysis of the respiratory organs. Death must have come to her quickly.

A month and a half after Carla's suicide, while his feelings were still, he said, "in sad disorder," Thomas Mann met Gustav Mahler. He had been hearing about Mahler for years from his wife Katia's twin brother, Klaus Pringsheim. Klaus had been studying conducting with Mahler for more than four years at the Vienna Court Opera as a volunteer "repetiteur" (conductor's assistant). Klaus said that for a premiere, up to the end of rehearsals, Mahler was always trying new solutions; he was never satisfied with even the highest achievement. He took for his motto "Better, more beautiful, more perfect." Mahler and Klaus had become friends, so that when Mahler came to Munich to conduct his Eighth Symphony, Katia and Thomas Mann were able to attend both the dress rehearsal and the concert at the Festival Hall on September 12, 1910. Right after finishing that score for singers and orchestra, Mahler had told Willem Mengelberg, "Try to imagine the whole universe beginning to ring and resound. These are no longer human voices, but planets and suns revolving." Mann had been thrilled by the music, and afterward by the composer. He thought Mahler "devouringly intense," and really the first person who had ever given him "the impression of being a great man." Later, Mann sent Mahler his most recent novel, *Royal Highness*, as "a poor exchange for what I have received from you," for it would be light as a feather in the hand of a man who embodied "the most serious and sacred artistic purpose of our age."

So the news in May 1911 that Mahler was dying came as a shock. Mann followed the Vienna newspaper reports on his condition until his death near midnight on May 18. Mahler had been suffering from a streptococcus infection of the throat, and Mann never forgot Bruno Walter's telling him that when he asked Mahler if he were in great pain Mahler had replied with a groan, "No, not pain, but it is so *unpleasant.*" Somehow that soreness of throat must have linked itself with the memory of poor Carla gargling to ease her burning throat. His still unresolved need "to come to some terms with poor Carla's action" pressed toward the realization that if he took up the dying—the dissolution, breakup—within a great artist like Mahler, one who embodied "the most serious and sacred artistic purpose" of an age, he might come to a more realistic conception of art, to a better understanding of what within Carla had led her to smash her own life, and with it those of her brothers. He saw that "all actuality is deadly earnest" and that both life and morality together do not let us "be true to the guileless unrealism of our youth." Long afterward he would say, "I regard my life work as the result of an extremely personal and very precarious coming to terms with art." Certainly *Death in Venice* had been.

For some time he had been deeply intrigued by the grotesque story "of the aged Goethe [seventy-four] and that little girl [the nineteen-year-old Ulrika Levetzow] in Marienbad whom he was absolutely determined to marry." Mann had been deeply moved by "all its terribly comic, shameful, awesomely ridiculous situations, this embarrassing, touching, and grandiose story, which"—so Mann said after he had written *Death in Venice*—"I may someday write after all." Mann had thought to make of it a "tragedy of supreme achievement," showing "passion as confusion and as a stripping of dignity." "Goethe's desire for order, moderation, and form" in art was, Mann knew, "an expression of his determination to control that potentially dangerous and demonically intense nature of his." It was the same battle that Nietzsche had shown between "the Dionysian spirit of lyricism," rapturous, irresponsible, and amoral, on the one side, and the Apollonian epic spirit on the other, "objectively controlled," and above all "morally and socially responsible." In *Elective Affinities,* Goethe had shown how an involuntary outbreak of passion could disrupt and destroy the lives of four rational and benevolently disposed people. So impressed was Mann by the objectivity and control with which Goethe designed this story that he read the book at least five times during the year of his writing *Death in Venice,* in order to maintain the right balance in his own story of disruptive passion. Both the story of Goethe's passion for Ulrika and Mann's understanding of the demonic force that Goethe habitually controlled merged in his mind with his profound feeling for the death of that other "devouringly intense" spirit Mahler to lay the groundwork for *Death in Venice*. But it was "a personal lyrical travel experience" on the part of Mann himself that brought the novella to life. It gave him a story eminently right for an investigation that could bring him to terms with Carla's suicide.

Ten months after Carla's death, Mann came to an impasse in writing his novel *Felix Krull*. *Death in Venice* begins with his writer-protagonist Gustave Aschenbach similarly blocked, taking Mann's own usual regenerative afternoon walk through the Munich English gardens to the North Cemetery, where he sees, as Mann actually did, a bizarre figure standing before the doors of the cemetery's Byzantine mortuary chapel. An instant after, he feels a sudden loosening of bounds and a thirst for exotic distances. Mann himself, like Aschenbach, had left within a couple of weeks for a Dalmatian holiday on the island of Brioni. It was there that Mann first read of Mahler's sickness in the newspapers and followed the bulletins until his death on May 18.

Of course, Mann had not set out alone like Aschenbach, but with his brother Heinrich, his wife Katia, and—although no mention is made of them in the *Sketch of My Life,* where he recalls this fateful voyage— perhaps with some of their children. Brioni had proved unsatisfactory, having no sand beaches like those Mann had learned to love in his childhood vacations at Travemünde, outside of Lübeck. So, just as Aschenbach in the story, he had changed plan and they had all taken the boat across the Adriatic from Pola to Venice.

Venice was a city that Mann had always "loved for deep and complex reasons," and one reason was certainly its strange resemblance to his native city Lübeck. Both had been great merchant republics, surrounded and invaded by the sea through canals, and as Venice had once ruled the Adriatic, Lübeck had ruled the Baltic. Mann always saw Venice as "Lübeck's southern sister." For him, the Gothic arcades of the Doge's palace summoned up those of the Lübeck Rathaus, and the whole shimmering Piazza San Marco became an enchanted dream of the marketplace at Lübeck. Even the duet between the sea beach at the Lido—recalling the beach at Travemünde—and the magical city nearby summoned up his childhood world divided between city winters and summers beside the eternal sea. Long years after he had written *Death in Venice,* he told his elder daughter and son, Erika and Klaus, who were staying at the Venice Lido: "In spirit I am with you leading that unique life between the warm sea in the morning and the 'ambiguous' city in the afternoon." Whatever its modern corruption—so Mann told them—"this musical magic of ambiguity still lives." Erika and Klaus thought that they were too late, for Venice must have been unspoiled in the middle of the nineteenth century. But even before then—so Mann replied—Platen had thought that all that was left of Venice lay "in the land of dreams." Yet Platen had "passionately loved it the way it was," even as had Byron and Nietzsche later, and as, still later, "your insignificant honorable sire." And were he there with them, Mann said, "my heart would be pounding." No wonder, then, if this story born of a Venice experience allowed him to come to grips with the beliefs out of his childhood that Carla's act had shattered.

When Mann spoke of a "lyrical" travel experience, he was using "lyrical" in the sense of Dionysiac, from Nietzsche's definition in the *Birth of Tragedy.* He was talking of an actual emotional outburst set off by a beautiful Polish boy who, with his family, was staying at the Hotel des Bains on the Lido when Mann arrived. More than a half century afterward, a Polish Count, who had just read Mann's story in Polish translation, sent a note to Erika Mann identifying himself as Tadzio, the boy of the story. When the Polish translator checked on it by interviewing Wladislav, Count Moes, the Count produced "undeniable proofs" in photographs and remembrances of that holiday in Venice. But after all that time there were places where the Count's remembrance was of Mann's story, not of any reality. Count Moes recalled that he and the Polish playmate (Mann's Jaschiu, in the story) at the beach had been conscious of "an old man" always watching them. That was the fictional Aschenbach, not Mann in May 1911, for Mann was then a *young* man and—far from being alone like Aschenbach, he had been seen usually accompanied by his beautiful wife and his brother, and perhaps some of his children.

Nevertheless, the lyrical impact of the adolescent Count Moes was certainly the experience that joined with Goethe's elderly infatuation and with the death of Mahler to give Mann his story. Just a little over a month from his return to Munich—that is, on July 11, 1911—Mann told Philipp Witkop that he was working on "a very strange thing that I brought with me from Venice," a novella about "an aging artist who falls in love with a boy."

The aging artist is certainly the image of Gustav Mahler as he looked to Mann after conducting his Eighth Symphony in Munich that last September. Gustave Aschenbach is a little "below middle height," with "a lofty, rugged, knotty brow," and an "almost delicate figure." Natalie Bauer-Lechner saw Mahler as "less than average height" with "an apparently delicate frame, being slight and lean in build." But she knew that "many a more powerfully-built person might envy him his extraordinary strength and suppleness." To Bruno Walter, Mahler was a "lean, fidgety, short man with an unusually high, steep forehead." Mann tells us that "the nose-piece" of Aschenbach's "rimless gold spectacles cut into the base of his thick, aristocratically hooked nose," that his "mouth was large, often lax, often suddenly narrow and tense; the cheeks lean and furrowed," and that he had a "pronounced chin." Mahler wore just such "stern and forbidding spectacles," and—as Natalie Bauer-Lechner declared—"Imperious is his hooked nose with its finely sensitive nostrils." Romain Rolland, too, saw the "strong nose," the "large mouth with narrow lips," and the "sunken cheeks" that could look, as Natalie Bauer-Lechner thought, "furrowed and aged" one minute and "youthful as a boy's the next." Finally, Mahler's chin was so pronounced that it appeared to be "stretched out" when he walked briskly forward.

This much of Aschenbach was pure Mahler, but his nature as an artist blends in Mann himself and also, quite palpably at the start of the story, Goethe (whose infatuation in old age had been Mann's original conception). It is really Goethe who lends the figure of Aschenbach its authority, dignity, and public honors. As with Goethe, Aschenbach's writings have been set as school models, and he himself has been made a nobleman. Mann might easily have made the art in question Mahler's music, for he had always seen himself as "half-and-half a musician," but the overlay of Goethe on his protagonist, along with his own desperate need to come to grips with the art he practiced, won out, and he made Aschenbach a writer.

In the austerity of his dedication, Aschenbach, like Mahler when he was liberated to create music from conducting it, seeks the mountains in the summer. From Klaus Pringsheim, Mann knew of Mahler's composing hut up a steep mountain path in deep woods, and he emphasized the austerity by making Aschenbach's "rude country house" his living quarters as well. Although Mahler actually had "a distaste for luxury and comfort," the house for his family was commodious. He alone rose at dawn to climb to his "work hut," where "on pain of death" it was forbidden to disturb him until noon. (Mann devoted the fresh morning hours to his work too, but isolated only by his study door.)

From childhood, Aschenbach has been pushed "to achievement." Always, he has been characterized by the clenched fist, never the relaxed hand, and his motto, taken from Frederick the Great, is "Durchhalten" (Hold fast). Out of his "loneliness," out of "bitter struggles," he has achieved his works. Indeed, the figure of Saint Sebastian, his vulnerable flesh shot full of arrows, his spirit triumphantly radiant and serene, makes a perfect symbol for Aschenbach: the artist and his achievement. Mahler had the same dedication to music. As a young conductor, he saw himself as entering "the lists to fight for what is holy." He always "set my aims high," "pledged all I have," and "did not spare myself." He saw his compositions as the pearl that the oyster creates out of his "terrible sufferings." His symbol for the creator in art was that of Jacob "wrestling with God" to "extort" a blessing. Everyone who saw him was impressed by "his dedicated seriousness, the severity of his whole manner and bearing." He was a man—so Catulle Mendes said—"whose entire appearance bespeaks powerful and nervous will."

Mann shared that dedication. He told Kurt Martens: "I am an ascetic insofar as my *conscience* directs me toward *achievement* in contrast to pleasure and to 'happiness.' " And he quoted Nietzsche's "Do I strive for happiness? I strive for my work." He knew that "one cannot serve both masters, pleasure and art." Before their marriage, he told Katia that writing never effervesces except "for the easily satisfied" who do not know "the pressure and discipline of talent." For him, talent was "the harshest scourge." His own motto was very like Aschenbach's "Durchhalten." He told Agnes Meyer: "I have always liked Andersen's fairy tale of 'The Steadfast Tin Soldier.' Fundamentally it is the symbol of my life."

So Mann himself, Mahler, and Goethe all entered into Aschenbach and his "tragedy of supreme achievement." But the plot, event by event, duplicates the actual facts of Mann's 1911 Venice trip (only with Katia and Heinrich and perhaps some of the children expunged, and with the protagonist in his fifties, as was Mahler when he died, and seeming even older from the Goethe overlay). Writing this story, Mann experienced "the clearest feeling of transcendence, a sovereign sense of being borne up, such as I have never before known." He was amazed "by the inherent symbolism and rightness for composition of even the most unimportant of the factual elements."

One of the extraordinary aspects of the story is the way the sheer facts became blended with memories of Carla's death in Polling. Mann himself said that nothing in the story was invented, not the " 'wanderer' at the Northern Cemetery" nor "the sinister gondolier" or "the rascally ballad singer." These three crucial figures bear a strange resemblance to one another. Physically thin—one blond and two redheaded—all are emphatically snub-nosed. The first has curled back his lips to bare "long, white, glistening teeth to the gums." The second also has "curled back his lips and bared his white teeth to the gums," and the third has a "grinning" mouth that reveals "strong white teeth." The wayfarer and the rascally singer have "two pronounced perpendicular furrows" in their foreheads over the snub noses. These two also have a strikingly "naked-looking" or "bald" Adam's apple. Very subtly all three summon up—probably not into full consciousness for most readers—the skeletal image of Death, with the bared grinning teeth, the bit of cartilage on the nose giving a snubbed appearance, and the two perpendicular sutures in the bones of the forehead. They recall Carla's death's head, the skull on her dresser. The unlicensed gondolier also takes on the associations of his "coffin"-black gondola, which arouses "visions of death itself, the bier and solemn rites and last soundless voyage."

The three have a brutal face. The wayfarer is described as "bold," "domineering," "ruthless," and the gondolier as "overbearing," "despotic." All stand outside the social and moral code—the gondolier actually is an outlaw, without a license. His straw hat is rakishly perched, and his gondola is redolent of "lawless, silent adventures." On Aschenbach, its effect is to produce a fatal relaxation—of purpose, discipline, moral boundaries. The third figure, the singer—coming as he does near the climax of Aschenbach's moral disintegration—takes on the lascivious connotations of Carla's death's head with its "scurrilous name." This lewd and mocking image of dissolution ends by making game of his audience, luring them into berserk laughter at themselves and then sticking out his tongue at them before vanishing.

A cholera epidemic had actually broken out in Venice before the Manns arrived, and it was being hushed up by corrupt authorities as in the story, so that at first the Manns had only suspected something wrong until an "upright clerk" in Cook's travel bureau revealed the truth and advised them to leave at once. In *Death in Venice* the first death's head (the wayfarer at the cemetery mortuary chapel) puts into Aschenbach's mind an alluring vision of a "tropical marshland" under a "reeking sky" and crossed by alluvial channels of stagnant water between hairy palm trunks revealing glimpses of crouching tigers. Decades before 1911, medical pathology books had already traced the devastating nineteenth-century epidemics of cholera in Europe to the Bengal peninsula, to "the hot, moist swamps of the delta of the Ganges," as Mann tells us. Aschenbach's vision looks into the source of the horrible disease. It also suggests the Venice salt marshes in sirocco, crossed by canals—without the tigers—for the city repeats the conditions that are favorable to the generation of the cholera bacteria.

The symptoms of cholera, which Mann gives in detail for their symbolic value, recall—to one who knows Carla's story—the outstanding facts of her death. Death from cholera is essentially, so Mann tells us, death by suffocation, as is death from cyanide poisoning. It is characterized by the bluish-black discoloration from congested blood of its victims, very like the blackish areas on Carla's face and hands when they found her. The "hoarse cries" of the cholera victims recall Carla's corroded throat. As a child, Carla had passed from convulsion to convulsion, as Mann tells us the cholera victims did. Curiously enough,

Mann suppresses from his account of cholera the three principal symptoms of the disease as described in all the medical texts: vomiting, diarrhea, and colic. It is significant that these excluded symptoms are precisely those that had no part in Carla's dying, in death from cyanide poisoning.

Memories of Carla also contributed to the unique atmosphere of alluring disease throughout the story, captured in the pervasive odor of carbolic acid that has been poured out as a disinfectant. At the third appearance of the death's head as the lascivious singer, he actually gives off the smell of it. He also recalls the cries of the cholera victims, speaking "hoarsely." In Aschenbach's appalling dream—signaling his ultimate moral collapse—a bacchanalian orgy desecrates his austere workhouse in the mountains, and in the dream the very attributes of disease and death transmute into those of sexual abandonment. Amid the hoarse cries of the delirious celebrants, the howling of Tadzio's name, as it sounded when he was called at the beach, echoes and re-echoes.

Following this dream desecration, Aschenbach lets go altogether and openly adopts the signs of corruption that he had shuddered at in the repulsive old homosexual on the Pola boat coming to Venice, with his red cravat, his rouge, his dyed hair. Even this dissolute painted "young-old man," who had actually been on the Pola boat, aroused Mann's memories of the early signs of the unhealthy in Carla's way of life. Speaking of her passionate devotion to the theater without real talent, Mann told of how she had resorted to "an artificial accentuation" of her person in private life by the use of "rouge and cosmetics, exaggerated hairdressing and extravagant hats." So the painted old man on the Pola boat was reinforced by poignant memory when Mann chose to present the final degradation and defacement of his artist Aschenbach as his resort to these artificialities that transform his majestic image into the shameful, pitiful, ridiculous figure he had looked upon with horror such a short time before.

Of course, the most important real event in the story, most important for his coming to terms with Carla's self-destruction, was the personal "lyrical," Dionysiac rapture he had felt at the sight of the beautiful Polish boy on the Lido. When questioned directly about "that emotional tendency," homoeroticism, by Carl Maria Weber, Mann said that he had no "wish to disavow" his particular understanding of it. But, he told him, "I am a family founder and a father by instinct and conviction." He loved his children, especially "a little girl who very much resembles my wife," and in this he knew that he was essentially "bourgeois." As he fully recognized, the bourgeois family founder had been consolidated in the image of his father, Senator Mann (and in the tradition of the Lübeck Manns). From Senator Mann, Thomas had received, as he was well aware, the austere discipline that went into his art—into his entire way of life. From all the Manns he had taken and put into *Death in Venice* the "Protestant, Puritan ('bourgeois') basic state of mind not only of the story's protagonist but also of myself; in other words, our fundamentally mistrustful, fundamentally pessimistic relationship to passion in general."

Yet he was subject to "unbourgeois intellectually sensual adventures," to what he saw as a yearning between mind and life, a kind of "eternal tension" perpetually unresolved between the two. For him, the "problem of beauty" lay in the fact that "mind feels life and life feels mind as 'beautiful.' " His experience of homoeroticism never emerged from that unresolved tension. In one such rapture (long after the one on the Lido) over the natural beauty of a young man, a gardener at work, Mann would reflect on "the unreal, illusionary, and aesthetic nature" of his inclination, for its goal lay in "admiring," and it required "no fulfillment at all."

He had always seen himself as in love with life, as on the side of common life. His identification with his father put him at one with bourgeois life, however far he was divided from it by his willingness as an artist to accept, even sympathize with, emotions, ways of life, antagonistic to the norm. In his novella *Tonio Kröger* (1903), his artist-protagonist had declared that it is not the "extraordinary and daemonic," but rather "the normal, respectable, and admirable that is the kingdom of our longing: life, in all its seductive banality!" Tonio Kröger sees "life and home" in the everyday German type, the blue-eyed ones, like his blue-eyed father. In *Fiorenza* (1904), Mann has Lorenzo di Medici turn upon Savanarola and condemn him the instant he realizes that the monk's choice of spirit over art is really a choice of death over life. "It is death whom you proclaim as spirit, and all the life of life is art." Mann's love and admiration for his respectable and respected father had led him, he was sure, entirely to life.

But in *Death in Venice*, Aschenbach's passion for the blond Polish boy is not Tonio Kröger's love for the blue-eyed Hans Hansen and Ingeborg Holm, nor does Tadzio stand as they do for the normal, the respectable. What Tadzio does stand for begins to emerge with Aschenbach's first glimpse of him in the lounge of the Hotel des Bains.

Aschenbach is struck by the contrast between the extraordinary beauty of the boy and the "cloister-like plainness" of his three sisters, dressed as they are with "pedagogic severity" in nunlike simplicity. In their formal reception of their mother, the young people show a "self-respecting dignity, discipline, and sense of duty" that speaks to Aschenbach. Altogether they remind one of "the stern, stark service of form" that he himself had always carried out as an artist. The aristocratic mother of the four young people echoes the simplicity of dress in her daughters, in pale grey, but she is rendered fabulous by a long three-strand necklace of priceless cherry-size pearls—those exquisite jewels created out of the disease and suffering of the oyster, as the work of art is born of the travail of the artist. The boy himself seems like a work from "the noblest moment of Greek sculpture," and Aschenbach's rapture at his perfection is the artist's "ravishment over a masterpiece." Indeed, Aschenbach looks upon him as a creator looks upon his work, thinking "What discipline, what precision of thought" went into the "tense youthful perfection of this form," and feeling in himself the strong will that had wrought it, like his own furious struggle to liberate the pure perfection of his works from the "marble mass of language." On a symbolic level, Tadzio, the beautiful boy, embodies spiritual beauty, the divine beauty of a great work of art. He is art. No wonder Aschenbach is stirred by him with something of a "father's" feeling.

But even by way of Tadzio's "pure and godlike serenity," in his recollection of the noblest Greek sculpture the boy takes on a symbolic meaning beyond art. Through that meaning, Mann learned the significance of Carla's action and came to a more realistic conception of the role of art in his life. At the beach, Aschenbach sees Tadzio silhouetted against sea and sky, against the immensities of space, and those immensities are as alluring to him as is the boy. He longs for the peace of the limitless, the eternal—indeed, of "nothingness." As he looks upon Tadzio running up out of the sea, a "virginally pure," austere figure, perfect as a young god, Aschenbach feels that the boy conjures up "mythologies." Only at the end of the story does Mann suggest a particular god and a particular myth. Mann's references to Tadzio's singular twilight grey eyes—eyes unlike other eyes, redolent of twilight, the fading of light into darkness—give the subtlest foreshadowing of the particular young god, the particular myth embodied in Tadzio. He is revealed fully only in the moment that Aschenbach passes out of the light into eternal darkness, looking at the slender god against an eternity of sea and sky and seeing him as a pale "Summoner," smiling and beckoning to him.

Thus Tadzio's identity is just suggested in the story, and only afterward, in a personal letter, did Mann say explicitly that symbolically Tadzio is "Hermes Psychopompos," Hermes the guide of souls to the underworld, Hermes der Seelenführer. Years later, Mann made a "private joke" in *Joseph and His Brothers* by having the Egyptian god Anubis say that he expects to lose his head. Anubis actually did lose his jackal head when he developed historically into Hermes Psychopompos. Mann had depicted Anubis sitting on a stone, he said, "exactly in the pose of the Hermes of Lysippus in Naples," for "I particularly love this statue, of which there is a fine copy in the old Museum in Berlin."

Long before *Joseph and His Brothers,* Mann had given Tadzio a resemblance to this elegant work of art out of the noblest period of Greek sculpture. When Aschenbach first sees Tadzio, he is sitting, as Lysippus depicted the god, with one foot stretched out. Like the statue, he is seen in half-profile, but he wears patent-leather shoes rather than winged sandals, and unlike the god, who needs no clothing, he wears a sailor suit. But Tadzio's "ringlets," the Greek line of his nose, and the winning mouth are surely as much a recollection of the statue as of the Polish boy. The real boy is in him too, sitting on a wicker chair, not on a stone, with his cheek resting humanly on his hand, but he is transfigured throughout by recollections of the statue of the god. Mann's reference to the lightness of Tadzio's tread recalls the winged feet of the swift messenger god, as the boy's perfection recalls the glory of the Greek statue, and the whole myth of Hermes Psychopompos.

The god and the work of art are one in the Lysippus bronze. So Tadzio is both art and, insofar as he is Hermes Psychopompos, death. At the finale of *Death in Venice*, Mann stood side by side with Carla. He had seen clearly the lure of death in her, and he had recognized the same lure in himself. He could no longer assume that art was necessarily on the side of life. Although he never made for a full self-analysis, the entire structure of his story gives evidence of an inner knowledge, outside of consciousness, that his homoerotic tendency came from the same source as the pull of death within him, and it was the same pull that had led Carla to kill herself. Where Mann identified with his father's discipline, his morality, he was directed to life. But where he felt only the profound love and admiration that had so suddenly, twenty years before, converted into grief, he was pulled as was Carla by a longing to join his beloved father in death.

The statements he made, the directions his art took after *Death in Venice*, show how consciously clear he had become of the pull of death within him, and how crystal clear was his realization that art in itself would not, could not, place him securely on the side of life. Right after finishing the novella, Mann felt only a "growing sympathy with death." A year and a half later he was saying that, as an artist, he would "never be able to obey the admonition to take the side of life against death." As to which was more distinguished, which was more repulsive, death or life, he could only answer, "I do not know." He was clear that *Death in Venice* had been a story of "death as a seductive antimoral force," a story of "the voluptuousness of doom," with a protagonist "who succumbs to lascivious dissolution." With the consciousness of the lure of death in himself, with his subsequent witnessing of the wholesale rush toward dissolution of his own fatherland Germany and of all Europe, which would culminate in the global suicide of World War I, Mann would be ready to write *Magic Mountain*. He would be ready to take up a protagonist "sensuously and intellectually infatuated with death." He would take him through a panoramic survey of contemporary philosophical and political thought in search of a foothold against sliding into the alluring grave. Finally he would bring him (although Mann would be clear on that only after he had written the book) to a first dawning conception "of a new humanity." So by solving one problem, Mann was faced with another. Although *Death in Venice* is complete and immortal in itself, it pushed Mann on to an ever-deepening understanding of life, death, and art.

The magic of *Death in Venice* came out of the blend of memories within it. The story had been set in action by Carla's suicide and the blow it gave Mann's belief that art, of itself, is on the side of life, preservative and supportive of life. Mann's entire way of life, his role as an artist, had partaken of Carla's smashing of her own life. No wonder memories of that disastrous event transfigured all the experiences of Mann's brief trip to Venice, out of which he built his plot.

The three real figures whom Mann had actually seen—the wanderer at the Munich cemetery, the unlicensed gondolier, and the singer at the hotel—took on suggestive power and meaning because the image of Carla's ubiquitous death's head, which she called by that "scurrilous name" (most probably the German contemptuous term for an old lecher), invaded their forms, endowing them with the ambiguity and horror of lascivious desire linked to the lure of annihilation. The same transfiguring blend of the convulsive delirium in cholera with Carla's cyanide poisoning, and of both with the sexual act, had created the unique poetry of the events. Similarly, the simple Polish boy whom

Mann looked upon at the Lido hotel had been lifted far beyond the actual young Count by his blend with all of Mann's memories of that transcendent work of art, the Hermes in Repose of Lysippus, both in its bronze original at Naples and the fine marble copy of it in the Berlin museum. Likewise, the grandeur of Aschenbach came of the blended auras of Mahler, Goethe, and Mann himself.

The entire push of the story had emerged from the realization—opening up as Mann wrote—that the lure of death in Carla was also within him and that it was inextricably allied to his homoerotic impulses. So art could not be counted on to support life. Out of art, Mann could take only truth, only self-knowledge, and in his case self-knowledge meant conscious awareness of the decadent pull toward dissolution that existed within him.

The discovery of that truth concluded the story, resolved the narrative with the problem that had impelled Mann to write it. But that resolution had not been a finale for the artist. If it had been, he would simply have killed himself, as Carla had, after writing it. Instead, he went on to a gigantic struggle by way of *Magic Mountain* to find an answer to the pull of death he had discovered within him and within all of Europe as it avalanched into the global suicide of World War I. In a lifelong writer of remarkable works like Thomas Mann, the resolution of one problem instantly presented him with another, so that he was impelled to move on to further works, each unique in the poetry of its particular blend of memories and each a stage in the growth of his own life-understanding, of his expanding wisdom.

2

The Real Treasure in
Treasure Island

When a writer sets out to create a book that will rake in "more coin" than he ever got before from what he calls "a low penny paper," no one expects him to produce a world classic. If his highest aim is to amuse a boy and he excludes women from his story simply on that same boy's orders, it seems even more unlikely that he will produce high art—especially if he is overheard exulting that writing boys' stories is "awful fun," for you need do no more in them than "indulge the pleasure of your heart." Yet all these unexalted purposes really have nothing to do with the value of what he creates. Far more profound purposes to which he remains oblivious may raise the meaning and impact of his final work infinitely beyond his preconceptions. This certainly was true of Robert Louis Stevenson—he who declared these lowly aims—when he started work on "The Sea Cook, or Treasure Island: A Story for Boys" in 1880.

Curiously enough, his first literary models—in themselves sheer penny trash—gave him the transcendent purpose that would lift his work above and beyond its inception as a boy's amusement. As a child in Edinburgh, Stevenson had found the "very spirit of my life's enjoyment" in Skelt's Juvenile Drama series, which gave the librettos, flamboyantly costumed cardboard figures, and stage settings for children's home theatricals. Long before Long John Silver was born in *Treasure Island*, Stevenson knew Skelt's "Long Tom Coffin." Long before he thought of Black Dog with his maimed hand, he had lived in the adventures of *Three-Fingered Jack, the Terror of Jamaica*. Years after, when his recently married friend Cosmo Monkhouse confessed that he had "fallen in love with stagnation," Stevenson exclaimed, "You will never be a Pirate!" The idea, for him, clanged a hollow knell: "—think of it! Never! After all boyhood's aspirations and youth's immortal day-dreams." For himself, he still dreamed of spending "any leisure I might have from Piracy upon the high seas" as the leader of a "great horde of irregular cavalry, devastating whole valleys."

A bronchial infection in early childhood had left Robert Louis Stevenson with permanently damaged lungs, diagnosed as "chronic pneumonia" or "fibroidal disease of the lungs" (what would now be called "bronchiectasis"), leaving him with episodes of uncontrollable coughing, cold sweats, fevers, persistent lung hemorrhaging. Afterward he confessed, "My childhood was in reality a very mixed experience, full of fever, nightmare, insomnia, painful days and interminable nights." Through all that agony, he had only his nurse, "Cummie," to comfort him, for—as he later put it—his mother was his father's wife, and "the children of lovers are orphans." Even in adult bouts of hemorrhaging, he would get the old feeling "of desertion and loss" in his heart and cry out "for the want of a mother." He had brought himself through that nightmare childhood of lonely suffering by projecting himself into an imaginary world in which he could face the very real danger of death threatening him and rise above fear and pain as a pirate or brigand or captain of cavalry who could confront dangers outside of himself and triumph over them.

As a result, all his adult life he was always glad to face external threats. His friend Sidney Colvin declared that for Stevenson "any kind of danger was a positive physical exhilaration." To George Meredith, Stevenson confided, "I was made for a contest, and the Powers have so willed that my battle-field should be this dingy, inglorious one of the bed and the physic bottle. At least I have not failed, but I would have preferred a place of trumpetings, and the open air over my head." That obscure battle against pain and sickness had taken all the courage of a cavalry charge, and he had fought it out as a boy by playing at cavalry charges. As a man, when life did not give him what he called the "bright face of danger," he made his fight against the fear of death by writing *Treasure Island*.

The real creative impulse behind that book lay entirely in Stevenson's need to struggle against and conquer the fear of death. That need became inextricably entangled with Stevenson's unresolved ambivalence toward his closest friend, William Ernest Henley, because in that friend he had found a second self, a person who had emerged out of the same kind of nightmare childhood darkened by disease and the threat of death, one who had struggled, even as he had, to transcend both.

Through the reality of its struggle and victory over the fear of death, *Treasure Island* rose above its genre and took on poetry through Stevenson's myriad memories out of his tormented childhood. He once confessed, "My horror of the horrible is about my weakest point," so disease, the horror against which he was pitted all his life, came to haunt *Treasure Island* from the moment the sabre-scarred, alcoholic, apoplectic old pirate Billy Bones comes to hide out at the Admiral Benbow Inn at Black Hill Cove and intimidates his landlord, already dying of galloping consumption, to collapse and death. In turn two emissaries from the pirates come to threaten Billy Bones into a "mortal sickness." The first, Black Dog, lacks "two fingers of the left hand," like Skelt's "Three-Fingered Jack," and he ends up running away, streaming blood from a shoulder and leaving Bones with his gory cutlass in such a rage that he falls in an apoplectic fit. A day after the landlord's funeral comes Pew, the blind beggar, "horrible, soft-spoken, eyeless," to tip Billy Bones the "black spot," which sets off a second stroke that kills him.

These maimed men are rendered more horrible by their mutilations, rather than less, for it is disease itself that Stevenson is battling through them. They all stand in terror of a more drastically mutilated man, a "seafaring man with one leg," for whom Bones has been paying the landlord's son Jim Hawkins to keep a lookout, so that the boy has come to share his anxiety. Jim tells us that on stormy nights when the "surf roared along the cove and up the cliffs" he would "see him in a thousand forms, and with a thousand diabolical expressions. Now the leg would be cut off at the knee, now at the hip; now he was a monstrous kind of creature who had never had but the one leg, and that in the middle of his body. To see him leap and run and pursue me over hedge and ditch was the worst of nightmares." Jim is thus entirely unprepared to recognize his dream terror in the treacherously sunny surface of the one-legged Long John Silver when he meets him in Bristol.

It was this figure who became fused with Stevenson's second self, his friend William Ernest Henley. Well after *Treasure Island* had appeared in *Young Folks* magazine and Henley himself had succeeded in placing the book advantageously with Cassell, Stevenson confessed to him, "It was the sight of your maimed strength and masterfulness that begot John Silver in *Treasure Island*. Of course, he is not in any other quality or feature the least like you; but the idea of the maimed man, ruling and dreaded by the sound [in body], was entirely taken from you." Like Stevenson, Henley had come out of early affliction—in his case from then incurable tubercular arthritis—so that before he was out of his teens he had already lost one leg, amputated just below the knee (not at the hip like Long John Silver).

In a way, Stevenson was overcoming the threat that had hung over both of them by playing pirates with his friend, taking for himself the role of the heroic boy in his story and giving his friend the equally attractive one of the terrifying pirate. In fact, the names of the boy Jim *Hawkins* and of the pirate *John* Silver give the complete name of that most famous English buccaneer (a legalized one at that), Sir John Hawkins. Stevenson did not feel he was violating his friend's privacy because, as he explained to Sidney Colvin, "The drawing of a character is a different thing from publishing the details of a private career." Besides, he was depicting only "one class of qualities—the warlike and formidable." He had performed a species of "psychical surgery" on Henley, cutting away "his finer qualities and higher graces of temperament to leave him with nothing but his strength, his courage, his quickness and his magnificent geniality."

Nevertheless, the character of Long John Silver took on depth and ambiguity in the writing, becoming prophetically endowed with just those negative qualities that, a good six years after *Treasure Island* first appeared in *Young Folks*, Stevenson would at last see clearly when he quarreled with this dearest of friends and broke with him irreparably. Indeed, Stevenson would find the same way of coping with this catastrophic finale to his friendship that he had already found for Jim Hawkins in *Treasure Island*. Clearly there was more at work in the writing of this book than ever its author so much as suspected, let alone put into words.

If Henley—alias Long John Silver—entered *Treasure Island* as a "Sea Cook," the disguise by which the pirate gets himself and his comrades taken on as crew for the treasure hunt voyage, he did because Robert Louis Stevenson first laid eyes on him in a back-kitchen. As Henley himself fondly recalled, " 'Twas a blessed hour for all of us, that day 13 years syne, when old Stephen brought you into my back-kitchen, wasn't it?" The back-kitchen no longer saw cookery, for it had been converted into a two-bed hospital room in the crowded old Edinburgh Royal Infirmary. Henley was in it because Joseph Lister—just coming into fame for miracle cures through his pioneering work in antiseptic surgery—was trying to save his remaining leg. Before that, Henley had been immured in the Royal Sea-Bathing Infirmary at Margate, and his doctors had decided to amputate his one remaining leg, because the bone had become necrotic. Crippled as he was and with almost no money, Henley betook himself to Edinburgh and succeeded in interesting Lister in his case. For eighteen months he had been stretched in an iron frame with a wide-open triangular wound cut in his ankle and having his foot bones scraped and treated daily with carbolic acid by Lister.

The "old Stephen" of Henley's recall was Leslie Stephen, the redoubtable scholar, critic, and editor of the *Cornhill Magazine* (whose daughter Virginia would surpass him in fame after her marriage to Leonard Woolf). Among his friends Leslie Stephen was called "Long Leslie Stephen," for, as Sidney Colvin said, "long he was alike of back, leg, and stride, of nose and beard (the fine forked and flowing auburn beard depicted in Watts's well-known portrait)." Stephen had been much impressed by the poems and essays Henley had been mailing to him at London, and, having come to Edinburgh for a lecture, he looked up the "miserable cripple" in his back-kitchen at the Royal Infirmary. Afterward he went to meet Robert Louis Stevenson, "Colvin's friend"—so he wrote back to his wife—"and told him all about this poor creature, and am going to take him there this afternoon. He will be able to lend him books, and perhaps to read his MSS. and be otherwise useful. So I hope that my coming to Edinburgh will have done good to one living creature." It was February 1875, and Stevenson never forgot that "black winter afternoon" when "Long Leslie Stephen, in his velvet jacket," had led him into the old back-kitchen of the infirmary where the "gas flared and crackled, the fire burned in a dull economical way; Stephen and I sat on a couple of chairs, and the poor fellow sat up in his bed with his hair and beard all tangled, and talked as cheerfully as if he had been in a King's palace, or the great King's palace of the blue air."

Two small boys occupied the other bed in Henley's hospital room, which Stevenson came to know well in the two months remaining until Henley was discharged, his leg intact but still tubercularly arthritic. Having identified instantly with the brave young cripple, Stevenson continued to visit him, bringing books and his friends with more books, even seeing to it that Mrs. Fleming Jenkin gave Henley free lessons in

German. Henley's roommate, before the little boys came, had been the seafaring Captain Boyle, and Henley was already courting—by no means to the Captain's satisfaction—his younger sister Anna Boyle, who had spent a lot of time in that back-kitchen in earlier months.

As Stevenson began his pirate story, memories of that reluctant ship captain and of the back-kitchen trailed into it along with the cheerful blonde giant Henley. So powerful and tall was Henley, according to Francis Thompson, that he looked like a "Viking chief." George Bernard Shaw never could criticize Henley, because, Shaw said, his physical disability, was so "heartbreaking in a man of his inches." By right Henley could be called "Long," and be taken on in the story as a sea cook by Squire Trelawney "out of pure pity," just as Henley in his kitchen was taken on by Leslie Stephen and Robert Louis Stevenson.

Jim Hawkins first sees Long John as the image of Henley, "very tall and strong, with a face as big as a ham" and managing his crutch "with wonderful dexterity, hopping about upon it like a bird." So Henley had hopped in the first weeks after he was released from the Royal Infirmary. Later he always had the support of a wooden leg as well as crutches. He had taken a room at Portobello, thirty yards from the Firth of Forth, and Stevenson came daily from Edinburgh to take him for carriage drives, always finding it "a business to carry him down the long stairs, and more of a business to get him up again." (In the book, Long John Silver is associated with the piratical Portobello at Panama, recalling Henley's Portobello.) Soon Stevenson had taken Henley into his world, shared all his friends with him, and, even when Henley transferred to London, surrounded him with his own friends, such as Sidney Colvin and Edmund Gosse, and even with family in his cousins Bob Stevenson (an art critic) and Bob's sister Katherine de Mattos.

Henley had grown up in Bristol (where, appropriately, Jim Hawkins first meets Silver), the son of a bookseller who soon went bankrupt. Although Henley, like Long John Silver, had had "good schooling," his early associates were all of a different caste than the gentlemanly group into which Robert Louis Stevenson was introducing him. Years later, when the rift came between Stevenson and Henley, one of their mutual friends, Charles Baxter, urged Stevenson to "make allowances" for Henley: "Let us remember the early associations, the early training and companionship, that we may cease to wonder at the elephantine tact, by which euphemism one is compelled to admit one means occasional lapses from the feelings and conduct of a gentleman."

The great companion of Henley's early years had been a coffeehouse keeper named Harry whom Henley always called "Old Nick" or "Demon." He it was who loyally sent him the small doles that kept him going in the Royal Sea-Bathing Infirmary and later in Edinburgh. When his remaining leg was threatened, Henley had written the "Demon": "And you know what that means. No more excursions with the Great Nick! No more walking between tavern and tavern in the night with him." At the Royal Sea-Bathing Infirmary, his pal had been a bricklayer who would join him in night escapades, hoisting him—as Henley later told it—"over walls, to the end that we might sit in daring and in state in unlawful gin parlors." If in a poem, "To W.R.," Henley saw "Life" as a prostitute and Death as the pimp who sticks you for her price, it was no doubt because on those escapades he discovered "Life" in that shape. So when Robert Louis Stevenson brought him into his circle of friends, Henley knew he was moving up. He wrote laughingly to "Old Nick": "I am going into good society: real aristo, my boy."

Very early in their friendship, Stevenson became aware of that breath from another world in Henley, underneath all his cleverness and wit and charm. Something of that double identity went into Long John Silver. Of course, Long John was also shaped in part by the very fact of his being a pirate. Stevenson had chosen to write of pirates rather than brigands or cavalry captains because the sea was as familiar to him as the sickbed. He had grown up knowing it as few boys did, coming as he had out of two generations of oceanic engineers. His grandfather had designed and directed the construction of the Bell Rock lighthouse on a rock outcropping in the midst of raging ocean—and when the tide was high, far beneath it. As supervisor of all Scotland's lighthouses, he had been in perpetual voyage around its perilous coasts. At one point he had taken Sir Walter Scott along with him, through the wicked currents and whirlpools of the Pentland Firth, to visit the inaccessible Shetland Islands beyond. In the next generation, Robert Louis Stevenson's father, Thomas Stevenson, had designed and constructed the equally perilous Skerryvore lighthouse. Robert Louis Stevenson himself had enrolled as an engineering student at Edinburgh University and had begun serving summer apprenticeships constructing defenses against terrific surfs at isolated rocky harbors, until it became clear that with his hemorrhaging lungs he did not have the stamina for such a life. If he had not known all about currents and tides and the intricacies of island oceanography, he never could have written *Treasure Island* with Jim Hawkins's extraordinary chase of the cut-adrift schooner in a tearing current amid shifting tides and winds.

So it is not surprising to find that Robert Louis Stevenson took part of the character of Long John Silver out of a family retainer and used an experience out of his father's boyhood for the way in which Jim Hawkins discovers that Long John Silver is really a deadly pirate—in fact, the one-legged seaman of his nightmares. When Robert Louis's father, Thomas, and his brothers were boys, they had often accompanied his grandfather on his voyages of inspection, so they had many opportunities to observe Captain Soutar, the commander of his ship, the *Regent*, who held—so Robert Louis Stevenson told it—"a stronghold in my grandfather's estimation." Soutar and old Stevenson had worked together in the dangerous construction of the Bell Rock lighthouse. Often only the Captain's great skill and utter fearlessness saved Stevenson and his workers from drowning. Just in the nick of time Soutar would succeed in maneuvering close enough to get them off the rock in boats before high tide swept over it.

In remembrance of those feats, old Stevenson would have Captain Soutar join him and the boys for Sunday dinner in the cabin, and they could see that the Captain knew how to "court and please" him with great "hypocritical skill." On weekdays too Soutar would come to the cabin—so Robert Louis Stevenson told it—"after dinner for a glass of port or whiskey, often in his full rig of sou'wester, oilskins, and long boots." Many times Robert heard his father and uncles tell how "insinuatingly" Soutar had presented himself, "artfully combining the extreme of deference with a blunt and seamanlike demeanour." With the "devilish penetration of the boy," the youngsters had not been deceived, and his father got certain proof. "He had crept one rainy night into an apple-barrel on deck, and from this place of ambush overheard Soutar and a comrade conversing in their oilskins. The smooth sycophant of the cabin had wholly disappeared and the boy listened with wonder to a vulgar and truculent ruffian."

Certainly Soutar was in Robert Louis Stevenson's mind when he depicted Long John Silver's bluff yet deferential air at the beginning of the story, and also in his mind as he had Silver's mask of the sycophant drop to reveal the vulgarity and hostility beneath. Yet if these attributes fitted so easily into his character, they did so because Stevenson had already sensed—as he would confess years later when the rupture between them came—a similar duality in Henley, who *was* Long John Silver. By way of this conscious conviction that he was dealing only with the two faces of his grandfather's captain, Stevenson could begin coping with the negative qualities he was not yet ready to recognize in the beloved friend. If Henley had a single fault, it was that of speaking out loud whatever came into his mind, with no thought of consequences. Since Stevenson had brought Henley into his own circle of friends, he came naturally over the years to hear from them some of the reckless and destructive things that Henley—quite innocent of conscious malice—had said about him and, worse, about the woman he came to love. By way of dealing consciously with the easily recognizable duplicity in his grandfather's Captain Soutar, Stevenson could begin to cope unconsciously in his writing with the painful double-dealing of that dear friend and the suppressed memory of some of the things he had said. From the point in writing *Treasure Island* where Stevenson had Jim Hawkins in the apple barrel overhear Long John Silver, all that troubled him in Henley began to flow into his characterization of the pirate.

Of course, a murderous pirate bent on rapine goes far beyond the duplicity of a sea captain like Soutar, let alone of a poet and editor like Henley. Besides, in this aspect of his book Stevenson had chosen—in place of Skelt's juvenile pirates—the brutal reality of real pirates whom he had learned about by reading Captain Johnson's *General History of the Pirates.* From quotes in it of the court testimony of actual pirates declaring they would rather blow up the ship than "be hanged up a-sun-drying, as Kidd's and Braddish's company were," came Long John Silver's fear of being "hanged like a dog, and sun-dried" at Cape Corso Castle or of "drying in the sun at Execution Dock." If Stevenson emphasized this gruesome custom of chaining up hanged pirates to decay publicly on the gallows, he did so out of his real struggle against the fear of death, not out of his conscious aim to amuse a boy.

Stevenson was particularly impressed by Johnson's account of how pirates punished offenders among them by marooning them on desert islands. Out of it he created the marooned half-wit on the treasure island who helps Jim Hawkins to ultimate victory over the pirates. Even the name of this character, Ben Gunn, came from Captain Johnson. Actually "Captain Johnson" was in reality the pen name of Daniel Defoe, from whom Robert Louis Stevenson had also taken—so he said—the idea from *Robinson Crusoe* of giving a parrot companion to Long John Silver.

The nightmare island itself, as well as the main plot, Stevenson constructed largely out of hints he found in Charles Kingsley's *At Last: A Christmas in the West Indies.* According to Kingsley, the islands Columbus had piously named for Saint Ursula and her martyred maidens had been given such unholy names as "Rum Island" and "The Dead Man's Chest" by the pirates. "The seed" of his story—so Stevenson said—lay in that island called "The Dead Man's Chest," for it suggested to him the discovery of a map to a treasure island in the sea chest of a dead pirate. It is that island that appears in the capstan chanty Stevenson designed to ring through the whole book:

> Fifteen men on the dead man's chest—
> Yo-ho-ho, and a bottle of rum!
> Drink and the devil had done for the rest—
> Yo-ho-ho, and a bottle of rum!

As a proper name, "the dead man's chest" should be capitalized, and someday it will be, if ever *Treasure Island* is taken seriously enough to be edited properly. Until now, generations of children and adults, reading the chanty as published, have had, at worst, delirious visions of fifteen men crowded onto a corpse's thorax, or, at best, of fifteen men balancing on a small sea chest—raising the question of what on earth they could be doing there.

Stevenson's island takes carefully selected images of various West Indian islands in Kingsley's book. Stevenson took for it the weird conical hills and mountains prevalent throughout the volcanic West Indies, as well as the "sad and desolate" appearance of Antigua despite the "blue sea leaping around" it and the "blue sky blazing above." Especially he took Kingsley's horror of Trinidad with its whole southern corner "utterly pestilential" from the "sickly smell" of a great mangrove swamp, which, no matter how "gay and green" the mangrove leaves were, was a "sad, ugly, evil place," suggesting, Kingsley said, the need for quinine "or some other febrifuge." Robert Louis Stevenson had the *Hispaniola* anchor near a great mangrove swamp, so that the already mutinous pirates land and camp right at its edge. Dr. Livesey immediately recognizes the danger of "that abominable anchorage." He reports, "The nasty stench of the place turned me sick," for he smells in it "fever and dysentery." In no time the pirates camped near it have gone from a roaring delirium of drunkenness to a raving delirium of fever.

To these features, Stevenson added memories of a terrible fever of his own, just a year before, in California. He had fallen in love with an American, Mrs. Sam Osbourne, a woman twelve years his senior with an almost grown-up daughter and a son (the very boy for whom he was writing *Treasure Island*), and he had followed her to the United States to see her through a divorce from her estranged husband so that he could marry her. As they had no money (it was before *Dr. Jekyll and*

Mr. Hyde opened all American magazines to his work), he and Fanny Osbourne had been camping like gypsies in the California mountains. There Stevenson had gone into such severe hemorrhaging that, he later confessed, "It was a toss-up for life or death." The doctors thought it must be "a galloping consumption," for he suffered, he said, "cold sweats, prostrating attacks of cough, sinking fits in which I lost the power of speech, fever, and all the ugliest circumstances of the disease." Very naturally, the California setting of that life-and-death struggle surrounded the fight for life on the island of Jim Hawkins and his friends. The first plants Jim sees on this West Indian island are California live-oaks and pines, and the first animal, an indigenous American rattlesnake. The chief botanical freak of Stevenson's Caribbean island is the species of tree from which the location of the treasure is to be calculated. The idea for such a tree, Stevenson was quick to point out, came from Edgar Allan Poe's *The Gold Bug*, where an exceptionally tall tree—a tulip—is the point from which to work out the position of a buried pirate treasure. In *Treasure Island* the tree has a trunk like a "red column as big as a cottage" and throws such an enormous shadow that a company of soldiers could easily maneuver in it. Clearly Stevenson had transplanted a giant redwood from California to his island.

Except for "chic" touches from Kingsley, Stevenson knew that "the scenery is California," but he never saw its connection with his own suffering, any more than he realized what a heavy aura of sickness and mutilation had entered into all the events and characters of his story. Yet instinctively he made the most admirable adult of his book a medical doctor. Even the character's name, Dr. Livesey, suggests that he is on the side of life. Morally he towers over the other leading adults, Captain Smollett and Squire Trelawney. Trelawney is marred by an uncontrollable temper and a very loose tongue—Stevenson having thought of him as seasoned with "a strong dash" of Walter Savage Landor. Captain Smollett—despite his sterling integrity—makes himself very disagreeable to the men he leads. Only Dr. Livesey stands serenely above the nightmare, courageously risking his life to go about among the murderously mutinous pirates, binding up their wounds and slaking their fevers. Something of Henley's view of the great Dr. Joseph Lister in his hospital poem "The Chief" went into Dr. Livesey, so that Stevenson saw him as Henley did Lister, steady and unyielding in a struggle against disease and death and hell. The treachery of the pirates—as Stevenson himself pointed out—gives Dr. Livesey's unswerving humanity and courage a "proper chance" to be seen.

Jim Hawkins's direct fight against dangers outside him are redolent of Stevenson's memories of his fight against dangers within. Because Stevenson was in reality fighting disease, those dangers bear its image. When Jim finally catches the drifting *Hispaniola*, he finds two pirates—who had been knifing each other—in a pool of blood, one in rigor mortis and the other, the coxswain Israel Hands, virtually moribund and calling for brandy. Even after Jim has dosed him liberally with it, he still looks "very sick." With this living image of sickness, the boy fights for his life. Treacherously set upon by Hands with a bloody dirk, Jim is forced to fly like a "sheep before this butcher." In the end he has involuntarily killed the pirate when his pistols go off at the moment that the pirate's dirk has nailed him to the mast. As Jim tears himself free, the "hot blood" streams over his "back and chest" in a strange surrogate for Stevenson's hemorrhages, except that the blood runs down outside rather than internally.

The most formidable image of disease is the maimed Long John Silver with his amputated leg. Throughout *Treasure Island* he retains something of the impossible powers of the one-legged monster who haunted Jim Hawkins's dreams, although he alternates them with the reality of Henley's lameness. Reporting for duty, Long John Silver swarms up the side of the ship "like a monkey for cleverness." Yet he then rigs up—in clear imitation of Henley when he first set up house-keeping alone at Portobello—lines and loops of rope ("Long John's earrings") so that he can lift himself and hand himself across spaces. At the beginning of the mutiny, Henley's handicap disappears, and Long John Silver can leap back "with the speed and security of a trained gymnast," then, catching the branch of a tree, make a javelin throw of his crutch at a loyal sailor, fell him, and leap upon him "agile as a monkey" to finish him off with his knife. A little later, in the scene of his parley with Captain Smollett, Squire Trelawney, and Dr. Livesey, Silver is once again William Ernest Henley, whom it had been a business for Stevenson to get up and down the stairway of his Portobello lodging, who could barely struggle up out of a chair, and who was once "nearly burnt alive in his bed" when a cigarette set fire to the sheets. After the parley in *Treasure Island,* all are so repelled by the outrageous treachery of Long John Silver that no one will help him to rise from the sand. He is forced to crawl—as Henley would have been—swearing all the way, "till he got hold of the porch and could hoist himself again upon his crutch." Yet not long after, Stevenson again forgets Henley's disability and says that the seated "Silver suddenly sprang up." Silver's disability continues to come and go near the end of the book when the pirates set out to get the treasure taking the captive Jim Hawkins along on a leash. At one point, Silver is plowing, panting through the sliding gravel, and Jim has to "lend him a hand" so that he does not slip backward down the hill. At another, Silver is moving so fast that Jim stumbles, and Silver plucks furiously at the line by which he is held.

Stevenson was more sure of himself in depicting Henley's masterfulness. Many of the writers who worked with Henley on magazines have described his domineering ways. Max Beerbohm announced sardonically that Henley was "as much loved by all who know him as he is feared by all whom he knows." Henley always received, it was said, such service from the young men under his editorship as only "great captains" call forth. One of those young men, William Butler Yeats, reported that Henley could terrify outsiders. "He terrified us also and certainly I did not dare, and I think none of us dared, to speak our admiration for a book or picture he condemned, but he made us feel always our importance," and no one could work well "and lack his praise." Henley made them "accept him as our judge," Yeats said, and they knew "his judgment could neither sleep, nor be softened." Once Stevenson had captured those qualities in Long John Silver, he never again saw Henley as separate from that incarnation. Not long after, representing Henley as "Burly" in an essay "Talk and Talkers," Stevenson labeled him "boisterous and piratic," a "loud, copious, intolerant" talker, who could "roar you down" with "thunderclaps of contradiction." Yet Henley and his opponent would somehow end up "arm-in-arm, and in a glow of mutual admiration."

As for Long John Silver, Jim Hawkins sees that "the crew respected and even obeyed him." He has a special way of talking to each, bestowing praise and a sense of importance. At their first meeting, he tells Jim Hawkins that he can see he is "smart as paint." Soon after, Jim hears him from the apple barrel using the very same words "smart as paint" to flatter a recruit to the mutiny. When the pirates try to depose him, Long John Silver harangues them "with a vehemence that shook the house," so that he finishes up wiping the "sweat from his brow." He roars so loud at one point that Jim Hawkins sees him as "a lion." In the end, Silver not only argues the other pirates down on all points, but also he persuades them to reelect him captain, which they do enthusiastically, cheering, "Barbecue for ever! Barbecue for cap'n."

Even small traits of Henley invaded the pirate. Rarely did Henley appear without his pipe. Similarly, throughout his conflict with the pirates, Long John Silver takes a "fresh light to his pipe" or complains that his "pipe don't draw." Also, he is as boisterous with his gestures as with his words. Silver not only roars, but stumps up and down "slapping tables with his hand." When H. G. Wells was interviewed by that "old giant" Henley, he saw him emphasize his remarks "by clutching an agate paper-weight in his big freckled paw and banging it on his writing table." When Henley first received the manuscript of Rudyard Kipling's "Danny Deever," he had barely started reading it before he was "flinging himself about and shouting for joy." Also, after his hungry hospital years, Henley developed a passion for gourmet dining (which put considerable weight on him in later years). His sumptuous dinners for his friends at Solferino's restaurant became legendary. Similarly, Stevenson had Long John brag that, apart from the hardships of voyages, he has always "lived easy" and "ate dainty all my days."

Certainly much more of Henley went into Long John than his strength, courage, quickness, and geniality. Most particularly, Stevenson's growing doubts and distrust of Henley went into Silver. As soon as Jim Hawkins walks into captivity—his friends having abandoned the fort to the pirates—his life depends on Silver, who is playing a perilous double game. He saves Jim from murder by his fellow pirates because he wants to negotiate a rescue for himself if the boy's friends win. But, as Jim sees clearly, Silver will sacrifice him in an instant should that be to his advantage.

As far as Silver's life depends on Jim, the pirate is safe, for the boy refuses to run away when he has the chance, because "Silver trusted me; I passed my word, and back I go." But being "already doubly a traitor," Silver may go back on the boy at any second. So Jim feels torn. At one moment his "heart" is "sore" with anxiety at the dark future awaiting the pirate. At the next he is angered by his lurking treachery. Silver himself keeps changing. At one moment he is "beaming with good nature," and an instant later he darts such a "deadly look" at the boy that it becomes evident he will "cut every honest throat about that island."

The same ambivalence characterized Stevenson's feeling for Henley as he wrote, although he did his best to suppress all consciousness of it outside the safe limits of his boys' story. The tension in their friendship dated from the time Stevenson first fell in love with Fanny Osbourne. Stevenson's friends, and Henley most of all, had reacted with dismay at his choice of a woman twelve years his senior—a married woman with encumbrances, but even more, an American whose first act was to drag him out of his own country where he was gaining foothold as a writer and carry him off into a primitive wilderness at the opposite end of the world.

Henley could barely trust himself to write Stevenson, being, he said, "too blasphemously given towards California and California things"—meaning, of course, Fanny Osbourne. Both Henley and Colvin hoped only to get him back quickly. As Colvin put it, if without Mrs. Osbourne "so much the better; if with her, then as the best of a bad job." When Stevenson's ship finally docked at Liverpool, on August 17, 1880, Colvin was there to meet him, distressed to find him so thin "you could put your thumb and finger round his thigh," but glad to see that he was "at peace" in his marriage. Only, as Colvin wrote Henley, it was another question "whether you and I will ever get reconciled to the little determined brown face and white teeth and grizzling (for that's what it's up to) grizzling hair" of the little woman whom they would see by his side.

Actually, Colvin would be the first to become more than reconciled to, positively enthusiastic over Fanny. All his life, Stevenson had been acutely aware of "how dear a hope, how sorry a want" had been his longing for a devoted mother in his afflicted childhood. He had dedicated his *Child's Garden of Verses* not to his mother but to his nurse, Alison Cunningham, "Cummie," calling her his second mother, his first wife, the angel of his sick infancy. With Fanny he had them all in one person—mother, nurse, guardian angel, wife. Indeed, one of her difficult problems was to protect Stevenson, without antagonizing him or his parents, from his mother's and father's blindness to his fragility. Colvin declared: "If ever I am hung it will be for throttling Mrs. T.S. [Thomas Stevenson]." Stevenson's mother and father had "crushed and exhausted" him with a three-week visit. Henry James had been in "high indignation" with them after witnessing three days of it. His mother had ended by infecting him with an influenza she had gotten—although Fanny had begged her to keep her distance. Afterward Fanny wailed, "If Louis dies of this it will be murder."

Like his old nurse, "Cummie," Fanny was often up all night caring for him. At one point she reported, "My back is broken altogether," for she had "to lift Louis in and out of bed ten times in one night. He was quite off his head and could not be contradicted because he was bleeding at the lungs at the same time, and got into such furies when I wasn't quick enough." No wonder Stevenson—when out of delirium—declared his wife to be true as steel. The only person as careless as his mother of sparing Robert was his dear friend, that "dynamite explosion," as Fanny called him, Henley.

Later, Colvin explained, "For all his crippled bodily condition, Henley was in talk the most boisterously untiring, the lustiest and most stimulating of companions, and could never bring himself to observe the consideration due to Louis's frail health and impaired lungs." If Fanny warned Colvin that unrestrained talks with Stevenson were out because "a very little of that brings on either a haemorrhage or cold sweat," Colvin was quick to cooperate. But with Henley—as Colvin himself saw quickly—the restrictions were "resented," and later Colvin was sure that they "sowed the first seeds" of all the trouble between Henley and Stevenson.

These seeds grew in the following years to become full-blown by 1888, when Henley—with his usual reckless unawareness of what he was doing—sent a letter to Stevenson who was staying in a forest cabin above Saranac Lake in the Adirondacks. This letter—which became the last straw for Stevenson—had been set off by a short story Katherine de Mattos had written earlier and that Henley had tried to place for her. Fanny had suggested that the plot would be livelier if Katherine made the mysterious woman in her story a water sprite. Katherine rejected the suggestion altogether and then Fanny asked whether she could try it with the undine should Katherine's version fail. As Stevenson recalled, "Katherine even while she consented—as she did to me with her own lips—expressed unwillingness; I told my wife so, and I asked her to go no further. But she had taken a fancy to the idea, and when Katherine had tried her version and failed and wrote to tell us so, nothing would serve her but to act on this unwilling consent and try hers. Hers succeeded."

In his disastrous letter, Henley had told Stevenson: "I read 'The Nixie' with considerable amazement. It's Katherine's: surely it's Katherine's? The situation, the environment, the principal figure—*voyons*! There are even reminiscences of phrase and imagery, parallel incident—*que sais-je?* It is all better focused, no doubt; but I think it has lost as much (at least) as it has gained; and why there wasn't a double signature is what I've not been able to understand." Actually, Henley had written this whole letter out of lonely longing for Stevenson. Quite unaware of his real hostility to the American woman who had taken him so far away, Henley had asked Stevenson, "Why the devil do you go to bury yourself in that bloody country of dollars and spew?"

Horribly hurt, Stevenson complained to Charles Baxter: "Suppose that I am insane and have dreamed all that I seem to remember, and that my wife has shamefully stolen a story from my cousin, was this the class of matter that a friend would write to me?" As Stevenson saw it, "Either my wife is innocent, and then I suppose even my enemy would hold his peace? or she is guilty, and then, O surely almost my enemy would try to hide it from me!" Responding to Henley, Stevenson asked him to "remember how very rarely a husband is expected to receive such accusations against his wife." He was sure that Henley would, on thinking, "withdraw what you have said to me." They had been merely "reckless words," uttered with no "clear appreciation of their meaning." Only he wondered that a friend "should have been so careless of dealing agony."

In reply, Henley told Stevenson his letter was "heart-breaking," convicting him, as it did, "of a piece of real unkindness unworthy of myself and our old true friendship," and Henley assured Stevenson he had not "struck to hurt." "It is your mistake, dear lad, to imagine that I've ever been any other than your true friend and servant. Twice before (I want you to remember) you put this same charge upon me: each time, as you know, to my astonishment." Yet not a word of retracting the accusation did Henley say.

All Stevenson's long-suppressed distrust of Henley that had flowed so powerfully into *Treasure Island* now burst forth, and he told Baxter, "I knew long ago how Henley tried to make trouble for me, and I not only held my peace when I had the evidence, I willingly forgave also; for I understand all his nature, and much of it I love." Nothing, Stevenson knew, could "make him close his mouth, even when he knew he could hurt me sorely, even to the friends whom he knew I prized: to you I know not; to others I do know and have long buried the knowledge." Years back he had told Henley he wished "your honesty were not so warfaring," and urged him to consider that in a few years they would both be "clay-cold and safe below ground, you with your loudmouthed integrity, I with my fastidious briskness."

Now Stevenson saw Henley exactly as if he were Long John Silver, treacherously concocting mutiny—this time, not among the pirates on the *Hispaniola*, but in the heart of Stevenson's family. While Henley had edited the *London Magazine*, he had lived near Stevenson's cousins in Shepherd's Bush, and they had become thick as thieves. Now Henley and the cousins seemed to Stevenson exactly like the drunken and mutinying sailors of his book. He told Baxter, "There is not one of that crew that I have not helped in every kind of strait, with money, with service, and that I was not willing to risk my life for: and yet the years come, and every year there is a fresh outburst against me and mine." He had "forgiven and forgiven, and forgotten and forgotten, and still they get their heads together and there springs up a fresh enmity or a fresh accusation." Stevenson declared: "When they get together round the bowl, they brew for themselves hot heads and ugly feelings." Just so had he portrayed them—unaware—in the fractious pirates of the *Hispaniola*.

As their leader, Henley had "corridor'd, and stewed, and Shepherd Bushed" behind Stevenson's back. That whole "clique" had had nothing from him but money, yet here again "they have sprung up one of their little cabals in my absence." There had been "too much hole-and-cornering, and cliquing, and sweltering," and Henley had carried it on too long. Stevenson had been "nettled and worried for years by his strange attitude behind my back," and he was, he said, "weary of it all—weary, weary, weary."

All this suppressed knowledge had gone into the cabal of the money-hungry pirates in *Treasure Island*, and into the ambivalence of Jim Hawkins for the masterful force behind it all, Long John Silver. The same ambivalence was powerful in Stevenson when the final break came. He knew that he still did "care for Henley," for he could not forget "all his fine spirit and courage and geniality and loyalty—though to me, of these late days, he has not been loyal." He answered Baxter's declaration of affection for Henley: "Lord, man, I can't help loving him, either. I would give a leg that this were blotted out, and I could sit down with him, as of yore." No matter how he suffered over Henley's "willingness to seethe up against me and mine in my absence," he suffered more because the loss of Henley "makes a damned hole in my life; I am always thinking of things I want to say to him."

At the time Stevenson began *Treasure Island*, he had no idea how he was going to end it. But as his combined admiration and distrust took shape in the ambiguities of Long John Silver, so also did the only possible solution for that dangerous friendship. At the end of the book, "drink and the devil" have done for all the pirates except Long John and three others who are too vicious to be taken on board. Only Long John Silver is rescued as a reward for saving Jim Hawkins, and he seems "the same bland, polite, obsequious seaman of the voyage out." But he escapes at the first port of call, and does not go empty-handed, for he has taken a sack of coins worth 300 or 400 guineas. "I think we were all pleased to be so cheaply quit of him," Jim Hawkins says. At the end he is infinitely relieved to say, "That formidable seafaring man with one leg has at last gone clean out of my life."

Appropriately enough, Stevenson made the same provision for Henley when he broke with him forever that he had made for Silver in *Treasure Island*. He saw to it that Henley did not go out of his life empty-handed. He told Baxter: "I shall have to get you to give the poor creature an allowance, pretending that it comes from Hamilton Bruce—or anybody but me. Desert him I could not." Before the year was out, he was sending Baxter money for Henley, asking him please to "tak' the credit o't, like a wee man!" So Stevenson parted from Henley, secretly helping him, always wishing him well, but knowing through all the years that "time has not diminished my fear of him." In the end he could say only, as Jim Hawkins might have, "I cannot describe the sense of relief and sorrow with which I feel I am done with him. No better company on God's earth, and in some ways a fine fellow, a very fine one." Although Robert Louis Stevenson's past had been full of Henley's "big presence and his welcome wooden footstep," Stevenson wanted no more. "Let it be a past henceforward; a beloved past, without continuation."

By way of *Treasure Island* and its ambiguous main figure Long John Silver, Stevenson had faced and forecast the inevitable resolution for his ambivalent closeness to Henley, who had fought the same battle against disease and fear that he had. Long John Silver shares with Jim Hawkins the chief struggle and victory in *Treasure Island*, and he goes off into a lifetime happy ending accompanied by his loyal wife, who is a "woman of colour," and his parrot. Jim Hawkins has an equally happy ending, liberated from his "dark and bloody sojourn" on "that accursed island," and liberated as well from the admirable but dangerous hero-villain of that sojourn.

Silver is a minor partner in the victory that Jim Hawkins wins, and the victory a reader of the novel wins with them—a victory over the fear of death. However redolent of fever, nightmare, pain, and blood, the story, the boy in it, rises above them. An adult reader faces with him the authentic horror conjured out of Stevenson's real battle, and triumphs, as Stevenson had, over it. W. B. Yeats told Stevenson that *Treasure Island* was one of the very few books his seafaring grandfather would read, and that he read it over again "upon his death-bed with infinite satisfaction." As for Stevenson, he brought himself by way of writing it to the total acceptance of the human condition that he would express soon after in his poem "Requiem." Gladly would he live, and gladly die and, when the time came, lie down most willingly.

No one could offer a greater contrast to Mann than Robert Louis Stevenson in the degree to which he remained unconscious of the creative process within him. Of course, Stevenson was perfectly conscious of his readings for *Treasure Island*, of his delight as a child in playing pirates, and of the fact that he was choosing in this book to play pirates with his dear friend William Ernest Henley. He was equally aware that he wanted the story both to please his stepson and to earn the money he needed to support his wife and her children. Beyond that, Stevenson remained oblivious to all that impelled him to write as he did and to all that impelled him to a joyous confrontation of external dangers in actual life or in the events of his fiction.

He had no conscious awareness of the inner battle he had been fighting throughout his childhood and was fighting against the real but intangible threat of death implicit in the fevers, deliriums, and perpetual lung hemorrhaging he was being assaulted by even as he wrote *Treasure Island*. The entire blend of nightmare memories that gave a mythical horror to the mutilated men of his story and to the catastrophic fever-ridden island where the treasure was buried remained for him a mysterious unexamined force. Also outside of his own awareness was the way in which his suppressed distrust of his beloved friend Henley, who had fought the same life-and-death battle as he had from childhood on, lent to Long John Silver the aura of ambivalence that gave him his large significance and fascination. Similarly unconscious for Stevenson was the process by which he foresaw and found through his characters the ultimate solution he would have to reach for that troubled friendship.

If—viewed through the whole of his life's work—Robert Louis Stevenson appears as a remarkably uneven writer, with peaks of greatness and sloughs of superficiality, the cause probably lies in the immense gap between his immediate conscious motives and the forces within him that lent validity, magic, and suggestive power to one work while keeping almost entirely absent from another. The greatness or mediocrity of what Stevenson wrote had nothing to do with his immediate rational aims. They depended on the extent to which his choice of theme opened up his psychological past and allowed him to cope with all his unresolved tensions, defenses, and hungers, without realizing that he was doing so.

Works like *Kidnapped* were transformed by the same inner need to confront danger and death that created the magic of *Treasure Island*.

Anything that awakened Stevenson's peculiarly Scotch sense of imminent evil, bred into him by childhood indoctrination in the primeval guilt and universal damnation of mankind, allowed him to write impressive works such as *The Merry Men, Thrawn Janet,* and *The Master of Ballantrae.* On the other hand, works such as his collaborations with his stepson Lloyd Osbourne never allowed Stevenson's transforming inner needs scope to work enchantment at all. So the blending of memories that gave splendor and symbolic significance to works like *Treasure Island* never raised them over the limited rational schemes that gave them birth. Only when the theme he found allowed him to resolve a major life-problem through a blend of memories, could Stevenson achieve the works that rendered him immortal.

3

FitzOmar: Live Eagle

One of the most widely read and lovingly quoted poems in the English language has for many decades been shut out of a place in English literature. In part, the fault lay in our uncertainty about what is great or original in art. Certainly Edward FitzGerald could not have written the *Rubáiyát of Omar Khayyám*, had he not learned Persian and read the epigrams of the eleventh-century Persian poet (also astronomer and mathematician) Omar Khayyám, but neither could Shakespeare have written *Macbeth* or *Anthony and Cleopatra* had he not read Holinshed and Plutarch. In recent years, anthologies of English literature have accepted the *Rubáiyát* as a native poem, but it also appears in world literature collections as a translation from the Persian. Can a translation transcend translations and become a great work of art? Even more of a question is what happened to FitzGerald—in this single notable work of a lifetime—to lift him, for one brief year among the gods.

The Life

Coming as he did out of the conventionality of a very rich Anglo-Irish family, originality was not what one would expect from FitzGerald. His mother, Mary Frances FitzGerald, was thought to be the wealthiest commoner in England—so much land and money had she inherited by her father's death, and it all came to her, for her older brother had died early and childless. Although rich in his own right, Henry Purcell, the first cousin she married, then took her name, FitzGerald, and she—with her striking beauty, her cleverness, and all that financial power—developed imperial ways. One of her eight children (five girls and three boys) recalled that their early life was made up of "extreme discipline and entire obedience." Edward FitzGerald remembered that his mother would come up from time to time to their nursery, "and we children were not much comforted." He would look up into his mother's beautiful face as a boy and wonder what in it gave away the not-so-beautiful aspects of her character. He decided that it might be a certain kink in her lips, "like that in—the tail of a cat!"

Talking about Richardson's tragic heroine Clarissa Harlowe, whose tyrannical parents had driven her into the power of a clever rake, FitzGerald declared that this "notoriously moral" story set at least one Frenchman to imitating the witty seducer, whom he took for the hero of the book. Similarly, "My mother read assiduously: and imitated the parents very effectually." Once, during his happy Cambridge days, FitzGerald's mother turned up unexpectedly at his college and sent for him. Panicking, FitzGerald sent his lackey to say that he could not come because his boots were all at the cobbler's. Of course, she insisted, and he came—in borrowed boots, or so he said. After his graduation, he made one heroic effort to pit his will against hers. The entire family was thrown into convulsions by it, so that his father—usually a beloved ally—declared that he was reducing his allowance from £300 to £200. This "wretched policy" to force him "to succumb to my mother," FitzGerald confided to his dear friend John Allen, defeated itself, for it showed to "what a stretch" his father was put. FitzGerald took refuge with his married sister Eleanor Kerrich, at Geldestone Hall, Beccles, the chief member of his family—so he said long afterward—whom "I cared much for, or who cared much for me."

Friendly advice induced him to submit, and he never again lifted his head in revolt. Instead he settled into the job—luckily part-time—of enforced Cicisbeo to his mother, for she demanded a male escort at all times in the absence of her husband, and her husband was often away at Manchester in his Pendleton Colliery, into which he had invested all of his own money, or with an opera dancer he kept.

In his days of liberty, FitzGerald lived the modest life he chose of friends, books, art, and music in his own humble lodgings on Charlotte Street. Otherwise, he was "pressed" into service at the majestic family town house on nearby Portland Place for his mother's sumptuous dinner parties. (Fanny Kemble recalled the gold dessert plates.) He also had to escort his mother to one high-society dinner party after another. The only two he ever liked were small parties given by the illustrious acting family, the Kembles—his mother having a passion for the theater. Edward's friend, William Bodham Donne, said that in his "state of innocence," FitzGerald had some of the "inconveniences" of marriage, not the least of them "accompanying Mrs. FitzGerald the round of the theatres."

She had a box on the third tier at the Haymarket Opera House, where she was often seen in a blaze of diamonds with her son Edward. Fashionable Brighton was also one of her places. Edward's friend William Makepeace Thackeray watched her come dashing into Brighton in her great coach drawn by four black horses and saw "an army of flunkies and lady's maids" unloading "mysterious" piles of luggage. Being young and impecunious, Thackeray thought: "There's a prospect of good dinners!" FitzGerald's letters relate incessant orders for him to appear at London or Brighton. One year he had to cancel his lodgings at Cambridge at a moment's notice because "my mother wants a gentleman at Brighton." In the end, FitzGerald decided that Brighton was the "hatefullest of all places," caught as he was there with the "roaring unsophisticated ocean" to one side of him, and four miles of "idle, useless, ornamental population" to the other.

Late in life, FitzGerald inherited a sketch of his mother by Sir Thomas Lawrence, which, he thought, bore an unnerving resemblance to the Duke of Wellington. The portrait ended up, "for want of room" (so FitzGerald said) shut up in a cupboard. In her last years, FitzGerald once confided, apropos of going to the opera with his mother one evening, "We get on very well together, by help of meeting very little."

If Edward FitzGerald became an affectionate friend, beloved by a wide circle of distinguished persons, he owed it to his father's warm heart. When in trouble, his sisters would rush to their father's arms, not their mother's, for comfort. As a small boy, Edward had his first real appreciation from his father, who wrote back from France that "little Edward" was keeping the entire party in good spirits "by his unfailing fun and droll speeches."

From among the "almost obliterated" slides of the "old magic lantern," FitzGerald remembered looking down from the nursery window of their mansion at Bredfield at his handsome father and Squire Jenney below on the lawn, surrounded by a yapping pack of harriers, about to set forth for the hunt. He also never forgot his father, resplendent in the uniform of "Lieutenant-Colonel in the Volunteers," or majestic as High Sheriff of Suffolk and Waterford, and as Member of Parliament for Seaford, Sussex (until the Reform Bill of 1832 knocked out his pocket borough). For eighteen years his father had been so busy as director of the Pendleton Colliery Company that Edward, when he came of age, took over from him the job of supervising the harvests on various of the other family estates.

Edward was also official escort to his sisters. As William Bodham Donne once reported, "Fitz" was "when he left me, under marching orders for Hastings to convoy certain sisters." One of FitzGerald's indelible memories was of coming up from Cambridge to London on the night mail coach, his head whirling with visions of medieval funerals from hearing Alfred Tennyson read him his latest poem, "The Lady of Shalott." At London, FitzGerald heard "wretched news" and was sent "upon an errand that has left its black mark upon me while I live." His next favorite sister to Eleanor, Andalusia, then a beautiful nineteen-year-old, had just had her first fall into the episodic psychosis that would, at intervals, darken her family's life, and Edward had been sent to her assistance. On more cheerful occasions, he was glad to join his sisters and his father. In 1842 he wrote Frederick Tennyson: "My father proposes to spend all next winter in London with my sisters: if he does, I shall certainly be here." He was always happy surrounded by the twelve children of his sister Eleanor Kerrich.

With all his admiration of his father, FitzGerald actually had more in common with his mother. When not in her service, he went right on "theatricalizing" by choice, except that he would take a seat in the pit, not a box. In his old age he became positively sentimental over seeing his mother's former box in the "dear old Haymarket Opera," and recalling the "grandeur" of Madame Pasta in Cherubini's *Medea*. His mother had loved literature too. Later he remarked that he had never known a woman who liked the poet Crabbe, "except my mother." One of his labors of love was an editorial job with scissors and paste on Crabbe's *Tales of the Hall*, to free the brilliant poetry from the dead wood. When the family stayed at Boulge Hall, Woodbridge, his mother often had the local Quaker poet, Bernard Barton, to dinner. FitzGerald made a lifelong friend of him. While his mother was living, FitzGerald was distressed to learn that Barton had read her some of her son's verses. He expostulated, "My dear fellow! You have no idea what FitzGeralds are."

He shrank from her penchant to push him into the limelight, for he had founded his poetry—his whole life—on a rejection of his mother's display. He said that books had given him "better idols than love of wealth and splendour and gentility." At twenty-one, he was already confiding to John Allen that he had "got all sorts of Utopian ideas into my head about society," but as he tried "the experiment" only on himself, he could do "no great hurt." He believed in living modestly. He always preferred "a little absurd lodging" to a "grave house" and spent his life in two or three rented London rooms during the winter. In the warm months, he took a thatched cottage at the outskirts of the family lands at Boulge Hall, Woodbridge, Suffolk, living in three rooms and leaving the rest for his housekeeper and her husband, the gardener on the estate. He even patched up the cottage so that he could stay there in winter when he wished. One December he wrote Frederick Tennyson that he seemed to have a "talent for dullness": "I really do like to sit in this doleful place with a good fire, a cat and a dog on the rug, and an old woman in the kitchen." Later, there were years when he had winter rooms at Woodbridge or Lowestoft and spent at least half the year sleeping in the cabin and living on the deck of his small boat.

When he could, he discarded upper-class formal dress. In his cottage he had only "smooth sailing," he told Frederick Tennyson, "No velvet waistcoat and ever-lustrous pumps to be considered; no bon mots got up." He liked to fling his "branches about him" naturally in conversation, instead of being "stretched on the espalier of London dinner-table company." After his mother's death, FitzGerald never again accepted a formal dinner engagement or wore formal dress. He liked a smoking party with two or three friends, to whom he served modest suppers of roast fowls and salad. When alone, he ate vegetables and bread and cheese. He did indulge a delight in going to auctions and pawnbroker's shops in London, buying for a few pounds, as one could then do, original masterpieces by painters such as Constable, Reynolds, Opie, and Crome. No matter how fine he thought the picture, he never went above a few pounds. Otherwise he believed in giving—and he gave—a good part of his income away to people who needed it more than he did.

He helped artists and writers, subsidizing with a regular pension Thackeray and Alfred Tennyson in their needy years. When Tennyson was finally awarded a Civil List pension, in spite of upper-class objections, he told FitzGerald that he knew him to be "one of those few friends who would still stick to me tho' the whole polite world with its great idiot mouth" were howling at him. FitzGerald also filled out Bernard Barton's small pension with weekly payments, and, with two others, supported the elderly Ipswich artist G. J. Rowe. He was always commissioning Samuel Laurence to do oil sketches of his friends, as well as finding other patrons for him, and he did the same for other artists such as Perry Nursey and Morris Moore and Thomas Churchyard. At the time of his death, FitzGerald was supporting a list of indigent old people in the Woodbridge area, for he left instructions in his will for their continuing care. He also was always finding jobs for people. Once when Bernard Barton had helped him to find a "situation" for a needy woman, FitzGerald said that if he had an offer from the powers that be "to write another *Iliad*" or to live his life in the "daily remembrance of such small charities, I should not hesitate which to choose."

He also spread enjoyment. His nephew, John de Soyres, Andalusia's son, told of how Uncle Edward would send "us little ones" into convulsions of laughter by his stories. A friend's child recalled that with FitzGerald at their dinner table, telling stories, the servants waiting on them would have to rush from the dining room so as not to disgrace themselves by bursting into laughter along with the family. After one of FitzGerald's visits to the Alfred Tennysons, Mrs. Tennyson declared that he had been "in delightful spirits and as amusing as man could be." He needed no entertaining, taking long walks over the hills and coming back with sketches, rare wild flowers, and bits of petrified wood. In the evenings "he would sit down to the piano and play one glorious air after the other." Sometimes he was enlisted to assist at rent-dinners by old Squire Jenney who—FitzGerald told Thackeray—"persists in thinking I can help to entertain the farmers."

James Spedding considered FitzGerald the "Prince of Quietists": "Half the self-sacrifice, the self-denial, the moral resolution, which he exercises to keep himself easy, would amply furnish forth a martyr or a missionary," Spedding decided. FitzGerald was a "most comfortable companion," for he made everyone else as "tranquil" as he was. He could even soothe Thomas Carlyle. After one evening in Chelsea with Carlyle fulminating away, FitzGerald was "delighted to get out into the street." Late as it was, an organ grinder was playing a polka, and—so FitzGerald reported—Carlyle was "amazed to see me polka down the pavement. He shut his street door—to which he always accompanies you—with a kind of groan."

If he was able, as he put it, to "sport a gentle Epicurism," FitzGerald could do so, as Spedding had perceived, only through "moral resolution." For he had suffered. As a young man, he had gone through severe "religious wanderings and despondencies" that were "very frequent and very distressing." He had been torn between "belief and disbelief." His brother Peter, who farmed their Irish lands, had converted to the majority religion of that country, Roman Catholicism. His oldest brother, John (heir to the estates)—prevented by poor eyesight from becoming a Church of England clergyman—had become an evangelical lay preacher (to the "eccentric" extent of delivering sermons on street corners and baptizing people in the Naseby reservoir).

FitzGerald's problem was that he could not believe literally in the Bible, even though he agreed with the "Exeter Hall war-cry," "The Bible—the whole Bible—and nothing but the Bible," because he did admire and believe in the ethics of the New Testament. Struggling to accept, he could tell his priest friend John Allen, "I may truly say that I improve every day in works, if not in belief and words." To all the theological theorists, he found he preferred the simple "commands of our Saviour. Who can say anything new after him?" But he wanted evidence to accept anything beyond them. He said that if anyone could prove to him that "one miracle took place," he would believe that "he is a just God who damned us all" because a woman ate an apple. He had been swept off his feet by "bare science," which he saw unrolling a "greater epic than the *Iliad*," in the "infinitudes of space and time!" Lyell's revelations of geological processes over immense sweeps of time, and of all the evidences in the rocks that there were "beasts and strange creatures acting and plunging about before *men*; and the fabric of earth rolling round the sun before beasts were," he found "wonderful, grand, and awful." He saw no end "to looking into this vista." Yet he went on believing in Christian ethics. When Carlyle wrote him about the essential goodness of the people of Derbyshire, coming out of the "funded virtues of many good humble men gone by," FitzGerald answered that Carlyle ought to have some mercy on what he called the "Hebrew rags," which had bound those virtues together, and he might even put up with "some absurdities in the form," for the sake of the spirit.

In spite of doubts, FitzGerald went on attending Church of England services, as his letters show. One Sunday—so he later wrote W. F. Pollock—"I mislaid this sheet in rushing off in a hurry—to church—not to where you supposed." In another letter, he told Frederick Tennyson he was bolting off for gloves, hat, and prayerbook, and added: "I always put on my thickest great-coat to go to our church in: as fungi grow in great numbers about the communion table." The next winter he talked of the morning church service, "where every one sat with a purple nose, and heard a dismal well-meant sermon." Even in the early 1850s he was meeting Frederick Tennyson at Richmond to take him to a chapel "where a good little man holds out."

When he learned from William Bodham Donne that a friend of theirs was about to be "m—rr—d," FitzGerald wrote W. H. Thompson asking, "When are you to be so, Thompson? I am sure you will be: for every man who is worth anything gets married when he can." By this time FitzGerald had himself come close to marrying, for during 1835 he had come to know—by way of his sisters—Elizabeth Charlesworth, daughter of the Reverend John Charlesworth at Bramford, very near Woodbridge. He told Thackeray that he was on the brink of asking a "plain, sensible girl, without a farthing" to marry him and wanted advice. But instantly he added that he would be "poor as a rat" and that he could no longer rattle merrily over to Paris "to see thee, old Will." Besides, the girl might not have him, for her family was "very strict in religion" and thought him "something of a pagan." Anyway, Thackeray would certainly not be for it: he would "hate to stay with me and my spouse, dining off a mutton chop, and a draught of sour, thin beer, in a clay-cold country."

A few months later, on February 4, 1836, FitzGerald wrote John Allen from Boulge Hall that the "young damsel" he had talked so much about had been staying with his sisters for the last fortnight and that he liked her "more than ever." She was "very pious, but very rational," with wonderful "sense and clearsightedness." She was "healthy, and stout, and a good walker, and a gardener, and fond of the country," and she thought everything beautiful, and could "jump over stiles with the nimblest modesty that ever was seen." She had the virtues of eating very little meat, drinking no wine, and understanding "good housekeeping" and children. But that made him wonder: "Should I dance round my room to the tune of Sir Roger de Coverley if I were married, and had seven children?" Eight years later, in 1844, he was referring to Elizabeth Charlesworth in a letter to Carlyle as the "famous girl (now 30) with whom I used to be slightly in love as I supposed."

Actually FitzGerald lacked the needed push of sexual desire to move beyond affection to marriage. In this particular period when homoerotic acts in England were seen not only as criminal but also as unspeakable, any proclivities in that direction usually remained—as they did for FitzGerald—perfectly unconscious. In effect, he was completely paralyzed by the conflict within him of contradictory directives. Realizing that he could not bring himself to marry, FitzGerald decided to "wrap myself round with the domestic affections of brothers and sisters and nephews and nieces." Besides, his friendships had always been "more like loves." At least once a year he would make a pilgrimage through England visiting in turn all his dear ones. It was during one of these pilgrimages, on the boat from Bristol to Tenby, Wales, late in August 1832, that he met the friend who became dearest of them all. FitzGerald had taken lodgings with two bedrooms at Rees's boardinghouse at Tenby so that his friend John Allen could join him there. On the packet, FitzGerald, then twenty-three, made friends with a sixteen-year-old boy, William Kenworthy Browne, who turned out to have rooms at Rees's too, so that the next morning and all the days after, Browne would appear, usually "with a little *chalk* on the edge of his cheek from a touch of the billiard table cue." From that time began the exchange of visits between them, Browne coming during the winter to take a room at FitzGerald's lodgings in London, and FitzGerald coming to Browne at Bedford beside the Ouse River for the summer.

Now that Thackeray was married—so FitzGerald told him—he could no longer write him persiflage, so he saved his nonsense for Browne, to whom he had written a circumstantial account of having just proposed to a young lady. Browne was sure to be taken in, and FitzGerald was looking forward to the letter of congratulations he would write. "You don't know what a good boy he is," FitzGerald said. He thought that perhaps the better English virtues had slipped away from the aristocracy and settled among the outside-of-London trading classes, from which Browne came. At eighteen, Browne was "quick to love and quick to fight—full of confidence, generosity, and the glorious spirit of youth."

By 1838, FitzGerald was telling Bernard Barton, "I am much in love with Bedfordshire." He had spent a "delicious" time there with "such weather, such meadows to enjoy; and the Ouse still wandering along at his ease through pretty villages and vales of his own beautifying." So pleasant was it that FitzGerald extended it by bringing Browne with him from Bedford to Lowestoft, with a "great black dog" named Bletsoe that Browne had given him. FitzGerald wrote John Allen that they were teaching the dog to fetch and carry, "playing with our neighbour's children, doing the first five propositions of Euclid (which *I* am teaching him!), shooting gulls on shore, going out in boats, etc." The happier he was with Browne, "the sorrier I am to leave him." Already his enjoyment was "darkened by the anticipation of his going." He told Allen he had thought once or twice "how equally happy I was with you by the sea-side in Tenby. You and Browne (though in rather different ways) have certainly made me more happy than any men living." To W. B. Donne—who was more likely to appreciate a joke than the serious preacher, Allen—FitzGerald sent a long paper with six lines of writing from Lowestoft, which instead of words, Donne reported, had something that looked like "an exercise in punctuation," all question marks, exclamation points, and semicolons.

In the spring of 1839 the huntsman Browne—his "Venator," FitzGerald called him—was staying with FitzGerald among the buttercups at Woodbridge, shooting "rooks and rabbits" and training dogs and horses. FitzGerald was again with Browne at Bedford in July, at his parents' house and garden, skirted by a "row of such poplars as only the Ouse knows how to rear—and pleasantly they rustle now," and he was writing a letter in a cool room opening into a greenhouse that led to the garden. In half an hour he would "seek my Piscator, and we shall go to a village two miles off and fish, and have tea in a pot-house, and so walk home."

To W. F. Pollock he reported that he had been in his "dear old Bedfordshire" that summer, "lounging in the country, lying on the banks of the Ouse, smoking, eating copious teas (prefaced with beer) in the country pot-houses," so that afterward he felt quite in "mourning" with "no river Ouse, and no jolly boy to whistle the time away with." In October he was taking Browne with him to Ireland to visit his uncle Peter Purcell at Halverstown, County Kildare. So the years went by and every summer FitzGerald was to be found "with a book and a colour-box by the side of the river Ouse" fishing with Browne, who was always the "best of good fellows, and absolutely wanting in nothing that may become a man."

When Browne's "screw of a father" was sending him off to be surveyor of taxes in Carlisle, FitzGerald mourned that there would be no one to call him "to the dear old Ouse—bless its idle windings." He felt that he could "cry, and spit in the face of old Browne at the same time." Instead, young Browne never did go to Carlisle, and FitzGerald became a close confederate of "old Browne." Clearly FitzGerald had solved the problem by subsidizing young Browne so that he could find his way in Bedford. By 1842, FitzGerald had involved both Brownes in his picture-buying hobby, for he said in one letter that "Mr. Browne the elder (long life to him!)" had stayed with him in London and "was pleased to express himself laudatorily of my Opie Fruit Girl." In another letter he said that young Browne, staying with him in London, had just bought a fine Venetian painting for £7 that came with a "most splendid carved frame that must have cost £80." By this time Browne was no longer a boy but a "whiskered man," a "man of business, of town-politics." Indeed, by the spring of 1844 Browne needed no subsidizing, for he was about to marry Elizabeth Elliot of Bedford, a very well-to-do young woman, and when FitzGerald learned "that they could not have less than five hundred a year, I gave up all further interest in the matter: for I could not wish a reasonable couple more."

He was apprehensive that "now my old summer swallow is going to pair off," and what with a "wife's hatred of the particular friend" he would have to lay by "my rod and line by the willows of the Ouse for ever." But Mrs. Browne turned out to be a "very good, quiet, unaffected, sensible little woman" and Browne "really domestic," so that their friendship and the old exchange of visits continued, as Browne became the "good Alderman Browne" and then "Captain Browne" in the militia, so that with his hunting, his farming, his business, his community service, his politics, he really became the image of Edward's father, as he had been in Edward's boyhood. Browne was "farmer, magistrate, militia officer—father of a family—of more use in a week than I in my life long," FitzGerald declared.

In admiration, FitzGerald wrote a song, taking the music from an old German melody. "Knowst Thou an Isle?" combined a tribute to England with a tribute to Browne as the best kind of Englishman. The island of the song, with its white walls rising out of the sea and its brave sons defending its ancient liberties, is unmistakably England. The second verse, specifying a "vale" within this isle "where poplars sigh beside a winding stream," clearly describes Browne's garden with its row of "such poplars as only the Ouse knows how to rear." So the refrain line about how this is the place where living he would be, "And, dying my Beloved, rest with thee!" expresses his love for living beside Browne in the valley of the Ouse, and his wish to rest beside him in death. This song—which they both sang, either solo or in duet, as they lay fishing on the brink of the Ouse or picnicking in its meadows—came to be associated inextricably with all those days, year after year, of happiness.

The Catastrophe

Into this easy life, which had given FitzGerald—as he himself said—neither the "strong inward call, nor the cruel-sweet pangs of parturition" that bring forth anything "bigger than a mouse," fell the disaster that transformed FitzGerald into a real poet. It came as part of an extraordinary chain of circumstances that actually gave time enough, a good seven years, for him to acquire the necessary knowledge of Persian that could join with his fine critical judgment and his experience in writing and compressing verse, so that he could answer the strong call for real creation when it came.

The disaster struck him in 1849. The reprieve—which kept the axe from falling until 1856—came by way of the sudden loss of his income in 1848. His father's affairs had already become desperate by September 1843. The colliery had suffered losses from runaway agents, and instead of drawing in, old FitzGerald had expanded. Tunneling into new land, he struck an underground stream, so that he was, as Edward put it, "drowned out" by an "influx of waters": "So end the hopes of eighteen years; and he is near seventy, left without his only hobby!"

By June 1848 his "poor father's affairs" had reached the "worst confusion," and he was bankrupt, his income in the hands of his creditors. The money being entailed, all his children were creditors, and Edward, who had lived on the interest of his share, was suddenly bereft—with his brothers and sisters—of an income. Luckily his mother's immense fortune was legally protected from involvement in the bankruptcy, so that when she died all her children would again be wealthy. With the help of his friend William Kenworthy Browne, Edward set about arranging an annuity on "literally iniquitous terms" for the reversionary interest in that money. He suffered, not for the money loss but for his father's tragedy, which led within a year of his bankruptcy to separation from his wife, then sickness, and then his death on March 18, 1852. FitzGerald thought him dead like "poor old Sedley in Thackeray's *Vanity Fair*, all his coal schemes at an end." It was this state of affairs—the removal of his income and his having to live on borrowed money—that gave him the respite of seven years, so that when the catastrophe of his life was precipitated in 1849 it did not fall full upon him until 1856.

FitzGerald was trapped by his own kindness and pity. His friend, the elderly Quaker poet Bernard Barton, died of a heart attack in 1849. A few years before that, FitzGerald had commissioned Samuel Laurence to do a portrait of Barton, telling him that the poet was a "generous, worthy, simple-hearted fellow: worth ten thousand better wits." Barton would be at his cottage waiting for them, FitzGerald instructed Laurence, with the tea laid out and "Miss about to manage the urn; plain, agreeable people." "Miss" was Barton's daughter and housekeeper, a big raw-boned woman a few months older than FitzGerald (who himself was six feet tall and weighed 14 stone—that is, 196 pounds). Lucy Barton had been teaching her own Church of England Sunday school for years, her grandmother having had her educated in that religion, rather than her father's Quakerism. With his habitual kindness, FitzGerald had helped her with her *Bible Stories for Children,* and perhaps she leapt to certain hopes from that, for in March 1847 Bernard Barton told W. B. Donne that as return for FitzGerald's gifts to her father, Lucy "all unknown to me" had knitted a silk purse for FitzGerald, of which Barton thought the chances were a "hundred to one he will never use."

After Barton's funeral, FitzGerald helped Miss Barton go through her father's papers, more "because it amused her, poor thing, to turn over all these things with one so intimate with her father," than because he thought anything could come of it. In order to put some pounds in her pocket, he set about making a selection of Barton's poetry and solicited his many friends to subscribe and get others to subscribe to it. As he told Richard Monckton Milnes, Barton had left his daughter "very slenderly provided for, I doubt. She always behaved very nobly to him: only caring for his comfort, without looking to her own future."

The work of editing came easily to FitzGerald. All the years of his life he had been reading poetry critically and amusing himself by improving it with big cuts and little interpolations. Out of Barton's nine volumes of poetry, FitzGerald produced two hundred pages, sometimes taking half a poem, sometimes taking a few stanzas from several and dovetailing them together, changing a word or even a line "to give them logic and fluency." He cut all the "diffuse and weary" passages and the repetitions, distilling "many pretty little poems out of long dull ones which the world has discarded." He did not pretend to be a poet, he said, but he thought he had "faculty enough to mend some of B.B.'s dropped stitches." Although he got Miss Barton to put her name to the book as editor, he ended by doing everything, including writing a memoir of Barton and proofreading the book, for Miss Barton was too "bothered and bewildered" with selling all her furniture by auction, "poor thing," and preparing to go as governess to the family at Norfolk of Hudson Gurney, a wealthy Norwich banker. FitzGerald thought it "noble" of her to insist on paying her father's debts and was glad that the book would virtually "clear" them. (Although he thought Barton's pious poems a "kind of elder nursery rhymes," he was sure no one would be the worse for them.) In fact, the subscription edition did so well that the publishers wanted to reprint it, and FitzGerald advised Miss Barton on arranging it so as to keep "out of all risk."

In the end the only risk had been his own. The danger of giving all that pity and admiration of Miss Barton's nobility did not become clear until he found himself—entirely contrary to his wishes—committed to marry Miss Barton when he should come into his share of the family fortune at his mother's death. So he emerged from his good deed with an axe hanging over his head, and in the following years, whenever he met Lucy Barton, he would try earnestly to persuade her that he was not made for marriage. Undeterred, she would defend him staunchly against his self-deprecation. Not for an instant did she suspect that all this talk meant that he wanted desperately to escape marrying her.

To no one did he reveal his predicament. It must have been in the summer of 1850 that he fell fully into it, for at that point a profound gloom creeps into his formerly cheerful letters, and he hints darkly at a threat hanging over him. Also he suddenly, very belatedly, becomes filled with regret that he had never married Elizabeth Charlesworth, for if he had he would never have been threatened with Lucy Barton. Elizabeth, at this point, was not to be had, for in 1845 a nineteen-year-old prodigy named Edward Byles Cowell, brought up as a merchant and working in a countinghouse, but already a self-taught master of a number of languages—Latin, Spanish, and Arabic, Sanscrit, and Persian among them—became a visitor at the Reverend Charlesworth's household and quickly became engaged to the thirty-three-year-old Elizabeth. Learning of it, FitzGerald wrote him: "You are a happy man and I envy you." As soon as she was safely married to Cowell in 1847, FitzGerald consolidated a friendship with Cowell and his lady, which developed, with the Barton threat, into a postmortem love affair on his part, full of romantic regret over the married woman he had allowed to slip through his fingers.

He sent Cowell one of Petrarch's sonnets to Laura in its original Italian telling of how the gleam of Laura's golden hair and the radiance of her angel's smile—which had once transformed earth into paradise for him—were now merely a handful of dust. Lovely as the sonnet was, FitzGerald suspected that Cowell would not care much for the love in it. He himself could care only for a love that was past in time and hope, which, he told Cowell, "makes me spoonily like spooney Petrarch." To Frederick Tennyson, with whom he had visited Elizabeth Cowell, FitzGerald wrote such a despairing letter that Tennyson wondered if he meant to drown himself. FitzGerald explained that the letter had acted as a safety valve for his "poor flame when sitting in the clean cheerful little parlour of that 'delightful grey-haired quadragenerial,' as you call her." He added that "not the loss of her alone" made him "hate myself for a fool, but other contingencies which may flourish into worse, and might make me prefer the pond." That was as close as FitzGerald came to telling anyone of the looming threat of marriage to Lucy Barton.

So commenced his friendship with Cowell and his past-tense love affair with Elizabeth, or, as he told Thackeray (to whom he had sent some of Elizabeth's poems) the "little Suffolk woman . . . who would have been my poetry if I had had wit enough." The regret was swelled by memories of other lost opportunities—recollections of the cousins of his friend John Allen, particularly Anne Allen with her light hair, her "China-rose" complexion, and the lilac dress she had worn. When Anne Allen died suddenly on November 4, 1833, he had written one of the most moving poems of his early years, expressing all his pain and loss in the sharp wind heaping up dead leaves at her father's door. As he told Anne's sister, at the precise moment the axe had fallen on him, he never had been able to take the tide at its flood, so everything went for him to "worse than waste."

Because Elizabeth's father, the Reverend Charlesworth, had been transferred to London at the time she married, she and Cowell were able to take over the cottage at Bramford. Soon there was hardly an afternoon that FitzGerald did not go over to see them. Memories of that "happy valley" became fused with those of the valley of the Ouse, and its winding river with the winding Ouse. Sweet to FitzGerald were all his arrivals at the "solitary home of household love," with the "lavender gown" running to welcome him at the gate, and Edward working within at Sanscrit. Thus he was shocked to learn that the Cowells were transplanting to Oxford because it was the "hope and dream" of Elizabeth Cowell's life—so she said—to see to it that her Edward took an Oxford degree. FitzGerald and William Bodham Donne both believed that a classics degree from Oxford would not help Cowell one bit toward getting a chair in oriental literature. Accordingly, FitzGerald overwhelmed Cowell with advice against Oxford. For once, Elizabeth gave a glimpse of her feelings during all those years of FitzGerald's flaccid courtship. Confiding in one of Cowell's friends, she spoke of the frightfully long letters FitzGerald was "rousing up his languid energies" to send them. (Cowell had pointed out to her that FitzGerald meant it kindly, being a man of the highest principle—insofar as a man could be, she added, who doubted that "Scripture be altogether the highest guide.")

As the Cowells prepared to leave for Oxford, FitzGerald asked Elizabeth for a keepsake—jokingly suggesting "either one" of Cowell's slippers, which he had been used to borrow, but then deciding seriously on a bit of green ribbon cut into a leaf shape that she had worn, so that he, "elderly knight" as he was, might take it as a guerdon, while he tackled her poems, which he was helping her to revise. When the Cowells invited him to Oxford, FitzGerald asked why he should go to see them "happy in Egypt," for, to his mind, they had made a reverse Exodus out of the "old land of milk and honey" into servitude. Nevertheless, he was soon with them in Oxford. In no time he took up Cowell's interests, really turning himself into Cowell (standing in his domestic shoes as it were, as when he had borrowed his slippers), so that he and Cowell were always in intensive communion over their studies. FitzGerald learned Spanish and began translating the plays of Calderón. Very quickly, he saw that he would have to make it a *free* translation, for "doing it slavishly," he thought, could only vulgarize it.

His great step came on a wet Sunday in December 1852, when Cowell declared that he could teach him the grammar of Persian in a day and set out to do so with Sir William Jones's Persian grammar. So interested did FitzGerald become in all Jones's quotes of the "delightful" poems of Háfiz that he felt actual *"love"* for Jones's text. By January 1854, FitzGerald was getting on splendidly with the poetry of Sádí, as he told Mrs. Cowell. He thought that Eastwick and Ross had translated his poetry wretchedly. They had both been very much on the wrong track in thinking that elegant Persian required elegant English. They would have done better to translate the Persian as the English Bible had been translated, remaining as oriental as possible in the metaphors but using the most "idiomatic Saxon *words*." FitzGerald had always been struck by what John Selden said in his *Table Talk* of the Bible's being the most strangely translated of all books, staying so close to virtually unintelligible oriental figures of speech. Yet it had succeeded, and so, FitzGerald thought, had prepared English readers for receiving other oriental writings done in that way. He advised Cowell to keep to the original names wherever he could in translating Háfiz, using "Shah" rather than "king" and "Suleymán" rather than "Solomon," so as to remove the words and names from European "prejudices and associations."

FitzGerald was strong at all times on using the terse Saxon idiom of the English Bible and of the great English authors—Swift, Cobbett, Dryden—for he knew that "vigorous language" necessarily implied "vigorous thought." He had always laughed at the French translation of Hamlet's "Thrift, thrift, Horatio!" into "Économie, économie, Horace!" In helping Mrs. Cowell to revise her poems, FitzGerald cut and cut, for—so he told her husband—"the shorter the better, in these days—and perhaps in all days." He was also very clear that her best poems came out of her girlhood in Bramford. Her more pretentious poems reminded him of his own works, which were echoes, he said, always recalling better poems, Alfred Tennyson's in particular, rather than "*growing* spontaneously" out of his own mind.

FitzGerald went powerfully to the aid of Cowell's translations from Háfiz, for he saw instantly where Cowell lost the suggested implications of an image and put a vague Victorian ideal in its place. Cowell had translated Háfiz's wish to keep the beloved's face free from the evil eye and followed up with the line "For all tenderness and truth to me are the looks it hath ever worn." FitzGerald told him that the implied meaning was "God ever keep the *Evil Eye* from that face which has ever look'd a *Good Eye* on me." Already he had the ability to plunge through a surface to capture and express tersely a sharply perceived idea. In the case of Cowell's translation, "The wine, my friends, the wine!" FitzGerald told him to let it read "Wine, friends, wine!" When Cowell did not dare to use the word "drunk" FitzGerald urged that Milton, Cowper, Taylor, and the translators of the Bible had all said "drunk," not "intoxicated" or "tipsy." Well before he had so much as seen Omar Khayyám, he had consolidated principles of translation that would allow him to use Khayyám's *Rubáiyát*, when he came to it, as a quarry for chips to construct an original mosaic.

FitzGerald received all the practice in Persian he needed by setting out to translate Jámí's *Salámán and Absál* in the spring of 1854. After an initial cry to Cowell that it was very hard, he found the work easier in the next two years. Giving all the credit for scholarship to Cowell, FitzGerald believed he had the "tact to dish up the poem neatly." Only after that did Cowell discover and introduce FitzGerald to Omar Khayyám. So it was that when the axe fell, and his first strong call came to overcome his anguish, FitzGerald had both the intellectual project and the skill necessary to answer it.

Certainly by 1856 the axe hung by a thread. Cowell had taken his Oxford degree and accepted a professorship of history and political economy at the Presidency College in Calcutta. The thought of his going to India, FitzGerald said, made his heart "hang really heavy at my side." At this point FitzGerald began to chant from the popular glee, which he would break into all through the coming catastrophe in his life, "When shall we three meet again?" His translation of *Salámán and Absál*, which he had meant as a "happy record" and pledge of his and Cowell's future "fellowship in study," he found darkened by the shadow of an eternal farewell. He gave Mrs. Cowell a green malachite brooch (recalling the leaf ribbon she had given him) as a recollection of green England on the banks of the Ganges. So ended his postmortem love affair just as the by-no-means-love affair that had been threatening him fell down upon him.

His mother had died in January 1855, and FitzGerald had been plunged instantly into conferences with lawyers and appearances in the Court of Chancery. When all was settled a year and a half later, he exclaimed to Alfred Tennyson at what a dry "remainder biscuit" had been left over after his forty-eight-year life voyage. He was winding up more than one piece of business in March 1856, *for better or for worse,* he said. His last liberty went in a trip down the Rhine with his dear friends Browne and young George Crabbe. He wrote old George Crabbe that he was looking with a "sort of terror" to the breakup of their party. After it, he made one last desperate effort—by way of Lucy's friend Mrs. Richard Jones—to convince Miss Barton that marriage with him would be a terrible mistake, trying, with all "delicacy," not to hurt her feelings. She—having no more delicacy than a steamroller—answered that she had no fears.

Only in his last month of freedom did FitzGerald inform his family and friends. He thanked John Allen's wife for her sanguine wishes—"sanguiner than my expectations!" To Stephen Spring Rice, he declared his coming matrimony a very "doubtful experiment," only recently fixed beyond change. Twice in this letter he stopped in mid-sentence, and at the second stop he declared that the sentence would remain "tail-less"—"a pretty pass English composition has got to." If a joke about castration came to his mind in announcing his marriage, surely the aura of his enslaved youth, helpless under the rule of his inexorable mother, had already laid a blight on all that was to come.

Besides, Lucy Barton had a genius for deciding to do exactly what he would least like—as foreshadowed by the silk purse she had once made for him. Of course, it was mere chance that made her choose November 4 as the marriage date, the anniversary of Anne Allen's death, with the dead leaves blowing, but she must have heard many times in all those years FitzGerald's repeated assertion that he "mortally" hated wedding celebrations, hated the crowd, hated the "hot rooms, speeches." She arranged a formal church wedding and a celebration with her family at Chichester, and she was not in the least put off by his not wishing to have even one of his family or friends present.

Her relatives were shocked to see that he was not wearing a formal frock coat on the fatal day and that he seemed like a sleepwalker, silent, with his head bowed. Offered blanc mange at the festivities, he waved it away saying, "Ugh! Congealed bridesmaid!" (Nobody laughed.) The climax came with the honeymoon; Lucy Barton had unerringly chosen six weeks at that "hatefullest of all places"—Brighton.

Apart from the rooms his wife found in London, FitzGerald kept his old lodgings, as he had in his mother's day, and was in them when he wrote his first letter to the Cowells in India. They would have been the last, he told them, to whom he would have revealed his approaching marriage, "for fear of utterly breaking down." There would have been no marriage, he let them know, had good sense won over "blind regard on one side." In the seven years Miss Barton had spent amid the wealth, the glamour of operas and parties in the family of the Hudson Gurneys, she had forgotten her father's Quaker simplicity. In fact, she certainly put pressure on FitzGerald, as his mother had, to accompany her in formal dress to the opera, to see and be seen by society. FitzGerald told the Cowells that she needed a "large field to work on," whereas he had only a "little garden of tastes and ideals," and a heart very dead to "better regards," by which he meant dead to the kind of display in high society that he had turned away from so strongly in his mother. He told young George Crabbe that his wife was, he feared, "given to profusion." (He had wanted her to "employ herself" in housekeeping after the example of Elizabeth Cowell, who had created such a simple, economical, happy little home around the needs of her scholar husband.)

William Bodham Donne described to Fanny Kemble the appearance of the dark, pretentious rooms that FitzGerald's wife had taken for them at 24 Portland Terrace, the Regent's Park, across from the zoo. Their apartment looked out—so FitzGerald had told him—into the wild beasts from the front and into a cemetery at the back. In this chamber of horrors, his wife looked—FitzGerald said—just like Lucrezia Borgia. William Pollock came away from a visit there reporting that FitzGerald had been suffering palpably every minute, and later, walking Pollock and Lady Pollock home, he was "very much the worse for some wine he had been taking," a condition in which Pollock had never seen him before. Certainly marriage had brought FitzGerald to excessive drinking, for Donne told of an evening at Gorlestone later, when George Borrow had visited and FitzGerald drank so much port wine with him that, after walking him home, he had lain down in the roadside grass and did not awaken until three or four o'clock in the morning. To the Cowells, FitzGerald confessed that "new channels" had been worn into his cheeks from the "many unmanly tears" he had shed, thinking of the days that were no more.

FitzGerald got through his marriage—brief as it was—only by constant flight from his wife. When he had not packed her off to comfort the Hudson Gurneys during a bereavement, or to find lodgings outside of London, he himself fled either to Browne at Bedford or to his sister Eleanor, or he neutralized his wife's vicinity by bringing back some of his beloved nieces to cheer him. He was always so ready to take all the blame for the failure of his marriage that few have realized just how dreadful that union was for him. It failed partly because Lucy Barton tried to push him back into the life of splendor and gentility he had revolted against in his youth, and even more because Lucy's strong will inevitably recalled his tyrannical mother. Long afterward, he confided to Mrs. Browne about his wife, "She was brought up *to rule*," and even though she might have submitted to be a slave, the price for her would have been too high, and "no advantage" to him. Only once after the separation, in a letter to Perry Nursey's daughter, Marietta, did FitzGerald talk of the sheer physical horror he had of his wife's rough voice and relentless grasp. Lucy had plagued him with four long visits to his Woodbridge vicinity in that single year, and he had accidentally run into her on the street. He would not have noticed her, he said, but "she rushed over the way, and put her claw in mine, and the terrible old *caw* soon told me." He had gotten away quickly, for, as he said, the "woman has no delicacy: and if one gives an inch will take an ell."

Through all of that terrible time, William Browne stood by him. When FitzGerald first fled to him in his agony, Browne exclaimed, "My dear Fitz, I would have kicked you to the Land's End, rather than this should have happened." Browne had not known about the engagement in time to awaken FitzGerald by kicking to the foolishness of letting himself be led like a lamb to the slaughter, but he did see at once that there was only one possible solution to his friend's anguish, legal separation. When FitzGerald separated from his wife in the next year and expected all his pious friends to turn away from him for doing so, it was Browne who stuck by him, giving "all friendly kindness and advice." In the end, FitzGerald settled the income from £10,000 on his wife for her life, which gave her an annual income of £300, leaving the formerly dependent governess very comfortably off.

He also did what he could to find someone else for her to take care of. When the Crabbe girls were bereaved of their father, he suggested sending them to his wife at Gorlestone. It would do them good, he said, and help to take the "poor soul" out of herself and give her what she pined for, "someone to devote herself to." On his recommendation, Browne sent for her as a "head nurse" during an illness of his wife and found her, FitzGerald said, so useful and agreeable that perhaps Browne was beginning to "wonder at my cruel bad taste." For himself, he expected to die homeless in the arms of Sarah Gamp. So ended his short and miserable married life, leaving him "older, duller, sicker, and sadder." He would find himself "settled" in the churchyard, he thought, before he found a place for himself out of it.

The Work

His salvation through the whole of that trauma was Omar Khayyám. Searching about in the Bodleian Library at Oxford in April 1856, Edward Byles Cowell had come upon the "Ouseley manuscript," dated 1460, containing 158 rubáiyát of the eleventh-century poet Omar Khayyám, and by July he had made a copy of it for FitzGerald. FitzGerald told Alfred Tennyson that he had spent a fortnight with Cowell, who was about to sail for India, looking through some curious old "Epicurean tetrastichs" that were as "savage against destiny" as Byron had been in *Manfred*, but also were full of "Epicurean pathos." From that time through all the excruciating misery of his marriage, Omar became his companion and support. In March 1857 he wrote Cowell that out of all the Persians, only Háfiz and "old" Omar Khayyám "ring like true metal." Flying from his wife to Browne in the spring of 1857, he put aside all books except Omar. Sitting among the breeze-brushed buttercups in Browne's paddock with a "dainty" racing filly "startling up" to snuff about him, he began, for sheer pleasure, to put Omar into Latin verse. "Omar breathes a sort of consolation to me!" he confessed.

Shortly after his arrival at Calcutta in November 1856, Cowell came upon another manuscript of Omar's *Rubáiyát* in the Bengal Asiatic

Society library, presenting more than 500 verses, and set about having a copy transcribed for FitzGerald. Receiving it on June 14, 1857, FitzGerald found that it abounded in verses as good as those in Ouseley, and he became convinced that Omar was the best of all the Persians. Shortly after, sitting at an open window at his sister Eleanor's and reading the Calcutta manuscript, FitzGerald was pierced by "Omar-like sorrow" to think that June was over. (July would bring him back to his wife at Gorlestone.) He saw the roses "blowing—and going" very much as in Persia. At Gorlestone, the roses were also blowing "as in Persia," and walking in his garden, FitzGerald began to think Omar into English—although in couplets—not yet in the quatrains rhyming a,a,b,a, like the Persian epigrams, which he would finally adopt. Thus at the exact moment when he decided—shattered and remorseful—to free himself from his devastating marriage by legal separation, FitzGerald was prepared to begin the creative project that would allow him to come to terms with its agony.

Nothing could be more unlike the poem he created than the materials he started with. The original rubái is a detached short verse epigram, self-contained, and deriving its effect from the pungency of its wit. The scribes organized their collections of rubáiyát by alphabetizing each rubái according to its rhyme word, so that the epigrams jump from bitter irony to farcical comedy without any connection of mood or meaning. In contrast, FitzGerald's *Rubáiyát* is a structured whole, not a random collection of verses. Later, when FitzGerald thought of adding some quatrains to give Omar's thoughts more time to turn in, he pointed out to Bernard Quaritch, his publisher, that the action takes place in one day, Omar beginning "with dawn pretty sober and contemplative," then growing "savage, blasphemous," and later sobering "down into melancholy at nightfall." In fact, the first verse comes at sunrise and the last at moonrise, with the protagonist moving from life into death, so that by the last verse he is gone, leaving an empty glass turned down.

Actually, the action follows the cycle of a year as well. It begins with the New Year and ends with the death of the old year, which is even more like a life cycle in the Persian calendar, where the New Year comes in spring with new life and ends with the ice of winter. At the start of FitzGerald's *Rubáiyát*, it is New Year and spring, then summer, and near the end of the poem, Ramadan, with fasting and penitence, concludes as the year draws to its end. In FitzGerald's Omar, no one can miss the parallel of spring to youth:

> Alas, that spring should vanish with the rose!
> That youth's sweet-scented manuscript should close!

Wine also binds the verses together, for, without losing any of its alcoholic reality, it comes to mean in FitzGerald, life, living, life-enhancement, just as it always has in the myth of Dionysus, who is god of both wine and life. Although FitzGerald certainly drank wine to soothe the pain during his marriage, the urgency for drink in his *Rubáiyát* does not seek oblivion, but life and life-enjoyment. From the beginning, where FitzGerald calls wine "life's liquor," through parallels of the bowl of wine to a "well of life," to the empty glass and death at the end, the larger significance of FitzGerald's wine is never in doubt.

Probably the strongest bond between the quatrains comes from their being the consecutive thoughts of one man in search of the meaning of life and death. Consistently (except where he is listening to the little drama of the pots), the thinker and speaker of the verses is Omar Khayyám, and Omar is unmistakably Edward FitzGerald. Once, as a joke, FitzGerald signed himself "E. FitzOmar," and the joke certainly revealed a heart truth, for his Omar really is Edward FitzGerald in the act of contemplating—by way of the speculation of Omar Khayyám—the mystery of human existence, of life and of death.

Long before FitzGerald read Omar Khayyám, he was already an Epicurean from all his readings of Lucretius, and he had seen wine as a symbol of life enjoyment from many readings of Anacreon. By the time he graduated Cambridge, he was already the "Prince of Quietists"—as Spedding had declared. He was sporting a "gentle Epicurism" by "natural inclination" long before his first lesson in Persian. When the Cowells were leaving Bramford for Oxford, FitzGerald turned to Lucretius for "comfort." In the full swing of his retroactive love affair with Elizabeth Cowell, in the full horror of his entanglement with Lucy Barton, he told Thackeray that he found life a "mess" and had become a "sad Epicurean," just trying to stay to windward of "bother and pain." No wonder he could say, once he knew him, that he had "great fellow feeling" with Omar. No wonder he could tell Cowell—in apology for appropriating Omar—that he was "more akin" to Omar, could "feel *with* him" in ways that Cowell, in his Anglican orthodoxy, never could.

No one can now say to what extent FitzGerald's Omar Khayyám came of the effect of Khayyám's ideas upon FitzGerald, and to what extent he came from the effect of FitzGerald's thinking and suffering upon his interpretation of the Persian poet. Only one thing is certain: FitzGerald emerged from writing his *Rubáiyát* different from when he began. In the process of working through Omar's ideas, his own long-suspended religious doubts were brought to conclusions he had not quite dared to reach before. Never again—after completing the *Rubáiyát*—did he attend a Church of England service, or that of any other denomination. Only a few months after he began studying Omar, he was already telling his very dear friend John Allen, then an archdeacon in the Church of England, that for all his delight in his company he was growing sure that "we walk in different ways," and he suspected that however well Allen had tolerated him in the past he might be less able to tolerate him now.

When young, FitzGerald's Omar has eagerly sought out doctor and saint and heard "great argument," even as FitzGerald had done at Cambridge and after, when he had tried so hard, with the help of John Allen, to accept orthodox belief. Old Parson Crabbe too had argued with him furiously, accusing him of pride because he could not stop asking questions. FitzGerald had struggled for belief, but like his Omar he had come out of all his religious searching, knowing only that he "came like water," and "like wind" would go.

In the midst of his marriage, he confessed to old Crabbe that he was paying in sorrow for his follies, and spending his days looking at a "poor little Persian Epicurean" who sang the world's religion of making the best of the day. Almost immediately after, he learned that "old Parson Crabbe" was bowing under a series of strokes, and his "brave old white head" would soon sink into the "church-sward." It made him feel his turn was coming. "Make way, Gentlemen!" he said, and he put this thought as a central theme into his Omar. FitzGerald's *Rubáiyát* is haunted by all the lovely heads that have merged with the earth. He sees them all transformed, as in classical myths, into the earth's flowers, roses or hyacinths. Even, it seems, the memory of that "China-rose" Anne Allen, one of the "loveliest and best" who had gone before him, merged into FitzGerald's immense vision in the *Rubáiyát* of the earth as crowded with all of the heads, the lips, the beauty of those who have died, made visible and almost speaking through every flower and blade of grass upon it. If his poem breathes *consolation*, it comes in great part from the poem's powerful sense of natural oneness with the fate of all life—flower or human—through all the centuries.

FitzGerald made his identification with Omar explicit by calling him "poor old Omar." It was a triple identification, for FitzGerald had emerged from his terrible marriage and separation feeling at one with the fate of his father. For many more years than his son, his father had suffered the terrible marriage, terminating in separation, followed quickly by sickness and death. FitzGerald had seen him as dead like "poor old Sedley" in *Vanity Fair*, "all his coal schemes at an end." After the funeral, he had told Thackeray himself that he had returned to Woodbridge "to bury poor old Sedley." With his own terrible marriage culminating in separation, he felt himself instantly "older" and "sicker," and likely to be "settled" in the churchyard before he could decide on settling himself anywhere else. He even came to calling himself "poor indolent old Fitz." If he thought of Omar as "old"—whereas he might have been any age when he composed the greater part of his epigrams—he did so not merely because Omar came out of the eleventh century, but largely because he felt himself old as he projected himself into Omar—as old as his father had actually been when he separated from his wife and died.

These interlocking memories, and especially those of "poor old Sedley," emerged in the five consecutive quatrains of FitzGerald's *Rubáiyát* that deal with the vanity and transience of "worldly hopes," whether they fail or prosper. Associations of his mother must have slipped into the quatrain about those who had "husbanded the golden grain," and of his father into those who had "flung it to the winds like rain," both having in the grave no gold about them that anyone would want dug up again. Recollections of his mother's grandiose display and high-society dinner parties must have slipped into those quatrains on the ruined splendors of Persian courts and vanished kings, as well as his advice to ignore the call to eat of that great dinner-giver of ancient Persia, Hátim Tai. Some remembrances of his hunter-father too may have haunted the quatrain about "that great hunter" Bahram, whose mortal sleep cannot be disturbed by the stamping of his former prey, the wild ass, over his head.

Where FitzGerald worked most intimately from his own interacting memories and treated the original Omar most freely and even cavalierly, was in the quatrains about sexual pleasure. Not only did he cut the proportion of such quatrains drastically, but he differed even more drastically in his conception of the subject from his originals. In a Mohammedan culture, where women are looked upon as domestic breeding animals and kept in careful seclusion to produce authentic sons, they are not thought of as companions. In the original Persian quatrains, love is mentioned ironically, for they recommend transitory sensual delight. So the boy wine-bearer, the "Saki," ready to fulfill all desires, is the traditional companion in pleasure among the epigrams of the Persian *Rubáiyát*.

FitzGerald accepted Lady Duff Gordon's innocent explanation of why only the masculine pronoun appears for the object of desire in Mohammedan poetry. She believed that it was used out of "decorum," because talk of women was Puritanically forbidden in Mohammedan society. Certainly, FitzGerald, no more than Lady Duff Gordon, would have thought that the object of such desires was actually masculine. Years after he had written his *Rubáiyát*, FitzGerald was astonished, reading about Henri Beyle (Stendhal) to learn his answer to a question about whether there was a love interest in a play he had written about Jesus Christ. Beyle had said, "Oh, beaucoup," not aimed at Mary Magdalene or the Samaritan woman, as FitzGerald might have imagined, but at Saint John, the disciple "chéri." "Could any but a Frenchman think of such a thing!" FitzGerald exclaimed. He thought it enough to persuade any Englishman to go back to the faith of his childhood and begin all over again with the catechism. He told Aldis Wright (Cambridge professor) that it made him feel inclined to go off to Trinity College Chapel to worship that very evening.

FitzGerald's ineradicable distaste for his tyrannical mother had crippled him for marriage, yet he believed in marriage, believed in heterosexuality, believed in begetting children. Homosexuality, to him, was the sort of bizarre absurdity that only a Frenchman would think up. He could love, but not lust after others, so that all his instincts were in direct opposition to his Persian sources. Always in his *Rubáiyát*, FitzGerald is talking of love, not of sensual enjoyment, and he is talking of one faithfully beloved, not of a transient series of boy Sakis.

Actually there is no way of telling the gender of the beloved in his *Rubáiyát* at all, for the loved one is never referred to by a third-person pronoun but only as "Thou," "we," "my Beloved," "Ah Love!" and "Moon of my delight." In this last oriental epithet, the moon is one, he says, that knows "no wane," so again he is speaking of enduring love, not passing desire. As a result, FitzGerald's *Rubáiyát* is one of the great romantic poems of the English language, for, man or woman, his reader can always see his own particular beloved in the verses and believe his love will last as long as life.

FitzGerald's beloved was the friend of almost a quarter of a century, William Kenworthy Browne, and so the poem is redolent not of arid Persia, largely desert, but of England's green and tree-shaded countryside, always at the brink of a river. His Persian garden with its roses and nightingales is really an English garden vibrant with the memories of all those summers of happy companionship out of FitzGerald's past.

Several Persian scholars have made studies of the originals of FitzGerald's images in the effort to determine the extent to which his *Rubáiyát* is a faithful translation, but what slips through their examination altogether is the extent to which, even when using Omar's image, FitzGerald invariably creates his own ambient and his own idea out of Omar's. It is precisely where he is using an image or two combined from Omar that he shows the originality of his *Rubáiyát*. Take, for instance, that best-known quatrain of his:

> Here with a loaf of bread beneath the bough,
> A flask of wine, a book of verse—and thou
> Beside me singing in the wilderness—
> And wilderness is paradise enow.

Literally the Persian reads something like this:

> If a hand should place a loaf of white bread,
> A decanter of wine, a sheep's thigh,
> And a young boy sweetheart amidst the desert,
> Joy unlimited will come, unknown to Sultans.

Translation demolishes the Persian wit. Although the hand, the thigh, and the heart remain, lost are the further pun allusions to parts of the body—all parts that will enter into the sexual entertainment of the picnic. Lost too is an implied comparison between the tender, succulent quality of the food and of the sweetheart. A Persian scholar, such as Arthur J. Arberry, skims over what he calls the "obscene echoes," in the Persian, but he does notice that FitzGerald's "bough" would not be found in a treeless Persian desert. He also is clear that no eleventh-century Persian gentleman, knowing, as he would, reams of poetry by heart, would lug a precious manuscript into the desert. He sees also that FitzGerald has excluded the mutton from the provisions, but he remains entirely deaf and blind to FitzGerald's two central images: the beloved's singing, and the glimpse of paradise—neither of which are in the original.

For FitzGerald, the Persian gave only an impulse to awaken personal associations of his own. He naturally excluded mutton from the picnic, just as he had once imagined Thackeray's horror if, married and poor, he had served him up a plebeian mutton chop. The book of verse came of his own love of poetry and of all the volumes of poetry he brought Browne each summer, from which he would read aloud to him while they lay fishing under the willows and poplars of the Ouse. The singing—of which there is no hint in the Persian—recalls the song "Knowst Thou an Isle?" which FitzGerald had written in praise of England, the valley of the Ouse, and Browne, the beloved of that song and of his *Rubáiyát*. Nor is this the only quatrain of his *Rubáiyát* that brings in a singer and a song not to be found in the Persian. Taking a hint from the description of old age in Shakespeare's *As You Like It*, as "Sans teeth, sans eyes, sans taste, sans everything," FitzGerald describes death in one quatrain as "Sans wine, sans song, sans singer, and—sans end!" Another quatrain shows that all along in memory FitzGerald is "lying on the banks of the Ouse," with Browne fishing, for he tells his beloved in it to rest lightly on the tender green that "fledges the river's lip on which we lean." Whether in uncultivated wilderness or in a garden full of roses, FitzOmar is always, with his beloved, somewhere "along the river brink," and the river is surely the Ouse.

Most intimate of all are FitzGerald's last words of his picnic quatrain, "And wilderness is paradise enow." The line links his love for Browne with his postmortem love for Elizabeth Cowell. Apropos of it he had quoted Petrarch's sonnet to Laura whose beauty (in death become a handful of dust) had transformed earth into paradise. In FitzGerald's quatrain, by way of poetry and song, love transforms wilderness into paradise, into a resplendent glory of spiritual beauty. So the quatrain is romantically opposite both in aims and in means to the entirely physical pleasure sought in the Persian epigram. FitzGerald's *Rubáiyát* celebrates happiness, not sensual pleasure; celebrates psychological fulfillment, not transitory desire.

Similarly transformed are the taverns in FitzGerald's quatrains, for they offer the wine of life-enjoyment, and FitzGerald tells us that a glimpse of life's meaning is better caught within a tavern than lost altogether in a temple. (For "Moslem temple" read "Anglican church" and recall FitzGerald's memories of the fungi, the dismal sermons, the purple noses of his local chapel.) Far from a mere winery, his *Rubáiyát* taverns pour out happiness, and they do because he associated London taverns with the same past happiness as the Ouse Valley. Within two years of finishing the *Rubáiyát*, FitzGerald lost his "poor Bedford lad"

Browne forever by his accidental death, and London became desolate for him. To one friend he confessed, "He and I were so much together in London, at the taverns," in the winter months that the city had become too melancholy for him. To another he declared, "W. Browne is too much connected with my old taverns and streets not to fling a sad shadow over all." From the time of Browne's death on, FitzGerald avoided London and never went into the valley of the Ouse again.

But Browne was alive when FitzGerald wrote his *Rubáiyát,* and so it radiates happy companionship. When FitzGerald came to lose that dearest friend, he could bear the bereavement with the help of "poor old Omar," who gave, he said, his own "kind of consolation for all these things." Throughout FitzGerald's *Rubáiyát,* life goes hand in hand with acceptance of death as intrinsic to it.

Not only did joy in living enter FitzGerald's poem, but also his remorse, regret, even despair, over his frightful marriage—emotions that are absent from the ironic Persian original. He worked through these emotions, and by way of one Persian epigram actually confronted the marriage itself:

> You know, my friends, how long since in my house
> For a new marriage I did make carouse:
> Divorced old barren reason from my bed,
> And took the daughter of the vine to spouse.

In literal translations of the Persian, Omar is divorcing "learning and faith" or "reason and faith." FitzGerald makes it reason alone and, by describing it as "old" and "barren," makes a private allusion to the elderly woman past childbearing he had married, combining a pungent comment on the sterility of reason with a comment on the absurdity of his marriage, sterile before it ever began. Also, FitzGerald's quatrain is filled with companionship, in the friends he addresses directly and the carouse that implies them, whereas in the Persian Omar takes a plentiful dose of wine all alone. As a result, FitzGerald's meaning—unlike the Persian—is that convivial companionship is better than fruitless philosophizing, not mere drinking. All along the way, FitzGerald recreates the meaning of whatever he takes from the Persian according to his own heart values.

One such transformed quatrain is full of FitzGerald's anguish at all that he had irrevocably failed to do in his life, and all that he had unfortunately done. The Persian original, literally translated, simply says that all is predestined and that the pen (meaning fate) writes "unhaltingly" with complete indifference to whether what it writes is good or bad, so that it is useless to grieve over the past or wish to change it. FitzGerald's verse reads

> The moving finger writes; and having writ,
> Moves on: nor all thy piety nor wit
> Shall lure it back to cancel half a line,
> Nor all thy tears wash out a word of it.

By talking about the moving finger rather than the pen, FitzGerald suggests to an English reader the ominous biblical writing on the wall, and adds his own images of the agonized desire to obliterate by crossing out or wiping away with tears. His verse brings into focus—as the Persian original certainly does not—all the futile agony of regret.

In this way, FitzGerald could come to grips with his feelings of guilt and remorse at having let himself be married against his will, and then at not managing to endure it. Many of his quatrains tackle the question of whether mankind is guilty of all the evil it has committed throughout the ages if all those doings were predestined from the beginning by an omnipotent and omniscient God. In one he arraigns the creator as follows:

> Oh, Thou, who man of baser earth didst make,
> And who with Eden didst devise the snake;
> For all the sin wherewith the face of man
> Is blacken'd, man's forgiveness give—and take!

Scandalized by this last line, Edward Byles Cowell accused FitzGerald of "making Omar worse than he is." Years after, Cowell told Aldis Wright, who was editing FitzGerald's letters, that there was nothing about the snake in the Persian and that FitzGerald's last line must have come from his misunderstanding of the Persian "give" and "accept" in what Cowell translated into a perfectly orthodox statement.

> O God, give me repentance and accept my excuses,
> O Thou who givest repentance and acceptest
>   the excuses of every one.

But FitzGerald knew what he was doing. At the time, he told Cowell that he had translated none of the quatrains "literally," usually having "mashed up two—or more—into one." He did not think he had gone "far beyond" Omar on the guilt of the maker in saying, "Let us forgive one another."

What with mashing up Omar's images into fresh ones and bringing perfectly disparate ideas in Omar together to shape new meanings, FitzGerald's *Rubáiyát* could not help becoming an original creation. He had been struck, early on, by what he called the *"Potter* tetrastichs," for the image of the pot and the potter as parallel to man and his maker is frequent in Omar and universal, as FitzGerald knew, in all ancient literature. So he decided to bring some together and construct a little drama out of them, set in a potter's shop, in which the pots try to come to some conception of the purpose of the potter who made them. FitzGerald even gave it a Persian name at first: "Kúza-Náma," meaning "Book of Pots." Some of the pots decide that they must be immortal because the potter, after going to all the trouble to shape them out of earth, would not want to stamp them back into it. One deformed pot wonders if the potter's hand shook when he made him. Another pot is sure that the "tapster" who poured life into him must be a good fellow and would not want to test or punish him, as some have asserted. A last pot, gone dry, looks forward to resurrection, for he might, if filled with the old juice, recover from oblivion "by and by." Finally, all the pots are jubilant to see by the new moon that the fasting and abstinence of Ramadan are now over, and they can fill up with wine—in its most realistic sense. Omar, along with the pots, accepts the wine of life, inseparable as it is from death, and after one last futile wish that the whole "sorry scheme of things" could be redesigned, he moves into night and death, his empty glass turned down.

FitzGerald had worked through all the pain of his life in his *Rubáiyát*. Through it, his mother's grandiose display had merged with the splendors of Persian dynasties that had already crumbled into dust centuries before, when Omar had been alive. The same dust had enveloped his father's pursuit of more gold with his failure and bankruptcy. Both his father's failed marriage and his own had been resolved, with all their pain and regret, when Omar divorced himself from barren philosophizing to cleave to life-enjoyment. FitzGerald had rejoiced with Omar in the great outdoors, and had rejoiced as Omar never did in loving companionship, in poetry and in song. He was ready to accept death, supported by the thought of all those others—flowers and fruits, women and men—who had come and gone in all the millions of years before him and who

would be coming and going after he too had accepted—unshrinking—
that darker drink, and turned down his empty glass.

Aftermath

Having finished his *Rubáiyát*, FitzGerald meant to go on and translate
the *Mantic* of Attár—but, he found, "My 'go' (such as it was) is *gone*."
Once he had drunk of real creation, he could not turn back at once for
even a free and cut-down translation like his earlier ones. He had given
John Parker of *Fraser's Magazine* some of the "less wicked"—by which
he meant less skeptical—of his quatrains from the *Rubáiyát*, but a full
year went by without a sign from *Fraser's*. So FitzGerald reinstated the
"wicked" quatrains and had 250 anonymous copies printed for him by
the bookseller Bernard Quaritch, a specialist in foreign-language books,
whom, he thought, "no wickedness can hurt." (Being Jewish, Quaritch
was invulnerable to attacks for deviating from Christian orthodoxy.)
FitzGerald took forty copies and gave the rest to Quaritch for sale.
A handful of reviews came—one good, the others indignant because
FitzGerald had let them know it was a free translation. Years went by,
and no one bought the slender book (at one shilling) from Quaritch. At
last he tossed it into his penny box outside his shop on Castle Street, off
Leicester Square.

Here fate brought the hero who single-handed saved FitzGerald's
Rubáiyát from oblivion. He was Whitley Stokes, a young barrister,
linguist, Celtic scholar (Irish, like FitzGerald). Both he and the friend
with him (John Ormsby) were struck enough by the anonymous English
Rubáiyát of Omar Khayyám in the penny box to buy several copies. On
July 10, 1861, Stokes gave one of them to his friend Dante Gabriel
Rossetti. At once, Rossetti rushed off to Quaritch's penny box, sweeping
Algernon Charles Swinburne along with him, both intent on buying
more. So the book spread among the Pre-Raphaelites and their friends.
William Morris, Edward Burne-Jones, even George Meredith and Alfred
Tennyson, had copies.

Meanwhile, Whitley Stokes, beginning a legal career in the Indian
Civil Service and still enthusiastic, had fifty copies privately printed at
Madras as Christmas gifts in 1862. Ten years later, when FitzGerald
learned of it, he joked about prosecuting "the Pirate." Actually, when
the *Rubáiyát* did begin to sell he told Quaritch to give his share to the

Persian Famine Fund. Probably "old Omar" would have done the same—FitzGerald added—had he translated "the works of yours truly."

In England the seeds Stokes had strewn among the Pre-Raphaelites went on sprouting. In 1863 John Ruskin read Burne-Jones's copy and left a note—to be delivered when the translator was discovered—saying that he had never before read anything "so glorious." Another who took fire from Burne-Jones's copy was the visiting American scholar-critic Charles Eliot Norton. A few months later, Burne-Jones told Norton that he had heard the translator was a Reverend Edward FitzGerald who lived in Norfolk and went out in boats. Norton asked Thomas Carlyle whether he had heard of him, and Carlyle cried, "Why he's no more reverend than I am! He's an old friend of mine." So it was that just ten years after Ruskin left his note with Burne-Jones, Norton gave it to Carlyle to send on to FitzGerald. FitzGerald thought a "sudden fit of fancy" must have hit Ruskin, but he told Carlyle it had been "kindly meant." Carlyle found FitzGerald's response typical of that "peaceable, affectionate, and ultra modest man," with his "innocent *far niente* life."

When Norton returned to America, he had his own copy of the 1859 *Rubáiyát of Omar Khayyám* and put a long review of it into the October 1869 *North American Review* (which he edited with James Russell Lowell), quoting many of its verses and telling his readers that this rendering by an "anonymous author" had "all the merit of a remarkable original production." Far from being a mere copy, it was a "redelivery" of the "poetic inspiration." It was unlike any other translation for its "value as *English* poetry."

One of the readers of Norton's book review, Mrs. Sarah Wister, became "intoxicated," she said, along with a whole group of young people in Philadelphia, by the quatrains Norton had quoted. Soon Quaritch was telling FitzGerald that orders were streaming in from enthusiastic Americans. One of them was from Horace Howard Furness (on the brink of publishing the first volume of his Variorum Shakespeare). He asked for two copies, and then almost immediately wrote back asking for eight more. In America, he told Quaritch, they all suspected that the "beauties of Omar are largely due to the genius of the translator." "They are a very odd people," FitzGerald commented.

Meanwhile, by the summer of 1867, the English Pre-Raphaelites had taken most of the copies, so that both Quaritch and FitzGerald began to think of printing some more. Inspired by the amazing news that Alfred Tennyson not only had a copy of his *Rubáiyát*, but actually liked it, FitzGerald thought of adding about thirty more quatrains. So came the four lifetime editions, the last of them with additions, subtractions, tinkerings, and finally even the name of the "translator." At the start, FitzGerald was uncertain about whether he should "leave well alone" and whether his additions wouldn't do "more harm than good." Usually, an author's final revision is assumed to be the one posterity ought to accept. But FitzGerald was a special case. After his first strong call of creativity had been met, his customary habits of self-suppression, self-denigration, and self-subordination took over.

Nothing is more illustrative of the dubious quality of his afterthoughts than one change he made for the third edition. Quaritch had told FitzGerald that his American clients, and he with them, preferred the first 1859 edition to the 1868 edition, which added thirty-five quatrains and altered many of the old ones. FitzGerald was for the later edition. Quaritch suggested that they might print both editions in one, bracketing the additions, but FitzGerald thought that made his poem "of too much importance." (In the end he would compromise by cutting nine of the added quatrains and restoring some of the 1859 readings.) While still in a quandary, he asked Alfred Tennyson if the edition he liked was the first or second. Tennyson could not find his copy, but he thought it had been the first edition, and he did recall: "I admired it immensely." He then made the fatal remark, "You stole a bit in it from 'The Gardener's Daughter,' I think." Instantly, FitzGerald thought he probably had stolen a passage from Tennyson, and asked Mrs. Tennyson which one "rankles in poor Alfred's mind," so he could relieve him at once. It turned out that Tennyson had been thinking of this quatrain:

> One moment in annihilation's waste,
> One moment, of the well of life to taste—
> The stars are setting and the caravan
> Starts for the dawn of nothing—oh, make haste!

The passage in "The Gardener's Daughter" describes a flirtation that came to nothing, speaking of the girl as a pilot who for a short while led the young man's heart, empty of love, to the "shores of nothing." The image has only the word "nothing" in common with FitzGerald's line, as Tennyson discovered to his "confusion" later when a friend (who had been to India and back with it) returned his copy of the 1859 *Rubáiyát*. Tennyson was sorry—he told FitzGerald—that he had ever mentioned it, for nothing could have been finer than that passage in the *Rubáiyát*, or indeed than almost everything in it. Tennyson even believed that

FitzGerald's poem must be "much finer" than the Persian, but his regret came too late. FitzGerald did not think it could matter what changes he made in his "immortal work," which might last at the most another five years. So the altered quatrain came out as

> A moment's halt—a momentary taste
> Of being from the well amid the waste—
> And lo!—the phantom caravan has reach'd
> The nothing it set out from—oh, make haste!

The changed verse—fine in itself but not nearly as suggestive as the original—points to one of the major results of FitzGerald's tinkering with his 1859 quatrains, as he moved further and further from the original Persian, which his failing eyesight could no longer make out, and still further from the desperate need that had made a great original poet of him. By the change, he clarified his image of stopping at an oasis, but at the expense of weakening the terror of "annihilation's waste" and the shock of his caravan's sudden arrival at nothingness.

Most of his revisions substitute clarity for resonance. Take the opening quatrain of his 1859 *Rubáiyát*:

> Awake! for morning in the bowl of night
> Has flung the stone that puts the stars to flight:
> And lo! the Hunter of the East has caught
> The sultan's turret in a noose of light.

FitzGerald had been working in it with an image taken from the warning signal among nomadic tribes (made by the reverberation of a stone thrown into a bowl), to take horse and fly. He had also used the Persian image of the sun as a hunter. Certainly FitzGerald was right in suspecting that the ordinary reader—uninformed by a note—would see the stone putting the stars to flight very much as a stone thrown into a pool, putting the fish to flight. So he obliterated the stone and the bowl along with the image of the hunter lassoing his prey and made it all a more prosaic statement about the sun.

> Wake! For the sun, who scattered into flight
> The stars before him from the field of night,
> Drives night along with them from heav'n, and strikes
> The sultan's turret with a shaft of light.

Even small changes are no improvement, as his bird of time with but "a little way / To fly—and lo! the bird is on the wing," which in the final edition becomes, "a little way / To flutter—and the bird is on the wing."

Some of his new quatrains seem to have been put in to neutralize the shock of his original to believers. He had been totally put off, by the alarm and distress of the pious Edward Byles Cowell when he received his copy, from distributing more than about three copies to his friends of the 1859 *Rubáiyát*. He submitted his subsequent editions to Cowell before publication, and not merely as a Persian expert. Some of the new lines certainly appear more orthodox. One speaks of the seas mourning "In flowing purple, of their Lord forlorn," and another talks of the "Master" whose "secret presence" runs through all the forms of creation: "They change and perish all—but He remains." Even his joke quatrain, which reverses the conventional shame in nakedness, although ambiguous, can be taken as belief in immortality of the soul.

> Why, if the soul can fling the dust aside,
> And naked on the air of heaven ride,
> Were't not a shame—were't not a shame for him
> In this clay carcass crippled to abide?

FitzGerald seems also to have taken to heart the rejection of his poem by early critics because it was a free translation. At any rate he expunged from his final version the three quatrains that could not even remotely be thought of as taking anything from the Persian. Also he cut out his non-Omar oriental epithet, where he calls the beloved "Moon of my delight." Other changes seem directed at reinforcing propriety, as his change of the famous quatrain "Here with a loaf of bread beneath the bough" into

> A book of verses underneath the bough,
> A jug of wine, a loaf of bread—and thou
> Beside me singing in the wilderness—
> Oh, wilderness were paradise enow!

He starts with the book instead of the bread to make it clear—so it seems—that he is speaking of an intellectual picnic, but he loses the lift of images going from the mundane loaf of bread to the effervescent wine, to the higher realm of poetry, and higher still to love and song, culminating with paradise. The revised verse goes down, passing from poetry to wine to bread, and then up to love and song and paradise, losing the original's spiritual ascent to a climax.

All these changes were made after the strange set of circumstances that allowed him to write his *Rubáiyát* was long past. Actually, the poem had been a miracle of chances that would not be repeated. Never again would he be pushed—as he was in the 1859 version—by the urgent need to resolve pain and guilt and to come to grips with the meaning of life. Never again would the circumstances come about that allowed him, for all his crippling modesty, to write original poetry without actually realizing that he was doing so. Had he never been threatened for seven years by the inexorable Lucy Barton, he would never have fallen into his postmortem love for Elizabeth Cowell that caused him to take up her husband's work of conquering and translating languages to learn Spanish and Persian and do translations from both. Had Cowell never dug up the Ouseley manuscript of Omar Khayyám, FitzGerald would have been caught up only by work like his translation of *Salámán and Absál*, which would straitjacket him in an alien mystical allegory and detach him from his own reservoir of memories, his own anguish, and his own search for meaning.

By astonishing luck, Omar conveyed a species of Epicureanism that could awaken and activate his own "sad" and "gentle" form of it and impel him to conclusions he had never before dared to reach. Only such a shapeless collection of epigrams, with absolutely no connection between one and another, would have given FitzGerald the opportunity to create his own structure, his own continuity, and through them to arrive at his own meaning. He certainly knew that he was creating his own structure, for he told Edward Byles Cowell that his *Rubáiyát* had been "most ingeniously tesselated" into an "Epicurean eclogue in a Persian garden." But he claimed no more for it than a little ingenuity in dishing up the original. He certainly knew that he had moved far from what he had found, for he scolded Quaritch for advertizing the poem as a "faithful" translation, "it being indeed, quite the reverse." He told a Boston critic that all his work, like his *Rubáiyát*, consisted of "things taken—I must not say, translated—from foreign sources," thus representing himself as a wayward translator at best. He saw no difference between his Omar and his other translations; he knew only that he had worked very hard on it. He told Cowell that few people had taken such pains with a translation as he had with Omar, but certainly not to be literal, for "at all cost, a thing must *live*: with a transfusion of one's own worse life if one can't retain the original's better. Better a live sparrow than a stuffed eagle." Could he have looked into the future, he would have been amazed to see the multitudes of readers of his *Rubáiyát of Omar Khayyám*, all of them attesting to the *life* of his poem and to the certainty that it was no sparrow but a true eagle, and a very high flyer at that.

From comparison with his poet friends, Edward FitzGerald knew that for the greater part of his life he had missed out on what impelled them: a "strong inward call" to create. No wonder that when, finally, for one brief year, the call resounded in him, he remained even more completely unconscious of where it had come from or what it was than did Robert Louis Stevenson in *Treasure Island*. More than merely an uneven writer like Stevenson, FitzGerald was a great writer once and only once, never really a writer before or after, although he tried sketching some poems and enjoyed editorial tinkering with the poems of others. He was so unconscious of the entire creative process within him that he never even saw himself as writing an original poem in his *Rubáiyát*, but conceived of himself as a translator from the Persian, and a far from faithful one at that.

Yet in a fragmented way he was conscious that there was nothing in his original like what he was doing. He certainly knew that the structure, the overall design, was his own, and totally foreign to the dissociated Persian epigrams. He knew that his images were fresh combinations, much altered from the Persian, and he knew that the "life," the *meaning*, of his poem was his own, not Omar's, although, with his usual self-annihilating modesty, he looked upon it as a mere commonplace sparrow's.

Certainly, FitzGerald never saw how the blend of memories out of his own past made for a fresh magic totally unlike anything in the Persian, or how the combination of immediate agony (in his mistaken marriage) and remembered happiness over many years (in the beloved valley of the Ouse) formed the unique flavor of his poem. His life story—his one brief flare into greatness—is extraordinarily revealing of the vagaries of creativity. In FitzGerald's case, what brought the creative push to life and what extinguished it are clearly visible. He created a masterpiece only through a complex set of circumstances that came together to give him both the pressing need and a way of working it out that freed him from his inhibiting modesty. If he wrote no more—except for some tinkerings, by no means improvements, on his sterling achievement—he stopped because his "go" was truly "gone." He had resolved the agony of his marriage and arrived at his ultimate life philosophy through his *Rubáiyát*, and he had no further to go.

FitzGerald is not the only writer whose creative élan came to life for only a year, more or less, of his life and then went out forever. The grandeur that lifted Samuel Taylor Coleridge among the great English poets really comes from three works written in a similarly astonishing year of creativity: *The Rime of the Ancient Mariner*, and the two fragments, *Kubla Khan* and *Christabel*. Just as FitzGerald could not have so much as learned Persian had it not been for his involvement with Elizabeth Charlesworth and her husband Edward Byles Cowell, so Coleridge could not have written *The Rime of the Ancient Mariner* had not William Wordsworth come into his life at exactly this point, liberating him from an outworn poetic diction, and even—through an abortive plan to collaborate on a narrative poem for money—given him what Coleridge's own chaotic mind invariably balked at, a clear-cut story structure into which his most urgent guilt and tensions could pour themselves. And Wordsworth would have effected nothing had he not come at a time when Coleridge's confused sexual identity, attested to by the nightmares confided to his diaries, and the tensions within his miserable marriage were not moving to a crisis, so that he would end up in flight from land to land, very like his mariner, in effect a warning to wedding guests other than the one in his poem, to stay away from marriage ceremonies. And if *Christabel* remained a fragment, it did because Coleridge became hopelessly entangled in his own sexual ambiguities as expressed in the man-woman figure of Geraldine, and he was helpless to resolve them. After the miracle year of his great poetry, Coleridge began his long flight from his wife and family, first to Germany, then to Malta, then to London, separating from them decisively and becoming a confirmed celibate for decades before his death.

The beginnings and endings of creativity in other writers are clarified by FitzGerald's history. After a notable initial sequence of novels (alive with frustration at the middle-class repression of the great god Pan), E. M. Forster lost his creative push at the moment he accepted his identity as a homosexual by writing (but not publishing) his novel *Maurice*. He managed, with great difficulty, to produce a final novel at the age of forty-five, *A Passage to India*, with the unresolved tensions of the two principal homoerotic loves of his life, both with colonials—one, an unconsummated devotion to an Indian, and the other, a temporary union with a humble Egyptian. Thereafter he wrote no more novels, only criticism.

FitzGerald's single masterpiece also throws light on books that lost their "go" and deflated utterly before their fictional conclusion—such a work, for instance, as Mark Twain's great vision of Huckleberry Finn and Jim, those two symbolic strugglers against all enslavement, as they swept down the majestic Mississippi River on their raft. As long as the story remained impelled by Twain's own inner striving for liberation and was fed by blended memories out of his own years on the Mississippi as a steamboat pilot, it retained its grandeur. The instant he ran his characters aground in the last chapters, it splintered up into slapstick and juvenilities. As the writing histories of Thomas Mann, Robert Louis Stevenson, and Edward FitzGerald show, the creative impulse can live only as long as the stress of unresolved problems propels it, and as long as it is nourished by blended memories.

4

War and Mir

If a writer sets a novel before his birth and relies on historical documents, he can be accused of sacrificing his intimate life experience for dead hand-me-downs. Matthew Arnold said he preferred Lev Tolstoy's *Anna Karenina* to *War and Peace* because a writer should deal with "the life he knows from having lived it" rather than what he may have learned "from books and hearsay."

Truly enough, *War and Peace* begins in 1805 and ends in 1820, a good eight years before Tolstoy was born in 1828. In it, Tolstoy relied—so he said—on letters and diaries and had his historical figures speak the words recorded in a mass of memoirs. Certainly Tolstoy never knew anyone in the Rostov and Bolkonsky families, for he modeled them on the families of his grandfathers, Count Ilya Andreyevich Tolstoy and Prince Nikolay Sergeyevich Volkonsky, both of whom had died before he was born. Tolstoy had no recollection even of his own mother—although she appears as the Princess Marya Bolkonsky, a major character in *War and Peace*—for he had not been quite two years old when she died.

Yet Matthew Arnold notwithstanding, *War and Peace* comes every bit as directly out of Tolstoy's life as *Anna Karenina*. There are ways, invisible to outsiders, in which an author's most urgent problems, his most profound experiences, can flow into a work. Without a word being

Tolstoy's sister Countess Marya Nikolayevna Tolstoy, model for the Princess Marya Nikolayevna Bolkonsky in *War and Peace*.

Tolstoy's maternal grandfather Prince Nikolay Sergeyevich Volkonsky, model for Prince Nikolay Andreyevich Bolkonsky in *War and Peace*, and in part for his son Prince Andrey.

Tolstoy's Decembrist cousin Prince Sergey Gregoryevich Volkonsky at the time of his immolation.

Alexander Herzen, a major model for Pierre Bezukhov in *War and Peace*.

Natalya Nikolayevna Goncharov at the time she married Alexander Pushkin.

Pushkin's wife, Natalya Nikolayevna, with her Ninon de Lenclos coiffure at the time she became the mistress of the Emperor Nicholas I.

said of them, an author's own times may haunt a novel set before they began. Even as abstract an element as a theory of history may come, as Tolstoy said of his theory in *War and Peace*, not invented but "painfully torn from my inside."

An epic with the immense scope of *War and Peace*—scores of characters and events—may derive as intimately from its author's feelings as does a lyric poem. After Tolstoy finished this book, he felt toward it, he said, something of the embarrassment of a man who looks on "the remains of an orgy in which he has taken part," an orgy into which he had thrown himself "heart and soul" so that "nothing else mattered beside it." The story of how this great novel came to life tells some of the secrets of how and why a man's life experience pushes itself into art and so lives ever.

Rostovs and Tolstoys

Tolstoy brings us into his grandfather Count Ilya Andreyevich Tolstoy's Moscow mansion—lightly disguised as that of Count Ilya Andreyevich Rostov—on a name day festival, with eighty guests invited to dinner and with a serf chef whom he has bought for a thousand rubles performing miracles of cookery, so that we see instantly the carefree prodigality that in reality as in the novel left his son Nikolay (Lev Tolstoy's father) with an inheritance entirely made up of debts. Like the family of Lev Tolstoy's grandfather, the young Rostovs consist of an older son (Nikolay), a younger son (Ilya in reality, Petya in the novel), two sisters (Alexandra and Pelageya in reality, Vera and Natalya in the novel), and an adopted distant cousin (Tatyana Alexandrovna Ergolskaya in reality, named Sofya Alexandrovna in the novel).

Tolstoy made it perfectly clear that Sofya—nicknamed Sonya—follows very closely the life story of "Auntie" Tatyana, who had loved his father and his father her from childhood but who had self-sacrificingly stepped aside so he could marry a wealthy heiress and repair the family fortune. No one was more influential in Tolstoy's life than "Auntie," who took over and mothered the five orphan children when Tolstoy's own mother died five months after giving birth to his sister Marya in 1830. Auntie Tatyana had been very attractive as a girl—so Tolstoy said—"with her crisp black curling hair in its enormous braid, her jet black eyes and vivacious, energetic expression."

He had first become aware of her when he was about five years old and she over forty, "short, stout, black-haired, kindly, tender, and compassionate." In those days he never thought of whether she was pretty: "I simply loved her, loved her eyes, her smile, and her dusky little hand with its energetic little cross vein." Once, as a small boy, he had squeezed in behind her on the drawing room sofa, and she had "caressingly touched me with her hand." Young as he was, he felt such "passionately tender love for her" that he caught her hand and covered it with kisses, weeping.

From her he had learned "the spiritual delight of love," not by words but because "her whole being" filled him with love. "I saw, I felt how she enjoyed loving, and I understood the joy of love." Even when he was twenty-four years old, he knew and said that the greatest calamity that could befall him would be her death or the death of his oldest brother Nikolay—"the two people I love more than myself." He was forty-six, with a wife and children, when Auntie actually did die, and he could say, "I lived with her all my life; and I feel frightened without her."

This profoundly beloved woman entered the Rostovs along with the image of Tolstoy's father, who had died when Lev was nine years old. With Tolstoy's grandmother, they are the only members of Ilya Rostov's family who owe their being to real Tolstoys, for the two Rostov sisters, Vera and Natalya, have only number in common with Tolstoy's aunts Alexandra and Pelageya.

It has been common knowledge from the start that Natalya "Natasha" Rostov took life from Tolstoy's sister-in-law Tanya, Tatyana Andreyevna Behrs, for Tolstoy told his wife's cousin Mikhail Sergeyevich Bashilov, who was doing illustrations for *War and Peace*, that he must not fail to use the daguerreotypes of Tanya when she was twelve, sixteen, and nineteen years old for Natasha's stages of development, and Tanya herself wrote recollections depicting herself as Natasha.

It is also believed that Tolstoy's oldest sister-in-law "Liza," Yelizaveta Andreyevna Behrs, suggested the coolly rational Vera Rostov. Tanya Behrs saw something of her own girlish comraderie with her young mother in Natasha's confidences with her older mother in the story, otherwise a portrait of Tolstoy's paternal grandmother (whom he remembered well). Even the youthful Petya Rostov—who stands in place of the crippled younger brother of Tolstoy's father, Ilya Ilyinich— appears to be a portrait of a younger brother of his wife, Petya Behrs (with touches of other boys). So the Behrs family certainly entered powerfully into the Rostovs, yet everyone has believed that Tolstoy left his wife out altogether (except for putting touches of her into Natasha in the "Epilogue" to the book).

Actually Tolstoy would not have dreamed of leaving out his newly wedded eighteen-year-old wife, any more than she, a girl riddled with jealousy, would have calmly accepted being overlooked. As a matter of fact, she knew perfectly well that she was safe from that, for, barely two months after her marriage, she wrote her sisters teasingly (November 11, 1862), "Girls, I'm going to tell you a secret, and don't mention it: perhaps Levochka will describe us when he's fifty!" Nor did Tolstoy make any mystery of what he was doing, for he used his wife's actual name for the character, "Sonya," intimate for Sofya.

What has blinded a century of critics is that he put his wife's personality and attractions into what he had explicitly declared to be his Aunt Tatyana's life story. In reality, the character is a composite, the girlish charm of the young Sonya coming from his wife. At the start of *War and Peace*, Sonya and Natasha are fifteen and thirteen respectively. The youthful attractions of these two girls, just emerging from childhood, make them joint heroines, both equally enchanting throughout the first parts of the book.

Tolstoy had watched his wife and her sister Tanya grow up, for he had known their mother all his life. One of his father's closest friends had been a nearby Tula landowner, Alexander Mikhailovich Islenyev who had a family of six illegitimate children called "Islavin." As a boy, Lev Tolstoy had been much in love with Islenyev's nine-year-old daughter, Lyubov Alexandrovna Islavin. Once he was so piqued at her for ignoring him that he gave her a push from a terrace, which later, as his mother-in-law, she would tease him about. After she had married Dr. Andrey Yevstafyevich Behrs, Lev Tolstoy would come to dinner at the Behrs in company with Lyubov's brother "Kostya," Konstantin Alexandrovich Islavin, either in Moscow, where the doctor's duties as "Physician to the Court," gave him an apartment in the Kremlin, or at their country villa outside Moscow.

At one dinner, when Lyubov's daughter Sonya was about twelve and Lyubov's youngest daughter Tanya was ten, the children had served at table. "What delightful, merry little girls!" he exclaimed in his diary. All his delight went into his portraits of Sonya and Natasha at the start of *War and Peace*, and as they grow up they give the Rostov home its atmosphere of youth, joy, and love. The charm of the fictional Sonya and Natasha grows as they grow, just as Tolstoy's delight in Sonya and

Tanya Behrs grew, until at the age of thirty-four he married the older girl, the eighteen-year-old Sonya.

Certainly it was Sonya as a growing girl, not the actual stout Auntie Tatyana in her forties, fifties, and sixties, who allowed Tolstoy to depict his Sonya as looking like a "pretty half-grown kitten" who will grow into a lovely little cat. With her eyes sparkling eagerly, she appears as if she were just about to jump down on her tender little paws and begin playing with a ball of wool "as a kitten should."

Auntie Tatyana's dark hair, "melting" dark eyes, and long dark lashes—reproduced in Sonya of *War and Peace*—were what Tolstoy had fallen in love with as a boy in the dark-eyed child Lyubov Islavin, and what he found enchanting in her children, Sonya and Tanya. If he fell in love with Sonya Behrs, he did because she aroused preconscious images of Auntie, who had filled him with a "passionately tender love for her" in his infancy, as well as memories of his later childhood love for her mother, Lyubov.

Tolstoy always thought of Lyubov, Sonya, and Tanya as "black" Behrs, and the fair-haired Behrs as "white" Behrs. Their fair-haired daughter Liza—and indeed the entire family—had thought at first that Lev Tolstoy was courting her. But after dining with them on September 22, 1861, Tolstoy confided in his diary, "L[iza] B[ehrs] tempts me; but she will not be the one. She is all reason, and has no feelings."

As for the black Behrs—so he told his wife Sonya—they were all indifferent to "intellectual interests," yet very intelligent. Their minds were asleep: "they can, but they don't want to." On the other hand, they loved passionately. If Sonya and Tanya were indifferent to intellect, it was because their mother, Lyubov, had always been "intellectually immature," Tolstoy said. The white Behrs cared greatly for intellectual interests, but their minds were "feeble and shallow." In *War and Peace*, Sonya and Natasha are black Behrs: both love all their dear ones passionately, but never—outside of lessons—read a book. When the Princess Marya Bolkonsky asks Pierre Bezukhov whether Natasha is clever, he answers, "I think not, and yet—yes. She does not think it worthwhile to be clever."

So strongly was Tolstoy's wife in the girlish Sonya of *War and Peace* that she blotted out Auntie Tatyana's characteristics with her own conflicting ones. The keynote of Auntie Tatyana was her prevailing self-sacrifice. Jealousy was foreign to her. But Tolstoy's wife Sonya, who had always felt shortchanged in her parents' love, was both possessive and jealous. She felt flashes of jealousy immediately over Tolstoy's affection for Tanya and wrote in her diary: "My jealousy broke out for the first time yesterday." Later she was saying such things as "I believe I shall kill myself one day out of jealousy." She thought that her husband's "whole life, his thoughts, must belong to me."

Tolstoy's Sonya has all his wife's jealousy at the start of *War and Peace*, so that she is instantly upset because Nikolay Rostov is chatting with the visiting Julie Karagin. Darting a "passionately angry look" at him, she rushes from the room. Nikolay has to run after her and exhort her not to "torture me and yourself because of a mere fantasy."

Sonya reaches her peak attraction at the New Year's masquerade when, with Nikolay and Natasha in the lead and several troikas full of house serfs transmuted into bears and Turks and clowns, they all dash off through the snow to bring delight to a neighboring landowner. One New Year during Tolstoy's boyhood love for Lyubov Islavin, Islenyev had come in this way thirty miles through the ice to burst in on them at Yasnaya Polyana with troikas full of his children and serfs all magical in costume. After this scene of love, Tolstoy's wife slips out of the character, leaving only the self-sacrificing Auntie.

The "joyful poetic period of childhood" was always sweet for Tolstoy, and especially so in little girls. "How charming little girls are at that age, both good and pretty," he exclaimed over his sister Masha's daughters when they were fifteen and thirteen, the ages of Sonya and Natasha at the start. Little girls were "pure poetry," Tolstoy thought; "feeding them is like throwing money out of the window, as the peasant said." His wife's younger sister Tanya in particular seemed to Tolstoy the essence of poetry.

In a letter to her, just a week after his wedding, Tolstoy told Tanya of his affection for her "wonderfully sweet nature with its laughter and its background of poetic seriousness. Such another Tanya would take a lot of finding, it's true, and such another admirer as L. Tolstoy." In the coming stressful years, he would urge Tanya to keep "your sweet, wild, energetic nature" when all went well, and "the same indomitable nature in misfortune." Out of Tanya's life-enjoyment came Natasha of *War and Peace*.

Like Tanya, Natasha is so wildly energetic as a child that she is called a "little volcano," and so indomitable that the formidable Marya Dmitrievna calls her the "Cossack." When we first meet her, she bursts into a "ringing fit of laughter," and from then on laughter is always with her. Catching sight of her for the first time running among the trees, Prince Andrey feels a pang at being outside her "bright and happy life," and he wonders, "What is she so glad about?" At her father's country house, he is moved by hearing her at the window above his telling Sonya of her rapture at the glory of the moonlit night. He sees Natasha as a "strikingly poetic, charming girl, overflowing with life." He finds her "brimming over with mystic forces" and admires her "frankness of soul," her "inner spiritual force."

Tolstoy portrayed Tanya's spiritual strength in Natasha by giving her one of Auntie Tatyana's girlhood acts showing how "resolute" she was. Young Tatyana Ergolskaya had been impressed by the Roman hero Gaius Mucius Scaevola, who demonstrated his indifference to pain by holding his right hand in the fire. The other youngsters (Tolstoy's father and aunts) knew they could never do such a thing, but Tatyana declared, "I will do it." S. I. Yazikov—who would later become Tolstoy's godfather—said flatly, "You will not." He heated a ruler red-hot in candle flame and applied it to her bare arm.

She did not pull away, nor did she groan until the ruler with her flesh was torn off. Telling of it in later years, Auntie Tatyana would show the boy Tolstoy "the scar of a burn on her arm, almost as big as the palm of the hand." In Natasha's story, Auntie Tatyana's unprovoked demonstration of fortitude is changed into a proof by Natasha of her loyalty to Sonya. "I burned my arm for her sake," Natasha says.

From the start, Tolstoy had planned to try his Natasha—the adored and sheltered child—outside the safety of the Rostov household. She was to be compromised by a handsome thoughtless "stallion" of a man, Anatole Kuragin, as a trial of the spiritual force in her and in the two men who have loved her enchanting innocence, Prince Andrey and Pierre. Tolstoy could shape these events with authority because, just in the course of living her young life in the next few years, Tanya Behrs showed him how Natasha would react. Without herself being compromised, Tanya contributed some of the more sensational details of Natasha's calamity.

At sixteen, Tanya felt herself exalted by the admiration of her brother-in-law Lev Tolstoy and also by the open admiration of Lev's older brother "Serozha," Sergey Nikolayevich Tolstoy. From boyhood Lev had always admired and wished to be like this brother for his "handsome appearance, his singing (he was always singing), his drawing, his gaiety and especially (strange as it may seem to say so) the spontaneity of his egotism." Always self-conscious, Lev saw himself as ugly and awkward. Serozha, in contrast, was "altogether himself, handsome, high-spirited, proud." So Tanya could see herself as surpassing her sister Sonya's excellent marriage by taking a much handsomer Count Tolstoy who shared her musical gifts. (Tanya had given her extraordinary contralto voice, with its unconscious power and velvety quality to Natasha.)

One obstacle stood in the way of Tanya's living happily ever after with Sergey Tolstoy (twenty-two years her senior). Back in 1851, Sergey had contracted a liaison with a beautiful gypsy singer, Masha Shishkina, and in 1863, when Sergey came into close contact with Tanya, Masha was pregnant with their fourth child. Sergey was torn between his long love for Masha and their children and his new love for this very young girl—also a striking singer—of his own social class. He did not know whether to make an acceptable marriage with Tanya Behrs or to shock society by marrying his loyal companion Masha and legitimizing his children. Tanya had always been highly susceptible, and Lev had warned her at the start: "Tanya, my dear friend, you are young, beautiful, gifted and lovable. Guard yourself and your heart. Once your heart has been given away you can't get it back again, and the mark on a tormented heart remains forever." In the midst of her anguish and uncertainty over Serozha—himself paralyzed as to which way to jump—Tolstoy urged her to think of all the "many friends who love you" and not to lose "control of yourself," for "you won't stop living, and you'll be ashamed to remember your lapse at this time, however it may turn out."

At this point—New Year 1864—Masha was in childbed, and for the first time Serozha was present. Tolstoy wanted him to decide yes for Tanya, but he was afraid "it will be no." Partly out of a sudden concern for Sergey's children, partly to avoid the humiliation of a refusal, Tanya herself broke the engagement. Two weeks after, in her agony, she swallowed a poisonous kitchen cleanser (alum), but became frightened and ran from her room, crying for help. Only much vomiting brought on by herbal teas saved her.

Tanya was going through a difficult period—so Tolstoy reported to his wife Sonya from the Kremlin where he was staying with the Behrs family while negotiating a price for the first part of *War and Peace* with Mikhail Nikiforovich Katkov of the *Russian Herald*. "Tanya cries day after day," Tolstoy told Sonya. In part, it seemed sheer boredom, for "after all the commotion" she was left with nothing but "the virtuous, but dull Liza" and her parents. Tolstoy said that he and Tanya were "booked for skating, we've made a lambskin hat, we've booked for a concert—but it's not enough for her." The least rumor that Sergey was about to marry Masha had her again "crying her heart out." (Luckily, by the time Sergey did marry Masha, Tanya was marrying an earlier love of hers, her wealthy young cousin, close to her own age, "Sasha," Alexander Kuzminsky.)

Tolstoy designed a very different story for Natasha, in which she is forced to wait a year before she can marry Prince Andrey Bolkonsky, and she is bereft even of his company, for he is in Europe undergoing medical treatment for a wound. After months she begins to feel the hysterical boredom that had beset Tanya after her break with Serozha, and she cries out that she wants her fiancé "now, this minute! I want him!" She feels bored with everyone, tired of everything, and asks herself frantically, "Where am I to go? What am I to do with myself?" She plucks at her guitar, and tears gush from her eyes. For a while she calms down in reverie with her brother and Sonya, but then, interrupted in her singing, she again bursts out "sobbing so violently that she could not stop for a long time."

The bored and tearful Tanya, as Tolstoy wrote home to Sonya, had calmed down in this way as she, Petya, Liza, and Lyubov Alexandrovna had reminisced and talked with Tolstoy. "Tanya assured us that the only thing she wanted was to live very high up in a tower with a guitar. Lyubov Alexandrovna contended that even in a tower you have to eat and go to the lavatory, and Tanya burst out crying in a nervous but hilarious manner as she did that time over the priest's daughter."

Tolstoy used this hysterical boredom as one of the causes of Natasha's vulnerability to the brainless Anatole Kuragin, along with the horrible reception she has just received from her fiancé's family. Wildly, she breaks her engagement to Prince Andrey and is prevented from ruining herself in elopement with Anatole only by the watchfulness of Sonya. She turns upon Sonya, who tries to warn her that the man must be dishonorable, crying, "I hate you, I hate you! You're my enemy forever!" (Tanya had responded to Tolstoy's warnings by calling him her enemy, and he had replied that her only "enemy is the twenty extra years I've lived on earth.")

Natasha is crushed to learn that Anatole is already married and so really had meant to ruin her. In her shame and despair, she follows Tanya's way by taking poison, then becomes frightened and calls for help, so that she narrowly escapes suicide. Thus the life Tanya Behrs was living even as Tolstoy was writing earlier parts of *War and Peace* entered into and shaped the fiction. Although the main story of the Rostovs follows that of the Tolstoys, the atmosphere and vitality of the family, particularly of the two girls Sonya and Natasha, emerged out of Tolstoy's profoundly intimate relations with the Behrs family in love and marriage.

Bolkonskys and Volkonskys

Never having seen so much as a picture of his mother, born Princess Marya Nikolayevna Volkonskaya, and having no recollection of her, Lev Tolstoy always thought of her as "so elevated, pure, and spiritual that often in the middle period of my life, during my struggle with overwhelming temptations," he had "prayed to her soul, begging her to aid me, and this prayer always helped me much." Everything he had learned of his mother, he said, was "beautiful." When he depicted her in the Princess Marya Nikolayevna Bolkonsky of *War and Peace*, he made her virtually a saint in loving-kindness and exalted self-transcendence.

He knew that the nun Marya Gerassimova—who, clad in a monk's cassock, had made pilgrimages as "Crazy Ivanushka" during her early years—had been made his sister Masha's godmother because of her prayers, which had been fulfilled, that his mother might have a girl after her four boys. Thereafter, Marya Gerassimova stayed as much with the Tolstoys as at the Tula convent. As a matter of fact, Lev Tolstoy's aunt, the Countess Alexandra Ilyinishna Osten-Saken, saw to it through the years after his mother's death that their house was filled with passing pilgrims, with religious devotees of all kinds, some of them staying for weeks at a time.

As a beautiful girl, this aunt had made a brilliant marriage to a wealthy Baltic nobleman, Count Osten-Saken. Almost immediately he became psychotic, and flying with her in an open carriage from enemies—entirely hallucinatory—whom he thought were attempting to ravish her, he panicked for her honor and shot her point blank through the chest (luckily missing vital organs). Afterward, with Osten-Saken incarcerated in an asylum, she lived with her brother, Tolstoy's father, at Yasnaya Polyana until her death when Lev was twelve years old. Aunt Aline, as they called her, spent her life in prayer, religious reading, service to others, and abstinence from luxury, even from comfort. As Tolstoy said, "She never had any money because she gave away all she had to those who asked."

Associated as she and her pilgrims were, through "Crazy Ivanushka," with his mother, this aunt became for him and his sister Masha a model of a truly Christian life. Tolstoy's ultimate philosophy of service and denial of luxury, and his later enjoyment of long conversations with pilgrims passing on the Tula road, harked back in many ways to her example. This aunt, plus all he knew of his mother, shaped the Princess Marya of *War and Peace*. She, like Auntie Aline, spends her time in prayer and conversation with pilgrims, nuns, and religious devotees.

When we first see her among her pilgrims, she is with an old lady and Marya Gerassimova during her "Crazy Ivanushka" period in a monk's cassock (except that Tolstoy erases the "Crazy," making her simply "Ivanushka," and deflecting the craziness to another pilgrim called "Crazy Kiril"). So much are these pilgrims an ideal for the Princess Marya that she keeps a rough pilgrim habit as a secret treasure, and only her devotion to her father and nephew stops her from going forth at once to beg her way from one holy place to another.

Of his mother's girlhood, Tolstoy had learned much from a first cousin of hers, Princess Varvara Alexandrovna Volkonskaya, whose father Alexander Sergeyevich Volkonsky, a widower like his brother Nikolay, took her for long visits to Yasnaya Polyana so that she saw much of what went on in that house. Tolstoy met this "dear old lady" in Moscow in the fall of 1857. Later he spent several weeks at her estate—"one of the pure, bright" experiences of his life, he said—where she fed him on her own homemade sauerkraut, marmalades, and cream cheeses and told him about his mother and grandfather.

Tolstoy also had direct access to his mother as a girl from a number of her letters that impressed him with the simplicity and honesty of their tone compared with the conventional artificialities of the early-nineteenth-century style. He knew that his mother had had a romantic friendship with a Frenchwoman, Mademoiselle Enissienne, which ended in disillusionment—probably at the time Mademoiselle Enissienne triumphantly carried off in marriage his mother's cousin, Prince Mikhail Volkonsky, whom she had thought of as her own suitor. In the novel, the Frenchwoman is Mademoiselle Bourienne, a pretty, vain, self-seeking companion to the Princess Marya, whose spiritual splendors she sets off. Tolstoy transplanted the romantic friendship from the Frenchwoman to a society girl, Julie Karagin, who also serves to set off by contrast the sincerity and spiritual force of the Princess Marya.

In his mother's letters, Tolstoy had been particularly impressed by a quality he had found also in his brother Nikolay, the ability to refrain from passing judgment on and condemning anyone. His Princess Marya shares it. In a story similar to his mother's of being cut out in love by her French friend, he had the Princess come upon her own suitor, Anatole Kuragin, embracing Mademoiselle Bourienne in the conservatory. Far from condemning her, the Princess comforts the tearful Frenchwoman, finds excuses for her, and even wants to further her happiness with Anatole.

These characteristics came from Tolstoy's conception of his mother as such a lofty spirit that he could pray to her as to a saint. Yet with all her spirituality, no character in *War and Peace* is more physically, tangibly realized than the Princess Bolkonsky. Tolstoy was able to transcribe every rush of blood to her face because he saw her in the form of his intimately known and loved younger sister Marya, next to him in age. In the novel he gave the Princess a brother and made their love for one another out of his and his sister Marya's.

Describing his sister in his earlier novel *Boyhood* as the little girl Lyubochka, Tolstoy tells us she is "small," and because she has had "rickets her legs are still crooked and her figure is very ugly. The only pretty thing about her face is her eyes, and they are really very beautiful—large and dark, and with such an indefinably attractive expression of dignity and simplicity that they are bound to attract attention. Lyubochka is natural and simple in everything." Later, in the third book of this series (*Childhood, Boyhood,* and *Youth*) Tolstoy tells us that Lyubochka had "begun to wear dresses which were almost long, so that her badly-shaped legs were hardly visible at all; yet she still cried as much as ever." Even in the last book, *Youth,* she is still called "tearful Lyubochka" with "her crooked legs and innocent prattle."

Just so would Tolstoy and his brothers talk of their sister Masha. Speaking in a letter of how innocently Masha had accepted their brother Sergey's liaison with the gypsy Shishkina, Tolstoy told Sergey, "That's what the pigeon-toed little Mashenka with the big eyes and rickets thought about it. How nice, how clever and what a wonderful heart." Tolstoy always felt toward his sister an odd mixture of jealous love, superiority, and pride in her. Meeting her as a married woman at the baths in Pyatigorsk, he scorned her pleasure in the "bad" company of the "local assembly rooms," and felt hurt at her seeming to prefer it to his own, but as he wrote his brother Sergey, "I can't help rejoicing to see her: how sweetly and simply and with what dignity she knows how to behave everywhere."

In *War and Peace* Tolstoy erased the childhood rickets, which his mother had never had, and spoke only of the Princess Marya's "thin face and weak, uncomely body," transfigured, as in the little girl of *Boyhood* by her eyes. They are "large, deep and luminous," and they seem to radiate "shafts of warm light." They are "so beautiful that very often in spite of the plainness of her face they gave her an attraction more powerful than that of beauty." Tolstoy also gave the Princess Marya his sister's tears. When her brother Prince Andrey returns to Bald Hills (Yasnaya Polyana) before setting out for the war, he tells her affectionately that she is the "same crybaby as ever." At the same time, he perceives "through her tears the loving, warm, gentle look of her large luminous eyes, very beautiful at that moment." Such were the eyes of Tolstoy's sister, described by V. P. Botkin as "large moist eyes full of deep feeling."

The deep feeling was certainly characteristic of Masha, and she, like Auntie Aline, was devoted wholeheartedly to Greek Orthodoxy, always ready to believe in the miracles that "God's folk" talked of. Tolstoy himself was skeptical of dogmas and miracles, but he respected the religious feeling of simple believers like his sister. In her sixties, Masha came under the influence of the elder of the Optina Monastery and entered a convent in 1891. It was his devout sister—not the mother he could not remember or the aging Aunt Aline of his childhood—whom Tolstoy saw when representing Princess Marya among her holy ones, and appropriately one of them is Marya Gerassimova, her actual godmother.

Tolstoy probably learned of his mother's unhappiness during her father's capricious senility from her cousin Varvara Alexandrovna Volkonsky and gave it to his fictional Princess Marya. But his representation of her as a perpetual victim, often looking "sickly" and blighted by an "unattractive martyrlike expression," came more likely of his own observation of his sister Masha's acute unhappiness and sickliness in the period when her unhappy marriage was breaking up.

Masha's martyrdom began some five years after her marriage in 1847 to Count Valerian Petrovich Tolstoy, a second cousin of hers and a nephew of Auntie Tatyana. As early as June 1852, Tolstoy was noting in his diary that Valerian wanted to separate from "Masha, who is wonderfully good." They staggered on together for another five years before the total smash came. Her suffering became mixed, both in her mind and in Lev's with their complicated feelings during and after it, for the novelist Ivan Sergeyevich Turgenev.

Turgenev spent most of his time abroad, usually in France, circling around his great love, the opera singer Pauline Viardot, but would return to Russia in the summer for a fairly long stay at his estate, Spasskoye. There, in October 1854, he met for the first time Count Valerian Tolstoy and Countess Marya, whose estate, Pokrovskoye, was about sixteen and a half miles from Spasskoye. He found this sister of the young writer Count Tolstoy—so he told Nikolay A. Nekrasov—"an enchanting woman, clever, kind, and very attractive." To Pavel Vasilyevich Annenkov, Turgenev confided that she was "one of the most attractive women I have ever met—charming, intelligent, and simple. In my old age (three days ago I was thirty-six) I have nearly fallen in love"—in fact, he was, he said, "smitten to the heart. I have not met so much grace for a long time."

Soon after, Marya made Turgenev godfather of her latest baby, and the "Turgenevo priest" christened it. Spasskoye being "25 versts" from Pokrovskoye, they met sometimes at Yasnaya Polyana, only 10 versts from Turgenev. Lev Tolstoy was then fighting in the Caucasus and the estate was a shambles. To pay Lev's gambling debts, Valerian had sold the beautiful mansion erected by Lev's grandfather Volkonsky, and it was being dismantled for erection elsewhere, leaving only what had been the servants' quarters, two bare detached wings.

At Pokrovskoye, Turgenev hunted with Valerian and read his own stories, as he finished them, to the Countess. She was a fine pianist, and he could share with her the love of music that had caught him in his futile lifelong devotion to the opera singer Pauline Viardot. Soon he was repeating the role he had played with the Viardots, except that he and Viardot were in the same boat, both pushed aside in favor of Pauline's great love, the portrait painter Ary Scheffer. But Marya Tolstaya— distressed as she was with the polygamously disposed Valerian—felt strongly drawn to the tall, handsome, blue-eyed Turgenev, sharing as he did her intelligence, sensibility, and interests. Yet Turgenev was already admitting to Annenkov, "As to the Countess, everything is finished and done with." He had explained to the Countess Lambert that for all her charm, Marya did not have beautiful hands, and for him hands were "if not everything, then almost everything."

In November 1855, when Lev Tolstoy escaped from the fighting at Sevastopol, having been sent as a courier to St. Petersburg, he went directly—in answer to an earlier invitation—to the apartment there of his sister's friend Turgenev. On arrival, as Turgenev reported to the poet Afanasy Afanasyevich Fet, Tolstoy had gone off "painting the town red. Debaucheries, gypsies, cards: and then asleep like a log till two o'clock in the afternoon." Turgenev wrote Marya: "You have quite a brother. I've nicknamed him the 'Troglodyte'—even the 'furious Troglodyte'—because of his impetuousness, wild stubbornness, and idleness—which doesn't prevent me from loving him from the bottom of my heart." He and Konstantin Islavin would discuss Tolstoy sighing, looking up to heaven, and shrugging their shoulders.

Tolstoy became steadily more rambunctious, disrupting a dinner party Nekrasov gave for Turgenev where all the assembled literati were adoring George Sand as the apostle of liberty and thinking women. Tolstoy "infuriated everyone" by declaring that her heroines—if real—ought to be "tied to the hangman's cart and driven through the streets of St. Petersburg as an example." Actually Tolstoy had admired some of her books, but he was desperately fighting the liberal opinions of his fellow writers at this point because he felt on the brink of adopting some of them himself.

Afterward, Turgenev told Tolstoy that much as he loved him as an author and person, he found it "more comfortable to keep my distance from you." Because Turgenev was back in France, he had no trouble keeping his distance. Before leaving, he had reported that Marya Tolstaya looked "sad and has lost weight." She seemed to be "ill all the time," whereas the adulterous "Count is flourishing like a peony." Recognizing herself in the heroine of the Turgenev short story "Faust," dedicated to her, Marya took fire and wrote Turgenev so enthusiastically that, frightened, he sent back (on January 6, 1857) a splash of very cold water.

While writing the story, he told her, "I was still dreaming of happiness," but "now I've given up on that forever." It had come at a turning point in his life when his whole soul "flared up with the last fire of memories, hopes, and youth." Never again would he feel that way, and it was no use "fanning the ashes." When he returned to Spasskoye in the summer, she and her brothers Lev and Nikolay could come stay with him and they would "begin living as merry, kind old folks."

By this time, Lev had finished fighting out his inner battle, and he began to swing toward liberalism. Turgenev kept receiving from fellow writers reports of a turn for the "better" in Tolstoy. Tolstoy himself felt the change as a new joy in the poet who inspired the revolutionary Decembrists, Alexander Pushkin. After a reading of him at V. P. Botkin's house, Tolstoy retreated to a sofa in Botkin's room and shed "blissful poetic tears," feeling "intoxicated by the rapidity" of his own "moral development—forward and forward." He wrote Turgenev announcing it, and Turgenev congratulated him on calming down, becoming more "free of your own views and prejudices," and on realizing that "a look to the left is just as nice as to the right." Turgenev concluded, "God grant that your horizons widen with every passing day!" Soon after, Tolstoy took his first look at Europe, landing on Turgenev's Paris doorstep in February 1857. To their mutual friends, Turgenev reported that Tolstoy was much better, much "smarter," but still "uncomfortable" with himself, and therefore with other people. Turgenev rejoiced to see him nevertheless, for Tolstoy was, he thought, Russian literature's "single hope."

One of the big changes in Tolstoy had come in his estimate of Alexander Herzen, whose criticisms of autocrat Russia he had once fiercely rejected. Now he had read Herzen's *My Past and Thoughts* with great admiration, along with some of his other works, and, as Turgenev reported to Herzen in England, Herzen's regards, sent through Turgenev, had made Tolstoy "very happy and he asks me to tell you that he's wanted to make your acquaintance for a long time—and that he loves you beforehand, just as he loved your works (though N.B. he is hardly a red)."

Tolstoy's feelings toward Turgenev remained as queasy as Turgenev's for him. From one day to another, Tolstoy thought Turgenev "vain and shallow," "kind and terribly weak," unable to "believe in anything," unable to love, or "nice, but he is simply tired." Yet on April 8, when he parted from Turgenev on leaving Paris, he suddenly began to weep and realized, "I am very fond of him. He has made and is making a different man of me."

Four months later, on receiving an S.O.S. from Tolstoy, who was ill and bankrupt from roulette in Baden-Baden, Turgenev rushed to his rescue. Within the day, Tolstoy gambled and lost all the money Turgenev brought. At this point came an urgent letter from Masha, telling Tolstoy that she could not live any longer with a husband who flaunted four mistresses in her face, and that she had fled Valerian's estate leaving a note saying that she did not want to be the "senior sultana in his harem." Reporting to V. P. Botkin, Turgenev declared that one of Valerian's mistresses, jealous of another of them, had brought the Countess a letter to the rival from Valerian, talking of what they would do when his wife died. Marya had been cut to the heart. From a friend in Baden, Turgenev borrowed enough money for Tolstoy to pay off his doctor, treating him for a venereal infection, and to rush home to help his sister.

After leaving Valerian, Masha placed her hopes on Turgenev. At a family conference with himself, Serozha, and Auntie—so Tolstoy noted,

August 11, 1857—"Masha told us about Turgenev," making him feel afraid for "them both." Auntie defended her, but Serozha was "touching in his perplexity." Without waiting for Lev and Nikolay, Masha went alone to stay with Turgenev at Spasskoye. Angrily, Tolstoy declared that she was "egotistic, spoilt, and narrow." Only later that winter did he begin to learn "to get on with Mashenka."

By that time, Masha was discovering—what had already become more than plain—that Turgenev had lost his initial enchantment with her. "Turgenev is behaving badly to Mashenka. The pig," Lev commented on September 4, 1858. Botkin asked Turgenev outright why he seemed to be avoiding Marya and Lev Tolstoy. He answered in all honesty, "She has changed very much in my eyes, and, on top of that, je n'ai rien a lui dire."

It was this double rejection, first by her husband and then by Turgenev that gave Tolstoy his image of the "wonderfully good" but cruelly hurt Princess Marya. From Masha, she takes both her "unattractive martyrlike expression" and her "thin face and weak, uncomely body." Lev Tolstoy and the entire family believed at this time that Masha was consumptive (luckily for her, erroneously, for she would end by outliving them all, including her husband Valerian, who died on January 6, 1865). Also in Princess Marya, Tolstoy put his sister's two distinct appearances. Unhappy, Princess Bolkonsky looks ugly, sickly, and awkward, but transfigured by loving-kindness she takes on "dignity and grace." Her large eyes appear radiant with a spiritual splendor more attractive than beauty.

So in this intimate novel whose characters came out of Tolstoy's nearest and dearest, his sister Masha became a major character, endowing the Princess Bolkonsky with her most powerful life experiences, although they were channeled through the life story of Tolstoy's mother. Nor did Masha's influence on the novel stop there. She was approaching a major event in her woman's search for love. Tolstoy himself had shared that search in the case of Turgenev, an older writer he admired. Like Masha, but on a different level, he had sought love from him and had been frustrated even as she. Tolstoy's sense of himself as ugly and awkward allowed him to enter into and feel within himself all his sister's pain and humiliation in love.

In the next years, crucial for both himself and Masha, they would share anguish and loss and a terrible fatality. Together they would suffer over the loss of their beloved brother Nikolay, after a terrible time when it seemed the whole family would die of consumption. Their brother

Dmitry had succumbed first. Masha and Nikolay seemed to be following him to the grave. Lev himself had nightmares that he had the disease and was dying with them. While Nikolay and Masha took the cure at Sodden, Lev worked in nearby Berlin. He was with them when they moved to Hyeres on the French Riviera, where Nikolay died on September 20, 1860. "Nikolenka's death is the most powerful impression that I have ever known," Tolstoy said. Hard on it came a decisive quarrel and severance from Turgenev for many years. So in different ways both his sister and he saw their affection for the senior writer end in evasion and rejection.

The culminating event in Masha's search for love came after all this—news of it reaching Tolstoy just as he was beginning to work out the design of *War and Peace*. Out of it he shaped what he would later call "the key point of the whole novel." It did not fit into his story of the Princess Bolkonsky, but it was just what he wanted for his character Natasha. He made it the decisive event in Natasha's moral development and in that of the two principal male protagonists, Prince Andrey and Pierre. For them, as for Lev Tolstoy himself, the event would become a test, a shattering of their lives and beliefs, demanding a cataclysmic restructuring of everything within them.

Prince Andrey

Through their spiritual growth, Prince Andrey and Pierre reveal much of the unfolding meaning of *War and Peace*. On the July evening in 1805 when the story begins, they stand together in sharp contrast to the courtly St. Petersburg society at Anna Scherer's soiree. At its end they are still linked, although Prince Andrey has died, in the book's "Epilogue," which gives a glimpse of Pierre and Prince Andrey's son as they mutually commit themselves to the secret societies that would bring on the December Revolt of 1825. Different as Pierre and Prince Andrey are in personality, they are both avatars of Tolstoy. Between them they argue out many of the questions within him, and they arrive, each in his own way, at answers he was seeking.

Although Prince Andrey ended as a central character in *War and Peace*, he came to life far from the nexus of memories that brought forth Sonya and Natasha and Princess Marya. Tolstoy picked him out of a letter written June 24, 1812, by a young girl, M. A. Volkova, to her friend V. I. Lanskaya, saying, "Prince Andrey has decided to set off for the war and is leaving his wife to cope with her childbirth as best she can." The girl's implied criticism and the name gave Tolstoy the germ of his Prince Andrey. At first, he was meant to be no more, for Tolstoy had merely needed—so he explained to his cousin's wife, Princess Louisa Ivanovna Volkonskaya—"a brilliant young man to be killed at the battle of Austerlitz," which, at this stage, was to begin the book. Then he brought Prince Andrey into his main story as a son of Prince Nikolay Bolkonsky and brother to the Princess Marya.

At once, he began to grow as a chip off Tolstoy's own Volkonsky stock. Interested, Tolstoy "took pity on him," and had him wounded, not killed, at Austerlitz. From a portrait of Grandfather Volkonsky in his prime, Tolstoy found his image of Prince Andrey as a "very handsome young man, of medium height, with firm clear-cut features." The same portrait, including his grandfather's actual wig, served for Prince Andrey's father as well. Bashilov's drawing of Prince Andrey, Tolstoy thought, failed, for he was "too tall," his features were "too big and coarse" and his "attitude and dress" not "dignified enough." He wanted a youthful and impressive image of his Grandfather Volkonsky, "a clever and talented, though proud man," with all his dignity as commander-in-chief of the Russian army. Prince Andrey is just as clever and proud, being described by the Royalist Vicomte at Anna Scherer's soiree as "that little officer who gives himself the airs of a monarch." His sister Princess Marya warns him that he has "a kind of intellectual pride," which is "a great sin."

On questioning the serfs at Yasnaya Polyana, Tolstoy heard severe criticisms of his father as a master, but "only praises of my grandfather's intelligence, business capacities and interest in the welfare of the peasants and servants of his enormous household." He gave Prince Andrey the same kind of "practical tenacity" and integrity.

Prince Andrey comes close to Tolstoy's intimate memories through the resemblance of the wife he leaves to Princess Louisa Ivanovna Volkonsky, who was married to Tolstoy's cousin Sasha, Prince A. A. Volkonsky, and whose short upper lip had charmed him through the winters of 1850–51 and of 1855–56 in St. Petersburg. Apparently she recognized both herself and her husband in Prince Andrey and his wife, for she asked Tolstoy about these characters when the first part of the story appeared. Tolstoy wrote back: "Andrey Bolkonsky is nobody, like any character by a novelist, as opposed to a writer of personalities or memoirs. I would be ashamed to be published if all my work consisted in copying a portrait, trying to find things out." Certainly Prince Andrey was a composite, but his enervated elegance probably did come from Louisa's husband, whose chronic debility had resulted in his death earlier that same year of 1865. Tolstoy instructed Bashilov to make Prince Andrey "more superciliously languid and gracefully supine." Death hangs over him throughout the book.

Prince Andrey took on real complexity as soon as Tolstoy received, at his own request, the criticism of A. A. Fet and also, through him, of Turgenev, whom, Tolstoy told him, "I dislike all the more, the older I grow," but who, he knew, "*will* understand." Fet's condemnation of Prince Andrey as being "tedious, monotonous, merely un homme comme il faut," Tolstoy accepted, adding, "It's not his fault, it's mine." At once, Tolstoy brought Prince Andrey vitality by giving him many of his own traits. Prince Andrey's strongest impulse—as well as that of his friend Pierre—is Tolstoy's own urgent need to grapple with the meaning of life. Back on May 23, 1856, in Moscow, Tolstoy had met Yury Fyodorovich Samarin and had taken at once to his "cold, flexible, and trained mind." He told Samarin that he was just the sort of friend he needed, "a person of independent mind, loving many things, but above all the truth, and seeking it." Tolstoy too was such a man, and all his life, he said, "I have loved the truth above all else, and have never despaired of finding it, and I go on seeking it." Their steadfast search for truth sets both Prince Andrey and Pierre above the "idiots" and "lackeys" to the tsar of the St. Petersburg society where they are first seen.

As Tolstoy told Samarin, "You are closer to me in the moral and intellectual world than any other person." So he made Prince Andrey and Pierre, and their intellectual closeness is chiefly what rescued Prince Andrey from his formerly evanescent role in the book to stand with Pierre as a channel through which Tolstoy could work toward solving the mystery of human existence. Tolstoy himself stood somewhere between the eminently rational Prince Andrey and the speculative, mystically inclined Pierre.

Disciplined rational minds always had an attraction for Tolstoy. Later he formed a similar bond with the highly analytical critic Nikolay Nikolayevich Strakhov (on whom he would rely absolutely to help cut *War and Peace* for its second edition in November 1873). "What criticism, judgments, or classifications can compare," Tolstoy asked Strakhov, "with an ardent, passionate search for a meaning for one's life?"

Even in small matters, Tolstoy gave Prince Andrey his own love of the truth and disgust with falsity. He had always suspected Turgenev's cordiality and tact as being, in reality, insincerity. Turgenev told E. Garshin of Tolstoy, "Any kind of emotion seemed false to him, and he had the habit, by the extraordinarily penetrating glance of his eyes, of piercing through the man who struck him as false." At the time of their great quarrel, Tolstoy's "penetrating glance," joined "with two or three venomous remarks," had exasperated Turgenev "to the verge of madness."

That quarrel had been set off by Turgenev's telling Fet and Tolstoy that the English governess he had provided for his illegitimate daughter had taught her to mend the clothes of the poor. Tolstoy burst out that, in his opinion, a finely dressed girl "handling dirty, stinking rags, is acting a false and theatrical farce." Taking this as a criticism of his care for his daughter, toward whom he always felt guilty, Turgenev lost his head and threatened to punch Tolstoy. They came within a hair's breadth of a duel.

Tolstoy was by no means blind to his own provoking traits. After the dinner party at which he had shocked the literati, he wrote in his diary: "Behaved disgustingly after dinner at Nekrasov's" and "I said unpleasant things to everybody." Prince Andrey has both Tolstoy's own sharp tongue and his distrust of emotional displays. On seeing each other for the second time in their lives, his sister and his wife fall into each other's arms weeping and kissing endlessly, Russian style. Prince Andrey reacts by shrugging his shoulders and frowning "as lovers of music do when they hear a false note." On parting with his wife, he turns to her "coldly ironic," saying "Well!" as if he meant that she could now go through her performance—which she does, screaming and falling into a faint.

In other scenes, Prince Andrey makes Tolstoy's "venomous remarks," declaring "with venomous irony" that German officers were court-martialing their Russian soldiers for foraging, "so as not to lay waste to the country we were abandoning to the enemy." By his "disagreeable ironical tone," Prince Andrey has tangled with Nikolay Rostov, who is telling how, at the battle of Schön Grabern, he had flown "like a storm" at the French square, cutting and slashing. Actually, in prosaic truth, going at a trot, he "fell off his horse and sprained his arm and then ran as hard as he could from a Frenchman into a wood." Prince Andrey's look of disgust drives Rostov—who really wanted to tell the truth, but could not avoid conventional patterns—to such a fury that he wants to provoke a duel. Even as he imagines making that "small and frail but proud man" fear him, he realizes that "of all the men he knew, there was none he would so much like to have for a friend" as this very Prince Andrey.

Real war, Tolstoy knew, was very different from the false ideas in the history books of his time. Reading Stendhal's *Charterhouse of Parma* had set him straight with its story of the adolescent Fabrizio del Dongo going off to fight for his hero Napoleon, only to find such chaos dashing about with a general and his staff (who end by taking his horse out from under him) that he wonders whether he has been in a real battle. Actually he has been in nothing less than the Battle of Waterloo. Tolstoy's fighting in the Caucasus confirmed for him the confusing nature of a battle, where, as he shows at the battle of Schön Grabern in *War and Peace*, a regimental commander cannot possibly know from what he has seen whether he has repulsed the enemy attack or the enemy had destroyed his regiment.

Prince Andrey sees that the real destiny of a battle lies with the regiments in combat, not with the plans of the top command. With Prince Bagratión at Schön Grabern, he sees that once the battle is under way, Prince Bagratión can give no orders because they will be obsolete by the time they reach his subordinates. His value lies in making it appear that all that happened "by necessity, by accident, by the will of subordinate commanders" is "in accord with his intentions," so that he calms and cheers everyone.

Tolstoy's war experience was in artillery. During the Crimean War, he was, from April 1 to May 15, "for four days at a time, at intervals of eight days," in "charge of a battery in the 4th Bastion," which was steadily "in serious danger." No wonder his two most vivid accounts of battle in *War and Peace*—Schön Grabern and Borodino—are seen from the viewpoint of an artillery battery under devastating enemy fire. At Schön Grabern, Tolstoy shows that the real hero of the battle is Captain Tushin, who, entirely on his own initiative, has his company fire incendiary balls at the village of Schön Grabern, setting it on fire, and who keeps up such an energetic cannonading that the French are afraid to attack, thinking that the Russian forces are centered around him.

On the report of a frightened adjutant, he is called up for reprimand. Luckily Prince Andrey has witnessed all, and can vouch that Tushin fought on with two-thirds of his men killed, two of his guns smashed, and no supporting battalions at all. They owe their success on that day, Prince Andrey declares, to the "action of that battery and the heroic endurance of Captain Tushin and his company."

Tolstoy's bastion at Sevastopol had shown similar courage and endurance, yet their commander, Captain-Lieutenant Korenitsky, had been brought up for court-martial afterward. Luckily Tolstoy had enough influence, because the new Emperor Alexander II had loved his Sevastopol stories, to give information and prevent a trial that might have ended disastrously for Korenitsky.

Although Prince Andrey is as little a careerist in the army as Tolstoy himself, he has Tolstoy's own passionate hunger for fame, for winning love and admiration. At only sixteen years old, Tolstoy already wanted to get "more power than others," to secure "a greater share of fame, of social distinction." He was afraid that he loved fame more than goodness and that given a choice he might easily "choose the former." Prince Andrey has the same hunger. He hero-worships Napoleon for rising from obscurity to heights of glory. He keeps waiting for his "Toulon," his "bridge of Arcola." On the eve of the Battle of Austerlitz, he is ready to sacrifice all he loves, "those dearest to me," for a "moment of glory, of triumph over men."

Actually he has his moment. With the sudden appearance of the French, a rout begins of panicking soldiers. Prince Andrey grabs a standard and, staggering under the weight of it, runs forward, so that an entire battalion follows him. A moment later he falls seriously wounded, as if bludgeoned, and has a revelation that entirely wipes out the "shouting and fighting," with all his dreams of glory. Above him he sees the peace and solemnity of an infinitude of sky with gray clouds gliding beneath it, and wonders why he never saw it before. "Yes! All is vanity, all falsehood, except that infinite sky. There is nothing, nothing but that." Melting into that "quiet and peace," he drifts into unconsciousness.

A similar mystical revelation of eternity that carried him above all earthly values, even above the fear of death, had come to Tolstoy on a hunt when he was attacked and knocked down by a huge bear, its slavering jaws gaping to get a bite through both his temples. Tolstoy could see "beyond the outline of that mouth, a patch of blue sky gleaming between purple clouds roughly piled on one another, and I thought how lovely it was up there." On the brink of "all-absorbing death," Tolstoy felt no fear, only a sense of peace. At Austerlitz, Prince Andrey has the same transcendent revelation Tolstoy had on that December day in 1858.

Tolstoy combined Prince Andrey's vision with the experience at Austerlitz of a cousin of his, Prince Nikolay Gregoryevich Volkonsky, who had taken his mother's illustrious name of "Repnín," at Alexander

I's order, to save it from extinction. He had fallen with a severe head wound, and the French, seeing he was a commanding officer, had him carried to the hospital tent. Napoleon had complimented him on his bravery, and Tolstoy's cousin had replied: "The praise of a great commander is a soldier's highest reward." In *War and Peace*, Prince Andrey witnesses this magniloquent colloquy, but Napoleon now seems to him "so mean," with "his paltry vanity and joy in victory," that he turns away to concentrate on the "lofty, equitable, and kindly sky."

Decembrists

If Prince Andrey took much of his vitality from Tolstoy's Volkonsky heritage, Pierre came directly out of it. He—along with the entire first conception of *War and Peace*—came to life on August 26, 1856, the Coronation Day of the Emperor Alexander II, when he granted a general amnesty extending even to the fifteen old men who were still alive of the 121 Decembrists who had been sentenced by his father Nicholas I to hard labor and permanent exile in Siberia twenty-five years earlier. Tolstoy's exiled Decembrist cousin, Prince Sergey Gregoryevich Volkonsky, was liberated with his comrades when his son reached him after traveling the 4,000 miles from Moscow to Irkutsk with the Emperor's decree. Nicholas I had tried to censor out all memory of the Decembrists, but they had become an indestructible symbol of hope.

Tolstoy came upon his freshly liberated cousin Sergey Volkonsky with his wife Marya in Florence, Italy, and was much struck with him during the two weeks of December 1860 he spent with him there. With his long white hair, the tall, gaunt, sixty-five-year-old former Prince Volkonsky—he had been stripped of his title when condemned—looked, Tolstoy said, exactly like "an Old Testament prophet," and he marveled over this "astonishing old man, the flower of the St. Petersburg aristocracy, nobly born and charming," who had spent many years of hard labor in the Nerchinsk iron mines, and more years as a Siberian farmer, working in his fields like a peasant.

To Tolstoy so electrifying was the life story of this former hero of the War of 1812, brother to the Prince Repnín who had been wounded at Austerlitz, that he immediately began writing a novel about him, "The Decembrists"—a book that would develop directly into *War and Peace*.

By the time Tolstoy reached Paris in February 1861, he had three chapters, which he read without delay to Turgenev.

Strangely enough, the story of the Decembrists—tragic, futile, exalted—would never be told in *War and Peace*, but it haunts its pages. Hardly a noble family of Russia was without a son, brother, or cousin among the Decembrists: Volkonskys, Trubetskoys, Bestuzhevs, Lunins, Muraviev-Apostols, Obolenskys. French, not Russian, being the language of the nobility, most of the Decembrists had been educated in French thought and had served as officers (thirty colonels and five generals among them) in Alexander I's elite guards regiments. During Russia's campaigns in Europe against Napoleon, they had seen governments made and broken, had compared the look of free men in Europe to their own serf population, and had watched their emperor grant constitutions to Poland and France, while they in Russia remained totally suppressed, without even a body of coherent laws.

As one of the Decembrists, Baron Vladimir Ivanovich Steingel, exclaimed to Nicholas I, "Oh, Sovereign, to eradicate free thinking there is no other means than to destroy an entire generation, born and educated during the last reign!" And Pavel Kakhovsky explained that their society had sprung out of "the spirit of the times," embodied in the United States of America, the republic that would "shine as an example even to distant generations." General I. V. Vasilchikov, Nicholas I's aide-de-camp, announced: "The entire contemporary generation is infected!"

The unexpected death of Alexander I had forced the Decembrists to action, for a coup d'état could be effected only between reigns. Yet they all knew they were doomed, for they could count on only a few regiments to join them. Prince Trubetskoy, their provisional leader during the revolt, declared it hopeless. He drew up their manifesto, standing for representative government, freedom of the press, religious tolerance, abolition of slavery, abolition of corporal punishment, and equality of all classes before the law. Then he simply disappeared, wandering off in a daze, not even appearing at the rallying point, Senate Square behind the Winter Palace in St. Petersburg. Kondratin Fyodorovich Ryleyev, the poet, told his companions they were sure to be destroyed, "but our example will remain. We shall sacrifice ourselves for the future freedom of our fatherland." Young Prince Alexander Odoyevsky kept chanting, "We shall die! Oh, how gloriously we shall die!"

On the morning of December 14, 1825, Staff Captain M. A. Bestuzhev marched some three thousand men into Senate Square, and there, in an icy wind, with the temperature eight degrees below freezing, they stood all day—without plan, without strategy, with nothing but the hope that, seeing them there, other garrisons would join them. Finally, in the arctic darkness of afternoon, the new Emperor Nicholas I had set up sufficient artillery and troops to mow them down with grapeshot. Everyone who could fled the square. Holes were cut in the ice of the Neva and some 200 bodies, many of them bystanders, were hastily thrown in.

Actually the police had already made a report on the secret societies, so they had no trouble finding those implicated. The leader of the southern societies, Colonel Pavel Ivanovich Pestel, had been arrested two days before the revolt. On learning of it, his close friend Prince Sergey Volkonsky felt "drained"—so it was reported—"of his very life-blood." Five hundred and seventy-nine were arrested, most of them confined in the icy dungeons—still wet from the flood of the Neva the year before—of the grim Petropavlovsk fortress, across the Neva from the Winter Palace.

Although Catherine the Great had abolished corporal punishment for the nobility, Nicholas I ordered many of them shackled with chains so heavy they could barely walk and kept on bread and water. When Lev Tolstoy saw those heavy manacles at the fortress later, he said, "I can't express the strange, powerful feeling I experienced." The irons accompanied the Decembrists throughout six months of interrogation, and through the first two years of hard labor in the Nerchinsk iron mines. When Sergey Volkonsky's beautiful young wife, the former Marya Raevskaya—one of the first Decembrist wives permitted to join her husband—reached him in his Siberian prison, she threw herself at his feet and kissed his chains before embracing him.

Nicholas I became prosecutor, judge, and jury of the Decembrists. He called back Mikhail Mikhailovich Speransky from exile to work behind the scenes setting up questionnaires, categories of guilt, and the punishments to be exacted—all as Nicholas wished them—along with a committee to take responsibility for the condemnations. Speransky had formerly been the most powerful figure after the Emperor Alexander I, until a cabal that was hostile to his liberalism destroyed him by a false accusation of conspiring with Napoleon.

In War and Peace, Speransky appears as an idol of Prince Andrey during a brief period when he naively believes, just as Tolstoy believed at the beginning of the reign of Alexander II, that he could work for reform by submitting a plan for a "reorganization of the army." Tolstoy had presented his plan to the Minister of the Interior, Count Sergey Stepanovich Lanskoy, and he had Prince Andrey submit his plan to Speransky and Arakcheev with equal futility. Later, Prince Andrey tries to mask his heartbreak at losing his fiancée Natasha by excitedly arguing that Speransky, just exiled, is innocent. Nicholas I knew very well that Speransky was innocent when he recalled him to organize the prosecution of the Decembrists.

Nicholas had many of the prisoners brought to him for personal questioning. All of them were led to believe that if they would confess fully they would come off lightly. Cooperative prisoners such as Kakhovsky—whom Nicholas had already slated for death as a "major offender"—were to be softened up by "privileged treatment," including hot tea. Others were to be treated with "the severity that befits a wretch."

Most of these officers were well known to Nicholas, for as Grand Duke he had been Guards Brigadier over them. He dangled the hope of a pardon before Prince Sergey Volkonsky if he spoke out, but Volkonsky thought only of protecting his comrades. Years afterward, the Emperor Nicholas was still raging at his reticence, pointing out that Volkonsky had always been "an absolute idiot" and had "stood before me with a sort of dazed look on his face—a revolting picture of flagrant ingratitude and arrant stupidity!"

On July 13, 1826, Pavel Pestel, Pavel Kakhovsky, Sergey Muraviev-Apostol, Mikhail P. Bestuzhev-Riumin, and Kondratin Ryleyev were hanged. In the days following, Alexander Pushkin filled his notebooks obsessively with sketches of the hanged men. He tried to accept the fact that "the dead are dead and cannot be brought back to life," but "When I think of those 121 friends, brothers, and comrades slaving away at hard labor," he told the poet Viazemsky, "I am filled with horror!" He managed to smuggle a poem to the Decembrists with the wife of one of them, Alexandra Muravieva, urging them to keep their "patience proud" until liberty triumphed, and Prince A. I. Odoyevsky got one back to him, laughing "in spirit over tsars."

For Alexander Herzen, the cruel fate of the Decembrists "shattered the childhood sleep of my soul." He was then sixteen, and he and Nikolay Platonovich Ogarev climbed to the top of the Vorobyev Hills outside of Moscow and swore to carry on the fight. Years later, when Herzen had escaped Russia and founded his own free press in England, assisted by Polish refugee printers who could smuggle its works into

Russia through the old Polish underground, he created a journal called *The Polar Star*, named after the almanac of Ryleyev and Alexander Bestuzhev, and on its masthead Herzen printed portraits of the five hanged Decembrists.

No wonder that Tolstoy, inspired by his cousin Sergey Volkonsky, went directly from Turgenev, who had also met Sergey Volkonsky and thought him "a very nice and good old man," to Herzen in London. As Herzen wrote Turgenev, "I am seeing a lot of Tolstoy. We have already quarreled. He is stubborn and talks nonsense, but is naive and a good man." For Tolstoy, his arguments with Herzen would trigger a transformation of the story he had started, "The Decembrists," into the very different book, *War and Peace*, that he wrote.

Herzen and he had argued over the meaning of history, of Russian history in particular. Official doctrine placed the cause of events in the will of the Emperor and celebrated Peter the Great as a god whose infallibility was embodied in his descendant, Emperor Nicholas I. All Russians were commanded to believe unquestioningly in the autocracy, in Greek Orthodoxy, and in Russianism. Herzen and Tolstoy argued over these shibboleths.

From Brussels, Tolstoy wrote Herzen: "You say I don't know Russia. No, I know my own subjective Russia, which I look at through my little prism. If the soap bubble of history has burst for you and me, this is also proof that we're blowing a new bubble which we can't yet see. And for me this bubble is the clear and sure knowledge of my Russia, as clear, perhaps, as Ryleyev's knowledge of Russia in 1825."

Herzen had given him as he was leaving the latest issue of *The Polar Star* with Bestuzhev's "Reminiscences of Kondratin Fyodorovich Ryleyev" and some letters of Mikhail Sergeyevich Lunin. "You can't imagine how interesting I found all the information about the Decembrists in *The Polar Star*," Tolstoy told him. "About four months ago I began a novel, the hero of which is to be a Decembrist returning from exile. I wanted to have a talk with you about it, but I didn't manage to. My Decembrist [called Pierre] is to be an enthusiast, a mystic, a Christian, returning to Russia in 1856 with his wife and son and daughter, and applying his stern and somewhat idealized views to the new Russia."

All the exciting new information from *The Polar Star* made Tolstoy decide to start with the Decembrist Revolt, so he moved his beginning back to 1825. Then he realized that the Decembrists could be understood only as a product of their experiences in the War of 1812, but he felt he could not present Russia's triumph over Bonapartist France, without describing "our failures and our shame" in the years before. So he decided to begin with Russia's defeats during the alliance against Napoleon with the hated Austrians in 1805, move on to the brief alliance with Napoleon, then to the War of 1812 against Napoleon, then to the Decembrist Revolt in 1825, and at last to the amnesty and return of the surviving Decembrists in 1856.

The astonishing shape of the final novel came of the impossibility of covering a half century of eventful history concerned with many intricately interrelated lives in a single book. Afterward Tolstoy confessed, "Neither my time nor capacity allowed me fully to accomplish what I intended." What had actually happened, although he was not consciously aware of it, was that he had succeeded by the time he reached 1813 in solving for his characters the questions on the purpose of life, on the meaning of history, and on the future of Russia with which he had begun.

So there he was with a central character, Pierre, whom he had been carefully delineating as a developing Decembrist only to have him reach illumination some thirteen years before ever the Decembrist Revolt began. Tolstoy had to take the odd way out of writing an "Epilogue" in which, during 1820, the secret societies are just getting under way with Pierre in the lead. In other words, he wrote a novel about a Decembrist without ever reaching the point at which he becomes one.

Once Tolstoy moved the start to 1805, he decided to "lead not one, but many heroes and heroines of mine through the historical events of 1805, 1807, 1812, 1825, and 1856." Nevertheless, the character he had started with, Pierre, remained dominant and kept his initial inspiration in the spiritual beauty of Tolstoy's cousin, the Decembrist Prince Sergey Volkonsky. As a young man, Volkonsky had been as Frenchified as Tolstoy made Pierre, who has grown up in Paris and returned to Russia at the age of twenty with a clipped head full of advanced French ideas. From childhood, Volkonsky, as Tolstoy knew, had been so very French in manner and thought that he was called "Monsieur Serge" by all his friends. At the beginning of *War and Peace*, everyone calls Tolstoy's protagonist "Monsieur Pierre."

Sergey Volkonsky had a reputation for being "simple," in the particularly Russian meaning of the word: "unpretentious," or "natural." By the time he returned from exile, Volkonsky's suffering had exalted the simplicity into a "superior inner artlessness." Tolstoy gave his Pierre just such a character. From the start of the story, when his naturalness frightens the artificial court lady Anna Scherer, Pierre's social gaffes are redeemed "by his kindly, simple, and modest expression." Pierre is also absent-minded—as were both Prince Volkonsky and Tolstoy himself—and for the same reason, because Pierre is a thinker, absorbed in philosophical inquiry rather than his immediate surroundings.

Of course, Tolstoy gave Pierre a background unlike his cousin's. Prince Sergey Volkonsky could not have been more legitimate. His mother, the Princess Sofya Volkonsky, was Mistress of the Robes to and a close friend of the Dowager Empress Marya Fyodorovna as well as of her sons, the Emperors Alexander I and Nicholas I. Likewise his father, Prince Gregory Volkonsky, dominated court circles. In contrast, Tolstoy's Pierre is illegitimate at the start of *War and Peace*, although he is a son of a grandee like Volkonsky. Thus his nickname, "Monsieur Pierre," appears as no joke, but a humiliating reminder that he is without name, rank, or expectations of inheritance. Only at the request of Pierre's dying father in his will does Pierre leap into legitimacy by the edict of the Emperor, take his father's name and title as Count Pierre Kirilovich Bezukhov, and inherit his father's wealth.

Illegitimacy was so common among nobles that Tolstoy needed no model for Pierre's, but as a matter of fact he had one very much in mind, who gave him much of Pierre's appearance, his reactions and attitudes, and even events in his life story. Pierre's identity is compounded out of Volkonsky with other Decembrists and also out of radicals of Tolstoy's day with Alexander Herzen foremost. Being illegitimate, Herzen was forbidden his father's name "Yakovlev," so he was called "Herzen," German for "hearts," which proclaimed only too clearly his origin as a love child.

In *My Past and Thoughts*, Herzen saw his ironic approach to society as a defense against the slights he suffered because of his illegitimacy. Pierre is equally sensitive. Even acknowledging his illegitimacy to a close friend like Prince Andrey, Pierre suddenly blushes "crimson, and it was plain that he had made a great effort to say this." He suffers from a sense of shame only, for he is indifferent to money and rank. Innocent and unaware, he moves among the plotting relatives trying to defraud him of his inheritance as his father lies dying.

With his wealth and connections, Herzen's father had been able to make him noble by buying a bureaucratic position for him that conferred nobility, so he was eligible to inherit land and serfs. In *My Past and Thoughts*, Herzen gave a vivid picture of his feelings as his father lay dying, and Tolstoy was inspired by its truth for his scene at the deathbed of Pierre's father. After receiving the sacrament, Herzen's father asked to be lifted from the bed to an armchair and pushed to the table. As Herzen told it, "He wanted to rest his head on his hand, but his arm gave way and fell as though lifeless on the table; I put mine in its place. Twice he bent a weary sick glance on me as though asking for help." When it was all over, Herzen said, "Everyone turned to me for orders. My new position was detestable, revolting to me—this house and everything in it belonged to me because someone was dead, and that someone was my father. It seemed to me that in this coarse taking possession there was something unclean, as though I were robbing the dead man."

In Tolstoy's scene, the dying Count Kiril is lifted, after receiving the sacrament, from an invalid chair into the bed, and while being turned, "one of his arms fell back helplessly and he made a fruitless effort to pull it forward. Whether he noticed the look of terror with which Pierre regarded that lifeless arm, or whether some other thought flitted across his dying brain, at any rate he glanced at the refractory arm, at Pierre's terror-stricken face, and again at the arm, and on his face a feeble, piteous smile appeared."

At any thought of his father's wealth, Pierre feels the same revulsion as Herzen, finding all such rapacity "very horrid." He is embarrassed and confused to see that the people around him are looking at him significantly, "with a kind of awe and even servility. A deference such as he had never before received was shown him." Understanding nothing, he decides he is "obliged to perform some sort of awful rite" and must accept the sudden services of those around him.

Pierre also takes from Herzen much of his appearance. This way, Tolstoy forestalled any recognition of his cousin Volkonsky in the character. Instead of having the "gaunt" figure of the old Decembrist, Pierre is a "stout, heavily built young man with close-cropped hair," wearing the "light-colored breeches fashionable at that time." He is "above average height, broad, with huge red hands." To the artist Bashilov, Tolstoy pointed out that Pierre needed "larger features," and something in his forehead "to suggest a greater disposition towards philosophizing—a wrinkle or some bulges above the eyebrows." The body had to be "broader, larger, stouter." Tolstoy wanted something like Malwida von Meysenbug's description of Herzen as "a thick-set powerful figure, with black hair and beard, rather broad slavonic features, and remarkably brilliant eyes."

When they parted, Tolstoy and Herzen had agreed to exchange

photographs, and the one Herzen finally sent must have been the very fine one of him as a writer and thinker, reclining at the edge of a sofa, next to a table, his elbow propped on a book and some papers, his head leaning on his hand, as he looks up thoughtfully, his magnificent forehead knotted in concentration. He is wearing an elegant dark waist-coat and jacket with the "light-colored breeches" of Pierre at Anna Scherer's soiree. Most likely Tolstoy had this picture in mind, as well as his own habit of reading stretched out on a sofa, when he suggested to Bashilov, "I wonder if you can do a portrait of Pierre lying on a sofa reading a book, or pensively and absent-mindedly gazing over the top of his spectacles, his attention distracted from his book—leaning on one elbow, with his other arm thrust in between his legs?"

Of course, Tolstoy was as reluctant to have readers recognize Herzen in Pierre as to have them recognize his cousin Volkonsky, so he added a flavoring of one other revolutionary—this time one he had probably never seen—the giant figure of Mikhail Alexandrovich Bakunin. Tolstoy knew well one of Bakunin's younger brothers, for he had recruited him to write for a military journal he had tried to establish while an officer in the Crimea, and he saw him often in Moscow at the end of 1856. Mikhail Bakunin is vividly described by Herzen, and Tolstoy heard a lot about him from Turgenev, who had been close to him in Stankevich's German-metaphysical circle. Together Turgenev and Bakunin had gone to Berlin to study the philosophy of Stankevich's favorites: Schelling, Kant, Fichte, and Hegel.

Bakunin's grandfather, a "State Counsellor" at the court of Catherine II, had been a "Samson," celebrated for his "enormous stature," his "muscular prowess, and his ungovernable temper." Once, the grand-father beat off a gang of robbers with nothing but a plank of wood he picked up, and another time, when a coachman spoke insolently to him, he lifted him out of the box and pitched him headlong into a river.

Bakunin had inherited his grandfather's dimensions, if not his de-monic strength. Tolstoy gave Pierre both. His father has been the Samson, and Pierre has his physique, his power, and also—when in-cited—his "ungovernable temper." His fellow rakes call him "Her-cules," and when two footmen cannot budge a window frame, Pierre instantly wrenches it out with a crash. Later, when a group of young men try to seize his arms, he shows himself "so strong" that all are "sent flying." Gentle as Pierre is, in a moment of passion he picks up a marble tabletop with a madman's strength and, feeling "his father's nature" rioting in him, he flings it down, breaking it, and shouts "Get out" in such a terrible voice that the "whole house heard it with horror."

As the novel advances, Pierre becomes more and more like Bakunin as Herzen described him in *My Past and Thoughts*. "His activity, his laziness, his appetite, his titanic stature and the everlasting perspiration he was in, everything about him, in fact, was on a superhuman scale. He was a giant himself with his leonine head and the mane that stood up around it." Pierre's father, like his son, has the "leonine head," and the "high, stout, uncovered chest and powerful shoulders." Pierre has the appetite, the laziness, the stature, and also, as Herzen said of Bakunin, "something childlike, simple, and free from malice about him."

So much of Pierre came of Volkonsky, Herzen, and Bakunin. Tolstoy, who had the strength (he also had been called "Hercules"), the simplicity, the goodness, the laziness, felt very comfortable in the character, and so Pierre, like Prince Andrey, became invested with the complex life of his creator. At the start of *War and Peace*, Pierre is caught up by the Kuragin family—Prince Vasily Kuragin being a connection of his father. Anatole Kuragin, Prince Vasily's son, has distracted Pierre from choosing a career, leading him into the usual pleasures of St. Petersburg nobles: gambling, drinking, and going the rounds of the brothels. Prince Andrey urges him to break with the Kuragins and all their dissipation.

At very much the same age as Pierre, Tolstoy had gone to St. Petersburg to find a career but had plunged instead into gambling, drinking, and debauchery, having been led astray by a family, in particular by the father, Alexander Mikhailovich Islenyev, who had been a close friend of Tolstoy's father, and even more by the youngest of Islenyev's illegitimate sons, Konstantin Alexandrovich Islavin. In *War and Peace* the Kuragins, father and son, are portraits of these two important people in Tolstoy's life, so they come as intimately out of his experience as did his heroines Natasha and Sonya, being modeled on their grandfather and uncle respectively.

Actually Tolstoy had already used his father's friend Islenyev as the father of the family in his first three books: *Childhood*, *Boyhood*, and *Youth*. Although he tried to differentiate his second use of him in *War and Peace*, anyone can recognize in the "bald, scented, and shining head" of Prince Vasily Kuragin the "bald head," "deliciously perfumed," of Irtenyev (a name only two letters off Islenyev), the father of *Childhood*. More important, Irtenyev is a man who knows how to "get the upper hand over everybody," as does Prince Vasily. Whatever brought him "happiness and pleasure, he considered good." Whether he had "any moral convictions it is difficult to say. His life was so full of impulses of every sort that he had no time to think about them."

Similarly, Prince Vasily Kuragin was not a man "who deliberately thought out his plans," but he always had "schemes and devices," which he did not consciously examine, "shaping themselves in his mind." No sooner has he failed to pocket Pierre's inheritance by destroying part of his father's will, than he sets out to take it in another way. "With apparent absent-mindedness, yet with unhesitating assurance that he was doing the right thing, Prince Vasily did everything to get Pierre to marry his daughter."

Old Islenyev seems very early to have led young Tolstoy into his own "governing passion," gambling at cards. So pernicious was his influence that Auntie Tatyana, who rarely passed judgment, wrote Lev a very severe indictment. "Why are you so set against Islenyev?" Lev asked her. "If it is in order to warn me against him, that is unnecessary as he is not at Moscow." But he agreed with her on "the evil of gambling" and made the first of many promises to himself: "I will play cards no more."

Within a few years of his marriage to Islenyev's granddaughter Sonya, the old man had become—as Tolstoy wrote Sonya from her parents' apartment in the Kremlin—"so loathsome to me—I could tell you why—that I can't look at him impassively." Just at the right time Islenyev had become ripe to play his reprehensible role as Prince Vasily in *War and Peace*.

The example of dissipation set by Kostya, Islenyev's son, had been particularly bad for Tolstoy, coming as it did after he had failed to find himself at Kazan University and needed to settle on a career. Just as Tolstoy had idealized his father and then his brother Sergey, so he worshiped in Kostya his self-possession and physical beauty. "Kostenka," Tolstoy said, was an "ideal love," before which he was ready for total "self-sacrifice." Only months later, on November 29, 1851, did Tolstoy realize: "My love for Islavin spoilt the whole eight months of my life in Petersburg for me. Although not consciously, I never bothered about anything else except how to please him."

But Kostenka remained an intimate friend for many more years, a companion in nights among the gypsies when they never went to bed at all but went to the Vorobyev Hills for breakfast at daybreak. Only after Tolstoy became a dedicated writer did he realize that "nothing will ever come of Kostenka. He does not believe that without work there is no success."

When Lev Tolstoy went off to fight in the Caucasus, Kostya took over his brother Dmitry, leading him from piety to "drinking, smoking, wasting money, and going with women." Long after, Lev noted that he knew only that Dmitry's "seducer was a deeply immoral man, very attractive externally, the youngest son of Islenyev." In late years, Tolstoy saw Kostya as "a lost soul, a drunkard, a glutton, an unhappy, lazy, and untruthful person." He had seen enough years before to make Kostenka in the character of Anatole Kuragin the prime seducer and deceiver of his novel *War and Peace*.

Anatole leads Pierre astray very much as Kostenka led Tolstoy, and Tolstoy gave Pierre his own "weak character," so that he rationalizes away the promise he made Prince Andrey to give up dissipating with Anatole, thus "nullifying all his decisions and intentions." Just so Tolstoy flagellated himself in his diaries, accusing himself of "indecision, inconsequence, lack of steadfastness, and inconsistency," of "want of firmness of character," and "non-fulfillment of resolutions."

Pierre cannot resist going to Anatole's, because the evening will end in a round of the brothels. "Women, my dear fellow; women!" he explains the lure of Kuragin to Prince Andrey. Because he did not marry until he was thirty-four, Tolstoy suffered, as Pierre suffers, from the whip of desire. He kept telling himself in his diaries, "Restrain thyself from wine and women."

Yet at Yasnaya Polyana he would find himself signaling to "someone in a pink dress," any serf woman, and would ravish her without even seeing her, thinking afterward, "All seemed foul and repellent, and I actually hated her for having caused me to break my rule." After a night at a St. Petersburg brothel, he would think, "Disgusting! Girls, silly music, girls, an artificial nightingale, girls, heat, cigarette smoke, girls, vodka, cheese, wild shrieks, girls, girls, girls!"

The night of dissipation Pierre spends with Anatole Kuragin and his fellow rakes comes partly out of Tolstoy's memories and partly out of what he learned of the exploits of young Russian nobles of an earlier generation. Among Kuragin's companions is the "notorious gambler and duelist" Dolokhov. This sadistic and revengeful, yet brave, resolute, and intelligent character came out of Tolstoy's cousin Count Fyodor Tolstoy—"The American," as he was called from once having been marooned on the Aleutian Islands for insubordination. Tolstoy knew him well in boyhood, his "handsome face, bronzed and shaven" and his then "white curly hair." Tolstoy always kept on close terms with Fyodor's widow, Avdotya Maximovna (a former gypsy like his brother Serozha's consort), and his daughter "Polenka," Praskovya Fyodorovna, who was married to "Vasenka," Vasily S. Perfilyev, a good friend of Lev. Fyodor's handsome face and curly hair became Dolokhov's, as well as his lack of mustache (in the novel because Dolokhov is an infantry officer, and an infantryman did not wear one).

Fyodor Tolstoy was—so Lev Tolstoy thought—an "extraordinary, criminal, and attractive man." He had been a great duelist, and once came close to a duel with the poet Pushkin, who thought he had calumniated him. Later, they had become friends, and Fyodor Tolstoy, knowing the Goncharov family, whose daughter, Natalya Nikolayevna, Pushkin was courting, had helped bring about Pushkin's fatal marriage.

Even Dolokhov's daredevil bet that he can drink a whole bottle of rum without pause while sitting on an outer window ledge (over a lethal drop) was typical of the exploits of young nobles of Fyodor Tolstoy's time. Pushkin himself had bet that he could drink a whole bottle of rum straight down without losing consciousness, and was considered to have won when at the end—otherwise paralyzed—he managed to wiggle the little finger of his left hand.

Pushkin and Pierre

In fact, Pushkin himself—that close friend of many of the major Decembrists—became a mine of facts for the life story Tolstoy created for his future Decembrist Pierre. After the Decembrist Revolt, Pushkin had been caught in a net by the Emperor Nicholas I, who personally interrogated him and then offered to become his patron and private censor, partly as a way of keeping him under unremitting surveillance by the "Third Department," of secret police, which Nicholas had established right after the Decembrist Revolt. The head of the Third Department, Count Benckendorff, acted as mediator between Pushkin and the Emperor Nicholas in what was really a plot to turn the influential poet into a eulogist of the autocracy. The situation became dangerously complicated by the all-powerful autocrat's infatuation with the fabulously beautiful young bride, Natalya Nikolayevna Goncharova, whom Pushkin married on February 18, 1831, "without rapture, without childish enchantment," he said—a step that led as inevitably to Pushkin's early death six years later, as would an infection with a mortal disease.

Tolstoy had been gathering knowledge of Pushkin from the time he came to a real understanding of the poet during his swing toward liberalism after leaving the army. It was then that Tolstoy began reading biographies and memoirs of Pushkin and became impressed by the splendor and truth of his poetry. In the winter of 1856–57, Tolstoy became particularly taken with "dear," "charming" Pavel Vasilyevich Annenkov, who had just finished a fresh biography of the great Russian poet, which Turgenev thought had "the great Pushkinian spirit, genuinely classical in its austere and youthful beauty."

In Switzerland during April and May 1857, Tolstoy became good friends with the "delightfully kind-hearted" Mikhail I. Pushchin (with the name so confusingly similar to *Pushkin*), who had known the poet because his brother Ivan had been a good friend of Alexander Pushkin dating from their boyhood days in the Tsarskoye Selo Lycee. Ivan had been one of the seriously implicated Decembrists sentenced to the Siberian mines, and Mikhail had been sufficiently under suspicion to be degraded to the ranks and sent to a dangerous outpost. So interested was Tolstoy in Mikhail Pushchin's reminiscences of the poet that he persuaded him to write them down.

Later in Baden-Baden, Tolstoy spent a few evenings, which he found "ridiculous and nasty," dining at the home of Alexandra Yosipovna Smirnova, who as a young maid of honor, Alexandra Rossetti, had known Alexander Pushkin and his wife well. Her memoirs record Natalya Pushkin telling her husband, "God, how you bore me with your verses, Pushkin!"

As a beautiful lady of the court, Natalya Nikolayevna Pushkina had been described by several contemporaries. Outstanding among them was Count Vladimir Alexandrovich Sologub, whom Tolstoy saw often during the winter of 1850–51 and through the following years. Sologub declared that he had known women as beautiful as Pushkina, women more fascinating, but that he had never seen "such perfection of classically correct features and figure. She was tall, with an incredibly thin waist, well-developed shoulders and bosom, and her small head, like a lily on a stalk, swayed gracefully on her slender neck: such a beautiful and perfect profile I have never seen, and then her complexion, eyes, teeth, mouth! Yes, she was a real beauty"; in fact, she was the "foremost beauty of the time." Reporting on her as seen at a ball of the Odoyevskys in 1833, one admirer declared, "I have never seen such a figure or such stateliness. . . . Her features were of classical nobility, and made me think of the Euterpe of the Louvre."

Her personality suggested marble as much as did her figure. Count Sologub declared, "She was reserved to the point of coldness and she talked little." Vera Nashchokina, wife of one of Pushkin's friends, admitted, "Certainly she always seemed to me to be utterly lacking in feeling." On the very eve of Pushkin's marriage to her, his friend Kisselov told Pletnev, "Pushkin is going to marry Mlle. Goncharova, who is, between you and me, a beauty without a soul."

Madly in love with her—so he said—young Georges d'Anthès, a lieutenant in the Horse Guards, confided: "This woman is generally supposed not to be intelligent. I do not know if love makes one intelligent, but no one could have shown more tact, grace, and intelligence than she did in our conversation." She had told him, "I love you as I have never loved, but do not ask me for more than my heart, because the rest does not belong to me."

After this woman, Tolstoy very consciously designed Helene (Elena) Vasilyevna Kuragina, whom Pierre is entrapped into marrying. Helene has a similarly "beautiful figure and shapely shoulders, back, and bosom." Tolstoy stresses her resemblance to a Greek statue, speaking of her "marble beauty," of the "wonderful classic beauty of her figure," or describing her as turning "her beautiful head" and looking "over her classically molded shoulder." After seeing a first illustration of her, Tolstoy asked Bashilov, "Can't Helene be made fuller in the chest? (Plastic beauty of form is her most characteristic feature.)"

Helene is also shown to be cold, silent, tactful, heartless, and unintelligent. She is totally unmoved as the Princess Drubetskaya pleads agonizingly with Prince Vasily to get her son into the Guards. As indifferently as a clock, she keeps reminding her father, "Papa, we shall be late." If Pierre thinks of her at all, he thinks either of "her beauty" or of her skill in looking "silently dignified in society." Reminiscent of Natalya Nikolayevna's "God, how you bore me with your verses, Pushkin," Helene responds to Pierre's talk of his ideas either by "a brief but appropriate remark—showing that it did not interest her—or by a silent look and smile."

Abetting Prince Vasily's scheme to get ahold of Pierre's fortune by marrying him to Helene, Anna Pavlovna Scherer breaks into a rhapsody to Pierre on how exquisite she is. "And how she carries herself! For so young a girl, such tact, such masterly perfection of manner! It comes from her heart. Happy the man who wins her!'' The extent to which Helene is all manner—untouched by mind or soul—appears as she listens to the Vicomte's story at Anna Pavlovna's initial soiree.

She takes great trouble in placing her arm on a little table next to her, and then sits upright, "glancing now at her beautiful round arm, altered in shape by its pressure on the table, now at her still more beautiful bosom on which she readjusted a diamond necklace." At crucial points she glances at Anna Pavlovna and adopts "just the expression she saw on the maid of honor's face" before relapsing into her usual "radiant smile."

This description must have been longer at first, for Fet had passed Turgenev's criticism of it on to Tolstoy and Tolstoy had replied, "Turgenev's opinion that you can't take ten pages to describe how N N placed her arm helped me very much, and I hope to avoid this fault in future." Why did Tolstoy call Helene Vasilyevna Kuragina "N N"? No matter whether she is translated as "Ellen" or "Helene," none of her initials comes out as *N*, and there is certainly no feminine "N N" in *War and Peace* at all. Fet must have been in on the secret that Tolstoy's Helene was a portrait of Pushkin's wife Natalya Nikolayevna, reduced to "N N" as Pushkin himself often referred to her. So Tolstoy spoke of Helene in a way that Fet would understand but no one else (at least no one else up to this point ever has understood it).

Yet for all the conscious portraiture of Pushkin's wife, which grows more and more unmistakable as the story advances, Tolstoy could not have dramatized as vividly as he does Pierre's misery and uncertainty in his entanglement with a woman he does not even like, had he himself not made an eleventh-hour escape from just such a trap. When Tolstoy returned from the Crimea, his friend Dmitry Alexyevich Dyakov advised him to marry Valerya Vladimirovna Arsenyeva, one of the daughters of a friend of theirs who had recently died, whose estate Sudakovo was very near to Yasnaya Polyana. Easily swayed for the moment, Tolstoy agreed it was the "best thing I can do."

Valerya seemed to Tolstoy "very charming" but "frivolous," and he began asking himself, "Do I love her seriously? And can she love for long?" At once he realized she was "extremely badly educated, and ignorant if not stupid." Although she was "a splendid girl," he knew "she certainly does not please me." After she had been away for a while, Valerya seemed to him "nicer than ever, but her frivolity and absence of care for anything serious is terrifying." Auntie Tatyana was all for the marriage, but Serozha was pouring "much cold water over me," Tolstoy said.

He himself found Valerya at one moment "simply stupid" or even "cruelly affected and stupid," and the next "not stupid" and even "remarkably kind." A little later she was again "sweet but, alas, simply stupid." At one meeting she was "simple and nice" and at the next "limited and incredibly futile," really "incompetent both in practical and in spiritual life." One day she was "a dear, dear girl, honest and frank," and the next day "terribly shallow, without principle, and cold as ice."

To get some sort of perspective on it, Tolstoy fled to Moscow, and after a while still further to Paris. By then he was telling Auntie Tatyana that he now knew he was "more than indifferent" to Valerya, that he could no longer "deceive either myself or her," and that he was sure "I have not only never had, but never shall have, the slightest feeling of true love for V." To Valerya herself, who still wrote him submissive letters, Tolstoy recalled, "I was always telling you that I did not know what kind of feeling I had for you, and that it seemed to me that there was something wrong."

Pierre is tortured by the same indecision—but does not escape. Guiltily he tells himself that he has been "deceiving yourself and her." Sleepless after being caught by her allure, Pierre thinks, "But she's stupid. I have myself said she is stupid. There is something nasty, something wrong, in the feeling she excites in me." A little later he argues to himself, "No, she is not stupid, she is an excellent girl." If she talks little, "what she does say is always clear and simple, so she is not stupid." Nevertheless, he is paralyzed by his feeling of guilt over how sexual lust is entangling him. As the "dreadful abyss" of marriage with her approaches, he asks himself, "What am I doing? I need resolution. Can it be that I have none?"

So much was Valerya associated with entrapment for Tolstoy that he used a recollection of her for Prince Vasily's attempt to marry his dissipated son Anatole to the wealthy Princess Bolkonsky, which comes right after the entrapment of Pierre. Her French governess, Mademoiselle Vergani, had engineered Valerya's attempt to capture Tolstoy, and the Frenchwoman's machinations had made him feel more and more caged in. On one occasion when he visited Valerya—so he wrote in his diary—"She had had her hair done up in a terrible fashion and wore a purple mantle *for me*. I felt pained and ashamed and spent a sad day." What angered him most, he said, was that he found himself "involuntarily" in the "position of a fiancé."

In *War and Peace*, Mlle. Bourienne and Prince Andrey's wife force upon the Princess Marya—who feels wounded and humiliated by the whole procedure—a new hairdo "arranged on the top of her head (a style that quite altered and spoiled her looks)" and a showy maroon dress to receive Anatole. Tolstoy's anger and shame at Valerya went into the Princess's suffering and her father's anger at this deforming getup.

Otherwise Tolstoy's ambiguous feelings for Valerya expressed themselves entirely through Pierre's distress and also through the changes they brought about in his original model for Helene, Pushkin's wife. Although Valerya had been far from a "depraved" woman, as Tolstoy made Helene, Helene's aura of wickedness came straight out of Tolstoy's inner ambivalence, his conflicting desire and disgust, and his nightmare sensation of progressive entrapment by Valerya. While visiting Moscow's menagerie, still very depressed over the whole Valerya episode, Tolstoy happened to respond disturbingly to a "lady with sensual eyes." With the guilty feeling that sexual lust alone had pushed his courtship of Valerya—even though she was not really attractive to him even sexually—Tolstoy wrote in his diary: "Thought with horror about Valerya apropos of the look of the lady with the sensual eyes."

So Pierre remembers with horror Helene's "languid passionate look" during their honeymoon. All of Tolstoy's worst impressions of Valerya during his ambivalent courtship went into his picture of Helene. After one uneasy visit, Tolstoy wrote in his diary, "The word *prostituer* which she uttered, heavens knows why, grieved me greatly and, added to my toothache, disillusioned me." Similarly, as Pierre becomes fully disillusioned with Helene, he thinks of the "coarseness and bluntness of her thoughts and the vulgarity of the expressions that were natural to her." Having been chilled by Valerya's "terrifying" indifference to anything but display in dress and the court doings for the coronation of Alexander II, Tolstoy told himself, "Am afraid hers is a nature that cannot even love a child." So he had Helene tell Pierre that she is not such a fool as to "want to have children" and she is not going to have any by him.

The rest of Helene and her story came largely out of the events in Pushkin's fatal marriage. One of Nicholas I's first moves aimed at turning Pushkin into a eulogist of the autocracy was to have him enrolled in the Ministry of Foreign Affairs at a salary of 5,000 rubles a year with access to the archives to work on Russian history—in particular on a biography of Peter the Great (to glorify the Romanov dynasty and thus Nicholas I). In order to have Pushkin's beautiful wife present at all the Anichkov Palace balls, Nicholas gave Pushkin a court position with obligatory attendance. The poet (in his thirties) was made a Gentleman of the Bedchamber (normally a role played by boys between fifteen and eighteen years old).

Pushkin wrote in his diary on January 1, 1834: "The day before yesterday I was made a gentleman of the chamber (which is quite improper at my age). But the court wanted N N to dance at Anichkov." From then on Pushkin would write ironically to his wife of the "agreeable mood in which you usually see me when I put on my magnificent uniform" or, more straightforwardly, of his "pitiable role and vexation" over it.

In *War and Peace*, Tolstoy had Prince Vasily Kuragin with his court influence announce to Pierre as soon as he has become Count Bezukhov that he has been "entered in the diplomatic corps and made a Gentleman of the Bedchamber." Actually Tolstoy had jumped the gun on this, for he put it into Pierre's story while Pierre is still young enough to be a Kammerjunker without ridicule, and also before Helene has an adulterous link with anyone at court. So, after announcing the position, Tolstoy dropped it until four years later in his story.

Having by then forgotten his premature announcement, Tolstoy made Pierre a Gentleman of the Bedchamber all over again, coming as close as he could under the censorship to the intimacy of Pushkin's wife with the Emperor Nicholas I. "Since the intimacy of his wife with the royal prince," Tolstoy tells us, "Pierre had unexpectedly been made a Gentleman of the Bedchamber, and from that time he had begun to feel oppressed and ashamed in court society."

At the same time, Helene is "enjoying the favors of a very important personage," being under the "special protection of a grandee who occupied one of the highest posts in the Empire." Thus Helene's climaxing double adultery comes veiled in circumlocutions and confusions to disguise the dangerous reality out of which Pierre's story emerged.

During her six years as femme fatale of court society, Natalya Nikolayevna bore Pushkin four children—two boys and two girls. Pushkin worried endlessly over her "girlish imprudence" while pregnant. "She dances at balls, coquettes with the Sovereign, and jumps off the porch. I must take the hussy in hand," he declared. He was afraid, he told her, she would go to the palace, and the first thing she knew she would "have a miscarriage on the hundred and fifth step of the grand staircase." In fact, at the end of a carnival season when there had been dancing at court twice a day, he found her "becoming ill" at the palace and got her home just in time to have a miscarriage.

The Emperor's patronage of 5,000 rubles a year did not begin to pay for Natalya Nikolayevna's court wardrobe. "I am rushing about in high society," Pushkin said. "My wife is a leader of fashion and all this requires money, money, money." He worried over money and worried about his honor. Half jokingly, half in deadly earnest, he warned her, when he had gone to the country to write, "Don't coquette with the Tsar or with Princess Lyuba's fiancé," and don't overdo flirtation. "Like a little bitch, you rejoice that male dogs are running after you with their tails like a poker and sniffing you in the ass; that's something to rejoice over!" The secret of coquetry, he told her, was just to look willing. "Where there's a trough, there'll be swine."

As long as Natalya Nikolayevna was flirting with the "entire diplomatic corps," and Pushkin could jokingly ask her for "a list in alphabetical order" of all the men who were courting her, he was not too troubled. But by 1836 she was being besieged intensely by two lovers, the Emperor Nicholas and a young, handsome, witty, and thoroughly unprincipled French lieutenant in the Horse Guards, Georges d'Anthès. It was these two—the Emperor Nicholas and Lieutenant d'Anthès— whom Tolstoy represented in the "grandee" and the "young foreign prince" in love with Helene.

D'Anthès had come to St. Petersburg through a love affair at nineteen with the fabulously wealthy middle-aged Dutch Ambassador to Russia, Baron Louis Beveriwaert van Heeckeren. Being childless, van Heeckeren adopted d'Anthès as his son and made him heir to his title and wealth. With that, St. Petersburg society went wild over the handsome, blonde young man. He was at all the court balls, and by January 1836 was declaring to his adoptive father van Heeckeren that he was "madly in love" with Pushkin's wife. Although he was sure that "she loves me," they were being kept apart, d'Anthès complained, because "her husband is disgustingly jealous." He was sure van Heeckeren would sympathize with his passion, "for I love you also with all my heart." From then on the Dutch Ambassador turned his ingenuity to assisting d'Anthès in seducing Pushkin's wife.

The tale of Pushkin, caught inextricably by the Emperor Nicholas's passion for his wife on the flypaper of corrupt St. Petersburg court society, and driven to destruction, haunted the story Tolstoy created for his protagonist, Pierre. Pushkin's tragedy moved Tolstoy very intimately. He had once told Valerya (when she had been flirting with her music master) that he feared marriage just "because I regard it too strictly and seriously." Should his wife so much as secretly allow another man to kiss her hand, he would, he said, "divorce her instantly and fly to the ends of the earth" out of respect for "my name" and "disappointment in my dreams."

No such flight had been open to Pushkin. He went through a year of torment, receiving hideous anonymous letters—which he correctly traced to van Heeckeren's homosexual set. Two of them would ultimately bring on his fatal duel with d'Anthès. Then, with the poet dead, and van Heeckeren and d'Anthès expelled from Russia, came the actual cuckolding by the Emperor Nicholas—some four years after Pushkin's death. Having met Pushkin's widow, become more beautiful than ever, visiting St. Petersburg to buy Christmas toys for her children, Nicholas I brought her back to court (1841), where she queened it until 1844, when she was quietly married off, under the Emperor Nicholas's aegis, to the recently widowed Major Peter Petrovich Lanskoy. The Tsar kept his intimacy with her through the birth of a child, which followed hard upon it, and catapulted Lanskoy, at forty-five, into a brilliant court career. Then Nicholas turned to a new mistress, Nelidova, and they all lived happily ever after.

For Pierre's story, Tolstoy reversed the chronology of these events, using Pushkin's story as a reservoir, not a model, and even freely swapping around, where needful, who did what. Within months of his terrible marriage to Helene, Pierre is being actually cuckolded, and receiving anonymous letters about it. His tragic marriage starts rather than ends as did Pushkin's, with a duel. Then he flees his wife, as Tolstoy would have done.

In order to give Pierre Pushkin's long-suffering and entrapment, Tolstoy had to bring him back to her, forced by social opinion (with pressure from the Masons). Only then does Pierre take on Pushkin's shame and suffering—although love for his wife has nothing to do with it. He lives with her under the same roof and gives her the social propriety of his presence at her receptions, but he has relinquished all physical contact with her. The shame and oppression Pushkin felt over his wife's position in the court is felt severely by Pierre only because he is forced to live a lie, and because he is blocked from fulfilling his real love for Natasha Rostova.

The most horrid anonymous letter to Pushkin (written, as was discovered years later, by young Prince Peter Dolgorukov, one of van Heeckeren's homosexual circle, who would make a career of anonymous calumny and attempted blackmail), announced to Pushkin that the "Most Serene Order of Cuckolds" and their "Venerable Grand Master," D. L. Naryshkin, had unanimously elected Alexander Pushkin "coadjutor of the Grand Master" and "historiographer of the order." The beautiful Marya Antonovna Naryshkina had been the official mistress of Alexander I for at least fourteen years, and her husband, Dmitry Lvovich Naryshkin, had been rewarded with a sinecure of 40,000 rubles a year. The implication of the anonymous letter was that Pushkin held the same position under Nicholas I and that his 5,000 rubles a year as historiographer from the Ministry of Foreign Affairs was payment thereof.

Tolstoy gives us no details of the anonymous letter that Pierre receives telling him he is a cuckold, but he seems to have been haunted by the implied parallel between Marya Antonovna and Pushkin's wife in the Dolgorukov letter. He put it into the St. Petersburg ball scene, in which he contrasts the freshness and delight of young Natasha at her first grand ball with the hard varnish of the more beautiful seasoned courtesan Helene, the "belle" of the ball to her husband's distress. Of course Tolstoy places the ball during the reign of Marya Antonovna, so she is there too, and the lady escorting the provincial Rostovs tells them, when Pierre's wife enters, "Ah, here she is, the queen of Petersburg, Countess Bezukhov. How lovely! She is quite equal to Marya Antonovna. See how the men, young and old, pay court to her." Aside from his own characters, Tolstoy mentions only the historical figures of Marya Antonovna and Alexander I and the actual French Ambassador Caulaincourt, but he brings in a special description of the gray-haired Dutch Ambassador, unnamed, who is making a bevy of court ladies laugh, very much after the style of the maliciously witty van Heeckeren—although this one comes historically long before van Heeckeren's time.

At this ball Pierre suffers intensely, for it comes at the beginning of Helene's double adultery, with its echo of Pushkina's double flirtation with d'Anthès and the Emperor Nicholas. At it, Pierre looks "gloomy and absent-minded. A deep furrow ran across his forehead, and standing by a window he stared over his spectacles seeing no one." Apparently Tolstoy was adapting an actual report of Pushkin at an Anichkov Palace ball where his wife was queening it, while he grew "more and more silent, absent-minded and moody. He stayed in a window recess, with pursed lips and dull eyes."

Observers thought d'Anthès was deliberately goading Pushkin by pursuing his wife. Being French, d'Anthès was, Prince Trubetskoy thought, "more daring with women" than "is permissible in our society." The Countess Fiquelmont said he violated "all social proprieties" by showing his admiration for Pushkina to an extent "completely inadmissible in the case of a married woman." And the Countess Stroganov, after watching d'Anthès courting Pushkina throughout an evening, declared that Pushkin "had such a terrible look that if I had been his wife, I would have been afraid to return to the house alone with him."

Similarly, Tolstoy had Dolokhov—the first to cuckold Pierre—address him with contemptuous familiarity at a banquet in the shameful toast "Here's to the health of lovely women, Petrusha—and their lovers!" Fully convinced now of the truth of the anonymous letter just received, Pierre feels something "terrible and monstrous" rise in him and challenges Dolokhov to a duel. In Pushkin's case, after d'Anthès had tried to get Natalya Nikolayevna—during a private rendezvous—to elope with him to France, and Pushkin had promptly received another anonymous letter declaring him thoroughly cuckolded, the poet was led to send his fatal challenge. Tolstoy's friend Count Sologub, who had been with Pushkin at the time, reported, "His lips trembled. His eyes were bloodshot. He was terrible to behold."

Tolstoy's telling of the duel rearranges the actual facts to achieve poetic justice, so that the innocent party Pierre comes out unscathed and the guilty party Dolokhov takes an almost mortal wound. In Pushkin's duel, which took place in deep snow, as Tolstoy placed Pierre's, destiny saved the rake and killed the great poet. D'Anthès fired first, before the two of them had reached the barrier, shattering the poet's pelvis and the interior of his abdomen, so that he fell in a pool of blood. The seconds and d'Anthès began to run to the barrier, but Pushkin called: "Wait! I feel strong enough to fire my shot." All bloody, he raised himself from the snow on his "left hand" and took careful aim. D'Anthès stood with "his body sideways" and with his arm "across his chest" to protect the heart. Pushkin's bullet went through his arm and flattened against a coat button, cracking two ribs, but the damage was slight.

In Tolstoy's account, Pierre—who has never held a pistol in his hand before—shoots before they reach the barrier, and Dolokhov falls in the snow. Filled with horror at what he has done, Pierre rushes with the seconds to his assistance, but Dolokhov calls out, "No, it's not over."

He wipes the blood off his "left hand" and, raising himself from the snow with it, takes careful aim. Perfectly careless of himself in his remorse and pity, Pierre stands "with his broad chest" fully exposed, although one of the seconds cries out, "Sideways! Cover yourself!" Only Dolokhov's weakness from loss of blood saves Pierre.

In Tolstoy's telling, the story emphasizes Pierre's awareness of the evil in dueling even as he is being caught up in it, very like Tolstoy's own belated recognition. At the time of their quarrel, Tolstoy challenged and Turgenev promised that as soon as he returned from Paris, he would give Tolstoy a duel. By that time Tolstoy decided he would just as soon do a dance on Tverskaya Boulevard "dressed up as a savage." Hearing that d'Anthès was recovering easily, the dying Pushkin said, "It's strange. I thought I would have liked to kill him, but now I think not." Pierre too in his new understanding tells Prince Andrey, "One thing I thank God for is that I did not kill that man."

Thus, in the great poet who inspired the Decembrists, Pushkin, who had been saved from joining their immolation only by chance, Tolstoy found and freely adapted a part of the story for his developing Decembrist Pierre, giving him a wife very like the one that destroyed Pushkin. Only, in poetic justice, Tolstoy saved Pierre and had Helene kill herself by her own stupid attempt to speed the abortion of a baby who is complicating her choice of which of her two adulterous lovers to marry. She takes too much of a dangerous drug and dies before help can reach her.

The story of one other revolutionary, Nikolay Platonovich Ogarev, Herzen's companion, contributed in part to Tolstoy's story of Pierre's unfortunate marriage. Ogarev came out of Tolstoy's childhood at Yasnaya Polyana, for his father Platon Ogarev had been a friend of Tolstoy's father and often visited from nearby Penza province. Of course Nikolay Platonovich was a generation older than Lev, but the boy knew him and much about him. From the time he had been a student at Moscow University, young Ogarev had attracted intellectuals by his charm and brilliance, so that he became the center of a circle and his wife Marya Lvovna Roslavlev became the hostess of a perpetual "open house, especially for intelligent men." Remembrance of that probably inspired Tolstoy to make Pierre's wife, the stupid Helene, hostess of a similar intellectual salon.

During the winter of 1839–40, Mikhail Bakunin, walking into the Ogarev drawing room in Moscow, came upon Marya Lvovna alone in a compromising contiguity with Katkov (afterward editor of the *Russian*

Herald and first publisher of *War and Peace*). It seems that Ogarev, who had early been orphaned of his mother and was subject to petit mal epilepsy, could not physically consummate his ardently idealistic love for his wife. At any rate, Herzen was soon calling her a "Messalina of the gutter," and she found herself a lover and exacted a cripplingly large part of the generous Ogarev's inheritance for a legal separation.

Helene agrees at once to separate from Pierre if he will give her "a fortune." He immediately turns over to her his estates "in Great Russia, which formed the larger part of his property." Ogarev had already liberated all his serfs (1,870 souls) on his estate, "Belo-mut," giving them the land (which they paid for over a ten-year period). Out of this early and far-reaching emancipation, Tolstoy modeled Pierre's attempts to free his peasants.

Ogarev had been so prodigal in giving away his immense wealth to anyone asking for it that he ended up destitute before he was forty, and Herzen supported him for the remainder of his life. Similarly, Pierre goes through a period—once shackled again to his adulterous wife—when "his purse was always empty because it was open to everyone." Ogarev's troubles, so Herzen said, all came "from wine—he has drunk himself to ruin." In Pierre's life too, "drinking became more and more a physical and also a moral necessity." So Pierre's story blended that of Ogarev with that of Pushkin, all compounded with crucial life experiences of Tolstoy himself.

The blending of all these disparate yet intimately personal memories into the central one of Pushkin's tragedy gave richness and intensity to Pierre's life story. A fresh insight into the grandeur of Pushkin's poetry had brought Tolstoy his realization that morality includes economic relationships as well as personal ones, as he had seen the night at Botkin's when he wept "blissful poetic tears," after the reading of Pushkin, at his own "moral development—forward and forward."

No wonder, then, that the tragic story of the poet who played such a strong role in his personal growth, Pushkin, comrade of the Decembrists, went into his story of his developing Decembrist Pierre. By the time Tolstoy finished *War and Peace*, he felt so closely identified with Pushkin that his next great project grew out of a slight opening for a story, never written, that Pushkin had once jotted down. Tolstoy found himself going on to visualize characters and plot, so that he ended up creating out of it another major novel, *Anna Karenina*.

The power and richness of great literature comes out of the distilled essence of a host of interconnected memories of the author's own life story, of the life stories of people he has known, even of people he has known only through reading about them. The magic and the originality lie in the blend and in the discoveries the author makes through it. Only if we have some knowledge of all the separate elements that fused to create the unique poetry of a work can we begin to appreciate the complexity of the creative process. Even the gaffes that appear in a creative work, such as Tolstoy's making Pierre a Gentleman of the Bedchamber twice over, can be perceived and understood by knowing the particular nexus of memories pressing upon him in the writing.

Out of the need to solve a particular life problem, a particular chain of memories comes together. So Tolstoy, trying to understand the meaning of his life, his family, his Russia, became filled with the tragic force of the Decembrists' stories (never overtly told in *War and Peace*), of Pushkin's story (used as a reservoir of events that could be swapped around freely), and of stories of revolutionaries Tolstoy knew—all blended into memories of his near and dear ones and his own life struggle. From this nexus of interconnected memories came the poetry of *War and Peace*, and through the clashes and mutual reinforcements of its elements emerged—as the story emerged—the answers Tolstoy was seeking.

Love, Brotherly and Romantic

Tolstoy had been "delighted" on reading Ogarev's "Fragment" from his "Confessions" in *The Polar Star* to learn that many of the leading Decembrists had been Freemasons. He felt "very proud," he told Herzen, that before he had known a single Decembrist, he had "instinctively divined the Christian mysticism" that inspired them. In the reign of Alexander I, Freemasonry had flourished, and young intellectuals like Pushkin had joined lodges. Many of his friends among the Decembrists—Ryleyev, Pestel, Muraviev, Küchelbecker—also became Masons. The very idea of a secret society was taken from the Masons. The "Union of Salvation," the first secret society, founded on February 9, 1816, in St. Petersburg, took from them their oaths of secrecy, their ideals of helping their fellow men, and their democratic structure, with the hierarchies of rank dissolved in brotherly love.

Tolstoy learned about the lodges through research at the Rumyantsev Museum in Moscow, for Nicholas I outlawed Freemasonry at the beginning of his reign. Those idealists both intrigued and depressed Tolstoy. He had Pierre at first interested, then disillusioned, so that at the end of the book he has dropped Masonry to become a leader in consolidating the secret societies that would make the December Revolt.

As a prelude to joining the Masons, Tolstoy had Pierre plunge into despair over the falsity of his marriage, asking himself frantically, "What is bad? What is good? What should one love and what hate? What does one live for?" After his mistaken courtship of Valerya, Tolstoy had asked himself just such questions. "Of what use am I? Whom do I love? No one." When Pierre arrives at the first posting station in flight from his wife, he is ready to accept almost any answer, and he is instantly impressed by the Mason, Joseph Alexeyevich Bazdeyev, whom he meets there, a character modeled by Tolstoy, with a change of only the first two letters of his name, on the historical Masonic leader O. A. Pozdeyev.

For Pierre the essence of Freemasonry lies in "the fraternity and equality of men who have virtuous aims." He cannot love death—as the Masons advised—for he really loves life. Nor is he attracted by the nebulous "important mystery" they wish to penetrate. What fills him with hope is the possibility of perfecting himself in his world. He really wants to help his serfs, and is prevented only by his tricky stewards, who go right on squeezing from the peasants "all that could be got out of them." In his new Masonic enthusiasm, Pierre arouses Prince Andrey from his depression and remorse over his young wife's death and awakens him to hope for the world. Pierre presents to Prince Andrey his own rapturous conception of Freemasonry as a form of Christianity "freed from bonds of State and Church, a teaching of equality, brotherhood, and love." Tolstoy had created his definition not out of Masonic beliefs but out of his own youthful dreams of hope for Russia.

Right after the bloody days on the bastions of Sevastopol, he had suddenly had a "stupendous idea" of founding a religion for modern man: "the religion of Christ but purged of dogmas and mysticism—a practical religion, not promising future bliss but giving bliss on earth." Through the struggles of Pierre and Prince Andrey to find a meaning for their lives, Tolstoy carried on his own search. "We must live; we must love," Pierre tells Prince Andrey, urging him to see himself not as lost in the evils of the world, but as a part of the whole universe—that is, of the infinite sky Prince Andrey had glimpsed at Austerlitz.

This talk marks the beginning of a "new life" for Prince Andrey. More practical than Pierre, he brings about the reforms that Pierre had fruitlessly tried to effect—abolishing cruel punishments and compulsory serf labor on his estates: in fact, putting his peasants on payment of quit-rent for the use of the land they farm, and paying them as free laborers for the work they do for him, the reforms that Tolstoy succeeded—after many difficulties—in putting into effect at Yasnaya Polyana after his return from the Crimea.

Because of Pierre, Prince Andrey is able to achieve a miraculous resurrection from despair like Tolstoy's when he fell in love with Sonya Behrs. Although Tolstoy found his love in September, he had always had his bursts of hope in the spring. In 1858 he wrote Auntie Tatyana that it was spring, and even though he was "an old frozen-out potato" he felt himself flowering along with all the plants burgeoning around him, growing "peacefully, simply, and joyously" in "God's world." All his regrets, repentance, all his vices seemed swept away, and in him was a "wonderful little flower which is budding and growing along with spring."

Prince Andrey's first delight in Natasha Rostov awakens in him just such a feeling. Traveling to the Rostov estate, Prince Andrey comes upon a bare old oak tree, "aged, stern, and scornful" among the fresh leaves of the birches around it. It seems to be telling him that spring is a fraud and a lie, and that his own life, like the oak's, is finished. But once he has been awakened to "youthful thoughts and hopes" by Natasha, he finds, on returning through the same woods a day later, that the old oak is "quite transfigured," fresh with unfurling leaves vibrating in the evening sun, and he is "seized by an unreasoning springtime feeling of joy and renewal."

Later he confides to Pierre his feeling for Natasha, saying, "Yesterday I tormented myself and suffered, but I would not exchange even that torment for anything in the world: I have not lived till now." So Tolstoy, in his first "irresistible" attraction to Sonya, had told her: "I would have died of laughter if I'd been told a month ago that it was possible to be tormented as I've been tormented, and joyfully tormented, all this time." And Pierre—who has really brought Prince Andrey to happiness through his own love both for the girl and for him—generously advises his friend, "Don't philosophize, don't doubt, marry, marry, marry."

Nothing sets off Prince Andrey's happiness as sharply as the simultaneous gloom into which Pierre is catapulted through having been persuaded—partly by advice from worldly Masons—to return to living in the same house with his wife, Helene. Pierre's growing disillusionment with the Masons stems in part from this, in part from seeing their lack of interest in assisting the poor or alleviating the conditions of their serfs, and in part from the contrast between their ideals and their actual worldly lives.

He is made Rhetor in charge of initiating into the Masons his wife's current lover, Boris Drubetskoy—who is joining because he hopes to further his ambitions through intimacy with wealthy and highly connected men. During the initiation ceremony, Pierre finds himself tempted—so he afterward writes in his diary—"to stab his bare breast with the sword I held to it." At the beginning of his wife's double adultery with both the "foreign prince of the blood" and the Russian "grandee," Pierre takes on the gloom of Pushkin in the last days before the fatal duel, and wanders through his wife's salon impressing everyone with his "preoccupied, absent-minded, and morose air."

The great trial both for Prince Andrey and for Pierre comes with the blow to them of Natasha's infatuation with Anatole Kuragin. In it Tolstoy worked with his own youthful infatuations for men serving as models to imitate, all of them replacements for the sudden loss as a nine-year-old boy of his handsome, charming, exquisitely dressed father. When Lev transferred his admiration of his father to his brother Serozha, he chose him as a model of charm and elegance, of being always "comme il faut." Later he chose his father's friend Islenyev with his aristocratic gambling, and then his son, the very attractive Kostenka, charming in social circles and a leader in debauchery with gypsy girls.

A stream of memories went into Natasha's infatuation with Anatole, which repeats his own infatuation with Kostenka. Among them was Tanya Behrs's enchantment with his brother Sergey, his sister Marya's betrayal in love by her husband and then by Turgenev, and even his own frustration in feeling for the admired older writer whose praise was so necessary for him.

When Tolstoy went on to Italy and met his cousin Prince Sergey Volkonsky, Marya had gone to Switzerland for her health. From that time until a year after his marriage to Sonya Behrs, Tolstoy really lost touch with her. So the letter that reached him at the beginning of October 1863 came to him as a shock and revelation. The love that had been so cruelly thwarted by Valerian and then by Turgenev found a return in a Swedish Viscount, Victor-Hector de Kleen, who was also in Switzerland for his health. The next two years they lived together in Algiers. On September 8, 1863, Marya Tolstaya gave birth to his daughter.

The news overwhelmed Tolstoy, and he wrote back at once: "My dear, dear thousand-times beloved Mashenka, I can't tell you what I felt as I read your letter. I wept, and am still weeping as I write." She had told him that her brothers could judge her as they wished, but Tolstoy passed no judgment on her. He felt, he told her, only "love for you—all that love which used to be somewhere remote—pity and love. No honest man will ever lift a finger to reproach you." He wanted to adopt her child, to keep the secret from everyone. She could be sure that he and Auntie Tatyana "will not pass judgment on you, and will do everything we possibly can for you."

Out of these strands came the key episode of *War and Peace*. As Tolstoy had Pierre trapped by the Kuragins, he had Natasha besieged by the same family, with Helene mischievously abetting her brother to seduce her into eloping with him. Being entirely thoughtless, Anatole needs the help of Dolokhov to work out practical details such as a fraudulent marriage ceremony to be performed by an unfrocked priest, a fur cloak in which to wrap the girl as she comes out of the house, and a wild coachman with a troika to whirl her out of Russia. Although Dolokhov tells Anatole the truth, that he cannot abduct a countess as if she were a gypsy, he knows no thought of consequences will stop Anatole in the pursuit of pleasure.

Of course, Tolstoy did not bring Natasha to anything like his sister Masha's illegitimate baby. She is rescued from this fate by the vigilance of Sonya and of Marya Dmitrievna, in whose Moscow house she is staying. The damage is psychological, like that of Tanya Behrs when her engagement was broken, and social as gossip spreads of her involvement with Anatole. From his own response to his sister Marya's disgrace, Tolstoy took his protagonist Pierre's self-overcoming. Tolstoy had come a long way up from his readiness to fly from a wife guilty of the slightest liberty. He felt only pity, love, and a wish to support her.

Pierre responds in the same way to Natasha's disgrace. After the first shock, he feels only an immense "pity, tenderness, and love." When Natasha speaks of herself with "shame and self-abasement," as one whose life is over, Pierre declares: "If I were not myself, but the handsomest, cleverest, and best man in the world, and were free, I would this moment ask on my knees for your hand and your love!" Both are in tears, and Pierre goes off in a rapture, looking up at the night sky over Moscow scintillating with stars, with the glowing white light of the great comet of 1812 shining above him like a symbol of the glory then "passing in his own softened and uplifted soul."

As Tolstoy had come to the practical assistance of his sister Marya (she and her daughters would be living with him in the following years), so he had Pierre work practically, sending Anatole Kuragin far out of the way so that neither Natasha's father nor her fiancé, Prince Andrey, would be endangered by a duel, and doing his best to stifle the gossip about Rostova. He even tries to fill Prince Andrey with his own forgiveness and love, but Bolkonsky is too bitterly hurt to forgive and too humiliated by the utter worthlessness of the man for whom he has been jilted. He tells Pierre that it would be "very noble" to be magnanimous, "but I am unable to follow in that gentleman's footsteps."

From then on, Prince Andrey is dominated by the determination to kill Anatole in a duel, feeling his life to be "narrow and burdensome and useless to anyone," with death only a further indignity. Just before the Battle of Borodino, Prince Andrey thinks he will be killed, not by the enemy but by one of his own serf soldiers. (Tolstoy himself said the Russian army was a "horde of slaves" whose "last spark of pride" had been extinguished in their training, and he pointed out the "large number of Russian officers killed by Russian bullets.") So Prince Andrey sees himself killed futilely, and he thinks that then the enemy would come "and take me by the head and heels and fling me into a hole that I may not stink under their noses," even as Tolstoy himself, on the Volynsk Redoubt in the Crimean War had seen the corpses "swung by their legs and arms and thrown over the parapet."

Death and destruction dominate this entire section of *War and Peace*, for the invasion of Russia by Napoleon is paralleled by disasters in the lives of the major characters. Prince Andrey sees his father's dying as one with the devastation of his native land. For Tolstoy the most "powerful impression that I have ever known" had been the death of his brother Nikolay, and he came to grips with it in this part of his book through the Princess Marya's feelings during the dying of her father who represents, as the dying of Tolstoy's Grandfather Volkonsky represented—he having been a former commander-in-chief of the Russian army—his country's mortal peril.

Just as Lev Tolstoy and his brother Sergey, knowing that Nikolay was doomed, had thought at first that the quicker he went the better, but realized after his death that "it is dreadful now to write it and to remember that one thought it," so he had the Princess Marya suffer from recalling that during her father's long ordeal she had been "wishing for his death." Tolstoy always recalled with pain that toward the end, hearing his brother Nikolay in his room coughing, he had wanted to go to him but had been kept back by false shame, and Nikolay had told him, "Needlessly, it would have consoled me." So Tolstoy had Princess Marya linger outside her dying father's door, afraid to enter, only to learn that he had been speechlessly "calling you all night."

But the great story through which Tolstoy would empathize with the dying brother whom he had, he said, "loved and *respected* more than anyone else on earth" came in his telling of Prince Andrey's mortal wound after the Battle of Borodino. At one point Tolstoy had been reluctant to kill any of these characters he loved so well, and had meant to save Prince Andrey's life and even give the whole book the happy-ending title "All's Well that Ends Well." In that version, Prince Andrey was to realize that Natasha and Pierre love each other, and so, like Sonya, he was to step aside generously for the welfare of the others, although nothing Tolstoy had put into this character made such a resolution appear likely. Actually, Tolstoy resolved the problem by giving Prince Andrey another great revelation of the meaning of life and death like the one he had had at Austerlitz, which places him at the same height as was Pierre the night he glowed like a comet in the spiritual triumph of forgiveness and love.

Coming to, after a frightful operation, Prince Andrey sees on one of the other operating tables in the hospital tent Anatole Kuragin, whom he had been so set on killing, and is filled with pity for him. Anatole has just had one of his handsome legs amputated, and feeble, miserable, sobbing, he is looking at the bloody limb and his irrevocable disfigurement. Long before this, the model for Anatole, Kostya Islavin, had told Tolstoy that he believed in committing "suicide from shame of disfigurement," and he had spoken so "well and expressively" that Tolstoy found himself advocating the idea until he realized it was "base." Very probably Anatole had been originally meant to kill himself as Kostya would have done, but because the censorship would not allow a Russian hero to break a church law, we are simply told in passing that Anatole has died.

Looking upon him, Prince Andrey feels a rapturous return of love for Natasha, an "ecstatic pity and love" for Anatole, and, through him, a sublime pity for all men—himself included—with their errors. So he passes from his pre-battle despair to an apotheosis of higher values.

In flight from the advancing French, when she with her family comes upon the wounded Prince Andrey, Natasha transcends the delightful spoiled child she had once been in noble devotion to the dying man and reaches new spiritual heights by participating in his dying. After Nikolay's death, Tolstoy had felt "torn" from life and knew he had approached "nearer" to his "own death." By sharing in that gradual detachment from life, Tolstoy had come to see that death was not "painful, but important, significant, and beautiful." By way of Prince Andrey's oneness with the infinite sky, by way of his detached pity and love for all humankind, by way of Natasha's sharing in his going, Tolstoy reached acceptance of his brother's death, of his own approaching death, and of the universal destiny of all life.

The Crimean War and the War of 1812

Tolstoy could put himself easily into the great changes brought about by the War of 1812, which turned a generation of young Russian officers into future Decembrists, because the same kind of changes had been brought about in him by the Crimean War. On the bastions of Sevastopol, on the redoubts of Borodino, Russians were fighting on their own land to repel invading foreigners. Suddenly smitten with patriotism, Tolstoy had asked to be sent to Sevastopol from the Caucasus. In fact, his idea of bringing Pierre to the Battle of Borodino as a civilian observer came not so much from hearing about such a spectator in the letters that gave him the germ idea for Prince Andrey, as from having been one himself in the Crimean War.

When Tolstoy got back to Sevastopol on August 27, after a command in the mountains, he was both interested in starting a military journal and eager to join in his country's defense. So he volunteered to go into the thick of the slaughter on that day of violent enemy assaults, and went about observing for his projected magazine as well as participating. Colonel P. N. Glebov watched Tolstoy with amazement and reported, "He moves around to various places like a tourist," and "as soon as he hears where the firing is, he immediately appears on the field of battle; the battle over, he goes off again as the fancy takes him, following his nose."

Similarly, at Borodino Pierre goes at once to the left flank because the fighting there is "frightfully hot," and his horse having been shot out from under him, he joins the soldiers on Raevsky's Redoubt at the moment it becomes the very center of the battle, "around which tens of thousands fell," where he paces up and down "as calmly as if he were on a boulevard" with the shells exploding all around him.

Before Tolstoy wrote his pages on the Battle of Borodino, he traveled to the battlefield and went over it for two days, reconstructing the events from his experiences at Sevastopol. From the Crimean War, Tolstoy came to conclusions very like those the young Decembrists reached from their experiences in 1812. "Russia must fall or completely reorganize herself," he decided. The whole army was misdirected, he thought. "The Cossacks want to plunder but not to fight. The Hussars and Uhlans consider military dignity consists in drunkenness and debauchery, while the infantry think it consists in robbery and money-making."

These ideas compelled Tolstoy to write a plan for reforming the army, and later on they directed his picture of the army in *War and Peace*. At Sevastopol, Tolstoy had talked with wounded French and English prisoners of war and had been struck by their self-respect and initiative in comparison with Russian serf soldiers, who had been disciplined throughout their twenty-five years of compulsory service with the knout. "With us," Tolstoy declared, "stupid drill for dressing the file and saluting with the musket, useless weapons, ignorance, and bad food" had destroyed in the common soldiers "their last spark of pride."

Parade-ground drilling had been the hallmark of Nicholas I's reign and one of the chief impulses behind the formation of the secret societies. Russia's young intelligentsia had been outraged by the brutal suppression of the Semenovsky Guards Regiment's "revolt," really a refusal of junior officers to carry out certain orders on October 16, 1820, which Tolstoy describes in his "Epilogue." In the years after 1812, this regiment had been reformed by its enlightened officers, who abolished "shameful corporal punishment" and created friendly relations between officers and privates.

To such martinets as Nicholas, then Grand Duke, and his brother Mikhail the regiment appeared "loose and extremely corrupted," so they saw to it that the commander, General Potëmkin, was removed and Colonel G. C. Schwarz put in his place to institute intensive drilling around the clock and severe flogging, averaging, on Schwarz's own calculations, 324 lashes to a man. When Schwarz commanded the flogging of soldiers wearing the Saint George cross, who should have been exempt, the officers refused to carry out his order. In reprisal, the Emperor disbanded the regiment, degrading its officers and sending them to dangerous outposts. Although *War and Peace* ends before the reign of Nicholas began, Tolstoy shows the parade-ground drilling from the first view of the Russian army. At the start of the book, a comically obtuse regimental commander is blundering against all practical purposes in his ardor to reach a field-manual ideal of perfection.

With all the ineptitude displayed at Sevastopol, Tolstoy was sure that the "terrible slaughter" was proving the "moral strength of the Russian people." He was sure that in the "passionate love for the Fatherland that is arising and flowing from Russia's misfortunes" a new spirit was being born in Russians that would inspire them to participate in "public affairs with dignity and pride" and stamp "self-sacrifice and nobleness forever on their character." Exactly such had been the effect of the War of 1812 on the generation who became Decembrists.

As one of them, A. D. Borovkov, put it, "Napoleon invaded Russia and it was then that the Russian people perceived their power," and then that "the feeling for independence" was "kindled in every heart." By the time Tolstoy wrote the first page of his prospective novel "The Decembrists," he was fully aware that this hope for a renaissance of Russia had come twice in the nineteenth century, "first when we gave Napoleon I a beating in 1812, and secondly when Napoleon III gave us a beating in 1856."

Without at first aiming consciously at it, Tolstoy gave Pierre's experiences during the French invasion a strong resemblance to the experiences of his Decembrist cousin Sergey Volkonsky in prison and then among the peasants on his Siberian farm. Pierre's imprisonment comes about because he takes up the historical Masonic interest in applying numerology to the interpretation of the "Book of Revelation." By giving arbitrary numerical value to the letters of Napoleon's name, they figured out that he was the Beast of the Apocalypse. Juggling the letters of his own name in a similar manner, Pierre arrives at the idea that he is destined to slay the Beast, so he remains in Moscow disguised as a coachman with the project of assassinating Napoleon.

In this, Tolstoy followed the story of one of the most extraordinary men who later participated in the December Revolt, Mikhail Sergeyevich Lunin, whom Pushkin had celebrated as a "friend of Bacchus, Mars, and Venus." While fighting in the "disastrous campaigns" of Austerlitz and Friedland, Lunin decided he could save the lives of thousands by killing one man, Bonaparte. He tried fruitlessly to have himself sent as an envoy to French Headquarters, where he could stab the tyrant "with a poignard which for a long time afterwards he kept hidden in his tent." Pierre has the same purpose and keeps both a knife and a pistol to carry it out.

In an earlier conception of the novel, Tolstoy had planned to put in an Italian whose life Pierre saves, which clearly evolved out of his cousin Volkonsky's comrade Poggio, who was beside him at the December

Revolt and later in Siberia. Perhaps at the time Tolstoy first met Volkon-sky he also came to know Poggio, who was in Italy with him, for Poggio's wife and five children had gone back there while he was in Siberia. (Poggio never left Volkonsky, spending the rest of his life in Russia on the Volkonsky estate in Chernigov.) Then Tolstoy decided to have Pierre save a Frenchman rather than the Italian, so that all that remains of the Poggio character in the final novel is an Italian prisoner of war whom Pierre helps after he is freed from the French.

Pierre's rescue of the Frenchman shows that his instinctive humanity is more powerful than his intellectual decision to become a killer. When Bazdeyev's insane brother picks up Pierre's pistol and tries to shoot a French officer who has just come into their house looking for quarters, Pierre throws his strength into diverting the shot, taking the pistol, and saving the man's life. Among the fires that break out all over the deserted wooden city left to a looting army, Pierre then saves a little girl—a by no means attractive child slobbering and fighting in her terror—and then throws himself into defending a beautiful Armenian girl being assaulted by plundering French soldiers.

Ironically he is then arrested as an incendiary by a French patrol that needs almost all its men to subdue him. As they take him off, they ask who the woman with the child is, and Pierre replies that she is bringing "my daughter whom I have just saved from the flames." In this seem-ingly "aimless lie," Pierre has defined himself correctly. By nature he is not the assassin he thought he could be, but a resolute father and protector of life.

From the lips of his beloved "Babushka" (Alexandra A. Tolstaya), Tolstoy first heard the story of V. A. Perovsky, whom she had known well. Perovsky had been taken after the Battle of Borodino, interrogated by Davout, slated for death, and then at the last minute reprieved to become a prisoner of war. To this story Tolstoy added parts of the Decembrist story from before he was born, and of the Petrashevtsy story, which came when he was twenty-one years old. ("Petrashevtsy" is the Russian term for the followers of M. V. Petrashevsky.) With Nicholas I's terror of the uprisings of 1848, he had unleashed a swarm of domestic spies on his people. In April 1849 they arrested M. V. Butashevich-Petrashevsky, a young official in the Ministry of Foreign Affairs, along with all the friends who met at his home on Friday evenings to talk—in particular about the immorality of private property and the inviolable dignity of the individual, which put them against serfdom and whipping. Although there was "no plot, no secret society," as the police later realized, and although the aim of the Petrashevtsy—as Petrashevsky himself put it—was merely "to fill out the thin ranks of those morally concerned for the future of Russia," they were cruelly punished.

Twenty-one of them, including the promising young novelist Fyodor Dostoyevsky, were sentenced to death, and another fifty-one were sentenced to imprisonment and exile. Usually the Emperor Nicholas had his judges give an extremely harsh sentence, and then, in "mercy," he made it a little less so. In this case he had the ingenious idea of having those sentenced to death led out to Semenovsky Square on December 22, 1849, and of having the death sentence read to them, a sword broken over their heads, shrouds put on them, and the first three tied to a stake and blindfolded before the firing squad. Then the drums beat a retreat and the men were told that in mercy "His Imperial Majesty" commuted the death sentence to life imprisonment in Siberia. (Dostoyevsky and the others regained freedom through the same 1856 amnesty of Alexander II that liberated the surviving Decembrists.)

Nicholas I's cat-and-mousing would have been of no use to Napoleon in punishing incendiaries, but Tolstoy managed to adapt it to his story. Pierre and the other prisoners are led out to be tied to the stake and shot in the Virgin Field. With "dismay, horror, and conflict," Pierre watches the five men before him being killed. Only then does he realize that he will not be shot, but taken as a prisoner of war. The number of men executed before him—five—comes, it seems, of a haunting recollection of the "five crucifixions," as Herzen spoke of them, of the leading Decembrists.

Into the horror of this scene, Tolstoy released the horror he had felt on seeing a murderer guillotined in Paris during his first visit there in 1857. In one instant he perceived the "stout white neck and chest" of the living man, saw him kiss the Bible and then in the next moment a bloody corpse. Tolstoy realized, he said, "not with my reason, but with my whole being," that nothing in the world "could justify such an act" and that even if all men believed it necessary "it was an evil thing." So, in criticizing a foreign government, Tolstoy reached a cataclysmic rejection of all institutionalized evil that would strengthen the upheaval in his own soul that was overthrowing his docility to the Russian government with its slavery and suppression.

Although he was overjoyed to get back from Europe to "delightful Yasnaya," Tolstoy felt depressed the instant he descended from the train at Tula and heard the screams of a serf named "Zorin" who was "being beaten." He confided to his diary: "Russia disgusts me and I feel how this coarse lying life begins to encircle me on every side." These experiences allowed Tolstoy to depict Pierre's horror at the relentless dehumanized killings he had seen enacted, and his feeling that "his faith in the right ordering of the universe, in humanity, in his own soul, and in God, had been destroyed."

For Pierre this experience, along with the frightful hardships he suffers as a prisoner in the demoralized, retreating French army, brings on a spiritual apotheosis. In fact, Pierre arrives at the same spiritual splendor that Tolstoy's Decembrist cousin Sergey Volkonsky achieved in his years of hard labor in the Siberian mines and his later years working like a peasant among the peasants on his farm.

The Decembrists had put into practice their highest ideals throughout their ordeal. In the mines, Volkonsky and his friends established an artel—a cooperative—in which they pooled all the money they received from home and then divided it so as to assist those among them who were entirely or almost entirely destitute. Perhaps the greatest saint and martyr among them was Mikhail Sergeyevich Lunin—he who, like Pierre, had thought once to assassinate Napoleon. After he was freed from prison, Lunin worked to let the world know the story of the Decembrists, smuggling his articles out for publication in Paris.

When this was discovered by the police, Nicholas I ordered Lunin's rearrest on March 6, 1841, and had him sent to the most terrible of the mines at Akatui, where all books were prohibited and the prisoners were chained to their wheelbarrows and the walls of their cells or knouted for the slightest offense. During this time, Lunin's thoughts were all for his fellow prisoners. When "Jeannot" (Ivan) Pushchin's brother came through inspecting prisons and asked what he could do for him, Lunin asked him to try to get the release of those of his fellow prisoners who were chained to their walls. To Sergey Volkonsky, he wrote asking for balm to soothe the lashwounds of his "poor comrades."

Tolstoy had read Lunin's letters published by Herzen in *The Polar Star*, and he used them for the ultimate wisdom achieved by Pierre. Out of the horrible mines at Akatui, where Lunin died on December 3, 1845, less than four years after his second arrest, he sent up hymns of praise for the gift of life. He declared, "One can find happiness under any conditions. Only the fools of this world are unhappy."

With his "bare, raw, and scab-covered feet," plodding through the snow on long, forced marches, Pierre achieves just such wisdom and sends up like praise. He learns, in just the way Tolstoy's great learning had come, "not with his intellect but with his whole being" that "man is created for happiness, that happiness is within him, in the satisfaction of simple human needs," and that whereas no man can be entirely happy or entirely free under any circumstances, "so there is no condition in which he need be unhappy and lack freedom."

At first, Tolstoy had Pierre achieve wisdom through himself, but he realized he could give him also the folk wisdom gathered through centuries by millions of enslaved Russian peasants, the wisdom his cousin Sergey Volkonsky had learned by working in brotherhood with his peasants on the land. So into this novel of nobles, Tolstoy put one great peasant character. On the very night when his entire faith in the ordering of the universe collapses, Pierre is soothed and healed by the presence of one of the fellow prisoners locked into a stable with him—a serf and man of the soil named Platon Karataev, who has undergone the cruelest fate that could befall a serf, that of being torn from his village and family and sent into strange regions to serve a twenty-five-year term as a slave-soldier.

From Karataev flows the strength of the people expressed in their proverbs and adages. "Don't fret, friend—'suffer an hour, live for an age!'" he tells Pierre. "Never decline a prison or a beggar's sack!" This globular Russian holds his arms "as if ever ready to embrace something," and he really embraces in loving-kindness all around him, including an absurd stray dog. He believes "the great thing is to live in harmony." All life to him is a holy ritual, as his words before sleep tell us. "Lay me down like a stone, O God, and raise me up like a loaf."

The Russian words for "Christian" and for "peasant" are similar, and Karataev pronounces both in the same way, so that they become one. He loves all that life brings to him, but without grieving at parting from anyone or anything. Moreover, he is self-sufficient and useful to everyone, being able to do all things. Tolstoy tells us, "He baked, cooked, sewed, planed, and mended boots." He was "always busy," and he sang "like the birds" spontaneously. Through his example, Pierre's shattered world is rehabilitated "with a new beauty and on new and unshakable foundations." Even in his acceptance of dying as a blessing and liberation, Platon presents the great philosophy, the real Christianity embodied in the Russian peasant.

When Tolstoy finally had Pierre liberated from the routed French, he had already brought him to a resolution of all his impelling questions on the meaning of life and of death, and so, except for tying up the marriages of Pierre with Natasha and of Princess Marya with Nikolay

Rostov, the book was really finished. All that Tolstoy had meant to discover and reveal through the ordeal of the Decembrists in prison and work, he had already revealed through Pierre's and Prince Andrey's experiences in 1812, a good thirteen years before ever the Decembrist Revolt took place.

To fulfill his original plan for "The Decembrists," Tolstoy had to put in an "Epilogue" to bring his readers to the start of the secret societies, with Pierre in the leadership and Prince Andrey's son Nikolay as his devoted disciple. But Tolstoy had really concluded the book he had been writing before he added the "Epilogue." So he found himself beginning what was really a new novel with essentially new characters about the meaning of marriage and the family. In fact, this "Epilogue" turned into a trial balloon for the next great novel he would write, *Anna Karenina*.

One of the most shocking surprises of the "Epilogue" of *War and Peace* is the transformation of the poetic, artistic, life-enjoying, well-beloved Natasha into a totally different person—a woman jealous, possessive, self-tormenting, and of-the-earth earthy. In fact, this woman is the very same Sonya whose jealousy and inner torment had taken over the character of Auntie Tatyana at the beginning of Tolstoy's book. Tolstoy's sister-in-law Tanya had not married and entered motherhood in time to serve in the "Epilogue" as a model for Natasha as the center of a family. So Tolstoy simply put his wife Sonya in her place.

"I took Tanya, beat her up with Sonya, and the result was Natasha," he later declared. Actually, no such amalgam of two such opposite personalities was ever feasible. Natasha is entirely Tanya throughout the book and then in the "Epilogue" she turns into that very different person, Tolstoy's wife Sonya, already endowed with the furious possessiveness, the jealousy, the hysterical outbreaks that would make her, far in the future, as Tolstoy would then say of her, "a stone tied with a rope around my neck and around the necks of the children." But in the "Epilogue," Natasha is above all the Sonya of Tolstoy's great happiness in love for her during the first years of his marriage, the "strong, handsome, and fertile woman" who was bringing him a steadily increasing crowd of delightful children. And as such she is still a positive figure.

Placed as the "Epilogue" is after the main characters have arrived at the wisdom Tolstoy had at first meant them to reach through the Decembrist ordeal, it comes as an anachronism. Pierre himself realizes that Karataev, his master in wisdom, "would not have approved" his work with the secret societies. Karataev would have been shocked by their futile sacrifice, standing as he did for—so Pierre says—"seemliness, happiness, and peace in everything." No wonder, then, that Tolstoy was disturbed by the difference between his book and the usual novel, "because I cannot and do not know how to confine the characters I have created within given limits," such as marriage or death. He could not, he said, "force my characters to act only with the aim of proving or clarifying some kind of idea or series of ideas."

Voyna i Mir

For all that, Tolstoy had achieved a great inner unity, a great resolution of all his questions on the meaning of history, of the intimate history of his family, of his fellow Russians, of all the important people in his life. Far from a novel about historical people he had never known, historical battles he had never fought, personal events he had never experienced, *War and Peace* came out of his most intimate struggles, his most intense experiences, the people he had been closest to and had loved best. Despite his Russian hatred of intellectual formulas and logical straitjackets, he had really, by the end of his book, arrived at the life-meaning and philosophy that only much later on he would try to translate into every act of his daily life.

In fact, when Tolstoy finally arrived at the right title for his book "Voyna i Mir"—as it sounds in Russian—in March 1867, he had really captured the essential meaning of the great experience he was writing about. Unfortunately, the words are hopelessly constricted in sense by translation into the English "War and Peace." Even a scholar like Reginald Christian, who knows Russian well, thinks in terms of the restricted meaning of the English words in talking of the book, so that he sees the basic contrast in the book as "inherent in the title," in which, as he defines the words, "war" means "military actions," and "peace" means "non-military actions."

The Russian words have a much wider significance. *Mir*, the Russian word, means not only "peace," but also "concord," "union," "community," and very specifically the Russian peasant community which is actually called a "mir." So the Russian title suggests not only "war and peace" but also "division and community," "discord and harmony," "conflict and tranquillity," "hatred and love," as well as "fragmentation and unity." For Tolstoy, the words also express the moral contrast in "evil and good."

Put to a definition of what is "good" or "moral" or "important" for human life, Tolstoy said, "That which unites people not by violence but by love: that which serves to disclose the joy of the union of men with one another, is 'important' 'good,' or 'moral.' 'Evil' and 'immoral' is that which divides them." Tolstoy thought that what was important for other people in art—in his art of writing—was anything that led them "to understand and love what they previously did not understand or love."

The major characters of "Voyna i Mir" come to a revelation of these meanings at the crucial points in their lives. Pierre's first excitement with the Masons comes of his seeing the "possibility of the brotherhood of men." Prince Andrey's awakening comes of sharing this hope with Pierre, and is further accentuated by the effect of his love for Natasha, which gives him his own vision of "mir." He decides that "Pierre, and that young girl who wanted to fly away into the sky, everyone must know me, so that my life may not be lived for myself alone," but may be joined to them all, and "they and I may live in harmony!"

The meaning of the Battle of Borodino for Tolstoy lies not in the mass slaughter of Russians and Frenchmen but in the mutually reinforcing visions of Pierre and Prince Andrey taken from it. Prince Andrey realizes that the secret of living is "compassion, love of our brothers, for those that love us and for those who hate us, love of our enemies," and that the great happiness of life is the "happiness of loving," of loving "everything."

For Pierre the secret comes—as it came to Tolstoy during the most perilous days on the bastions of Sevastopol—out of his happiness in brotherly love for the soldiers facing death with him at the Battle of Borodino. Tolstoy noted in his diary on April 12, 1855, that in the midst of bursting shells he actually felt happy: "The constant charm of danger, observing the soldiers with whom I am living, the sailors" was "so pleasant that I do not want to leave here." So, on the Raevsky Redoubt, Pierre wears an "unconsciously happy smile," feeling with the men around him "a common and as it were family feeling of animation." In fact, his "whole attention was engrossed by watching the family circle" these men had formed among them.

After the battle, Pierre has a sublime moment sharing in the mash of three common (serf) soldiers, and he thinks to himself ecstatically, "To be a soldier, just a soldier!" To be able "to enter communal life completely, to be imbued by what makes them what they are." Afterward, sleeping outdoors in his coach, he sees a dream vision of the meaning of community—*mir*—of the uniting of all people, which becomes mixed with the words of his coachman awakening him, so that he thinks, "Yes, one must harness; it is time to harness." As the dream slips away, he is left with the nebulous realization that everything in life must be harnessed, linked.

The most intense vision of "mir" comes to Natasha after her humiliating and crushing experience with Anatole Kuragin, when she decides, as an act of purification, to take Communion and then participate in the Mass in special prayer for victory. Here Tolstoy makes a direct pun on the word *mir* as meaning "peace," "concord," "community," and "union." Echoing the priest who has said "In peace [*mir*], let us pray," Natasha thinks, "In community [*mir*], without distinction of class, without enmity, united by brotherly love—let us pray!"

The most expansive and beautiful vision of "mir"—of peace, harmony, concord—is that which Tolstoy gives to the boy Petya Rostov the night before the guerrilla engagement in which his young life will be wiped out. Between sleep and waking, Petya hears a great orchestra playing a sweetly solemn hymn with instruments all blending, separating, blending again, and as the music becomes more joyful, men's and women's voices join in with "harmonious triumphant strength" that fills his heart with awe.

So he achieves symbolically the understanding of life that Karataev has imparted explicitly to Pierre: "The great thing is to live in harmony." With such wisdom, Tolstoy emerged from the great "orgy" of his reexamination of his own life, the lives of all the relatives he had known personally or merely heard about, the lives of all the people he had been close to, and history understood not as the will of a few people but as "the development of humanity as a whole." In concord, harmony, brotherhood, community—in "mir"—all would be ultimately resolved.

No one understood better than Tolstoy how far beyond immediate conscious goals the real impetus of art lies. At one point, he refused to write for a newspaper, declaring that its practical aims were "millions of miles away from genuine artistic" activity, were as far from the "business of poetry" as the "painting of signboards" was from art. He could not write "just for the sake" of writing; he could write for no purpose but the "satisfaction of an inner need." He saw art as the "highest manifestation" of the human spirit. He believed that art "directs all human activity" and so cannot be directed. Clearly, he understood that real art, great writing, arrives at knowledge beyond the conscious awareness and directive plans of the artist at its inception.

Certainly when Tolstoy began his gargantuan and complex novel *War and Peace* as a book about the Decembrists, he could not have expressed the need that impelled him to reexamine his own purpose in life as well as the meaning of the lives of all his loved ones, relatives, friends, and forebears, particularly those who lived through and took part in the Napoleonic wars. So powerfully was he directed by unconscious inner needs while writing, that he completely altered his initial plan of episodes extending from 1805 through the 1856 return from exile of his Decembrist cousin. In fact, he did not even cover a decade of it. By the time he reached 1813, he had already resolved for his major characters all the problems that impelled him. So he was left with a story about a developing Decembrist that was over—fully concluded—more than a decade before he became one.

The strange structure of *War and Peace* resulted from the practical necessity of dealing with that paradox, which Tolstoy managed by adding an "Epilogue" which leaps ahead to 1820 and shows his major character, Pierre, at the point when he has taken leadership in organizing the secret societies that would immolate themselves in December 1825. But he could not limit his "Epilogue" to that, for by the time he wrote it he was already strongly directed by a fresh impelling question fed by a new nexus of memories: the problem of the meaning of love and marriage, which would become the force behind the next novel he tackled, *Anna Karenina*. Like Mark Twain's *Huckleberry Finn*, *War and Peace* is therefore a novel that has lost its original impetus before its conclusion. Luckily the loss appeared only in the "Epilogue" so it disrupted only that afterthought. In the resulting vacuum, the "Epilogue" became charged with a new impetus, departed upon a new story, and altered the principal characters beyond recognition. As it came out, Tolstoy's "Epilogue" serves as much to confuse the reader as to complete the buried Decembrist theme—of which very few, if any, readers have ever been aware.

Another oddity in the structure of *War and Peace* came about through Tolstoy's conscious purpose of finding a more truthful theory of history than the official Russian imperial theory that events are brought about by the plans and actions of great men. This official theory was closely allied with the government program of fostering idolatry of Peter the Great, and thus of the whole Romanov dynasty, particularly of its present incumbent, Emperor Nicholas I. Tolstoy's fresh theory of history had taken off from his admiration for the thought of the philosopher Nikolay Stankevich (to whose German metaphysical circle in Moscow Tolstoy's friend Turgenev had belonged, and on whose inspiration Turgenev, along with Mikhail Bakunin, had spent months in Berlin studying the ideas of Schelling, Kant, Fichte, and Hegel). Stankevich's basic ideas were that history is not concerned with the doings of great men, but with the "development of humanity as a whole"; that art is the unique way to grasp the "essence of things"; and that knowledge lies not in the disparate facts but in a unifying conception of the whole.

From these ideas, Tolstoy went on to arrive at his own theory of history. From his observations of fighting in the Caucasus and in the Crimean War, he came to the conclusion that the outcome of a battle is determined not by the strategic plans of its commanders but by the mass of soldiers in the fighting. From his work with history while writing *War and Peace*, Tolstoy came to the conclusion that emperors—such as Alexander I and Napoleon—do not direct the course of events but are actually swept along helplessly by larger forces that determine their decisions.

Because Tolstoy arrived at these ideas through writing, long stretches of *War and Peace* came out as straight argumentation. Only at the end of all the writing did Tolstoy realize that most of this exposition was extraneous to his story and clogged the action, so he cut it all drastically. But he could not bear to throw away all those hard-won ideas. In the end he solved this problem by adding a second "Epilogue,"—all of it a debate in favor of his theory of history, made up of what he had cut from the body of the novel.

No wonder the structure of this very great novel with its complex epic scope has baffled so many of its critics. No wonder Tolstoy believed that art directs everything, but cannot be directed. Certainly, structure, conscious theme, scope had all changed magically in the course of writing, transformed by what Tolstoy had to put in to resolve his impelling life problems—of which need he remained, for the most part, unconscious. And that resolution brought him an understanding of life and his world that he did not have when he began and thus that could not have directed him at the start.

As for the novel about the Decembrists he had meant to write, he was still haunted by it. But he was more urgently propelled by the whole question of the meaning of love and marriage that had taken over the first "Epilogue" of *War and Peace*, so he turned to working on *Anna Karenina*, which dealt with that problem. Only after that did he make another attempt to write a book truly centered on the Decembrists. But by that time (1878), Russia had changed. Hope of reform had died, and a new generation—the product of many years of repression and feeling totally blocked from constructive action—turned to destructive terroristic acts as the only means left to them.

As Tolstoy told his friend Strakhov, there was no need to look far to see what lured revolutionaries to murder. "An overcrowded Siberia, prisons, wars, the gallows, the poverty of the people, the blasphemy, greed, and cruelty of the authorities—these are no excuses, but the real causes of temptation," he said. Having no sympathy with these acts of violence, yet realizing that they were the form protest was taking in these times, Tolstoy lost his enthusiasm for setting up the Decembrists as an appropriate example. Besides, Tolstoy himself had been refused government permission to examine the archives on the Decembrists, so he dropped all the research he had done on them after *Anna Karenina* and looked about for other ways of working for the future of his country and of humanity.

Far from losing touch with the life he had experienced by writing about a period preceding it in *War and Peace*—as Matthew Arnold had supposed—Tolstoy had been most vitally nourished by that experience. All his research on the times before his birth had blended with the most intimate events and people of his life to create the great human experience of that book. If Tolstoy never saw Moscow in flames, never looked upon its occupation by Napoleon's troops, he did weep to see Sevastopol burning and the French flags flying on the bastions he had defended.

Pierre turned out to be a titanic figure in *War and Peace* because within him a generation of struggling individuals came vividly alive: several important Decembrists, their inspiration and comrade, the poet Alexander Pushkin, and those who came in their footsteps—Herzen, Ogarev, Bakunin, the Petrashevtsy. These human stories blended with and became one with Tolstoy's own many-sided character, with its contradictions, pains, joys, and hopes. Out of life came the great art of Tolstoy's *War and Peace*. Out of life came also those other great writings by Thomas Mann, Robert Louis Stevenson, and Edward FitzGerald. The creative process begins in life and results in a fresh strength for living both for the authors of great writing and for the readers who partake of their work.

Tolstoy himself was always aware of what fiction can achieve that an explanatory treatise is powerless to bring about. A reader of a novel receives an experience, relives in himself, Tolstoy said, the emotion "which moved the man who expressed it." By way of fiction, a single reader, walled into his one, narrow life experience, breaks out to live another life and to receive from it a fresh perspective he could not have come to by himself. He emerges from his reading with an enlarged understanding.

If a great work of art is born of an urgent inner need to come to grips with certain of the immense problems of living, then the value of reading such a work is the same in kind as the value of writing it. By struggling and experiencing with Mann, Stevenson, FitzGerald, and Tolstoy, a reader emerges as did those writers: wiser, enriched, better equipped to live his life.

Appendix:
Who's Who in Chapter 4

Russian Names: There are a chaotic number of ways that a Russian name may be transcribed into English. In my text, I selected the spelling simplest to pronounce and recognize for an English reader who does not speak Russian. I preserve the Russian patronymic and use the feminine form of the family name (Tolstaya for Tolstoy) where I can, for atmosphere. Because translations of the novel usually give the English form without gender in the family name, I do the same for names of characters. For Russian authors in the notes, I give the spelling in the publication used.

Annenkov, Pavel Vasilyevich
  Russian writer, friend of Lev Tolstoy, biographer of Alexander Pushkin.
Arsenyeva, Valerya Vladimirovna
  Neighbor's daughter whom Lev Tolstoy courted for a while and who contributed to his picture of Pierre's courtship of Helene Kuragin in *War and Peace*.
Bagratión, Prince Peter Ivanovich
  Commander of the Russian army in the Napoleonic wars who appears in *War and Peace*.

Bakunin, Mikhail Alexandrovich
Anarchist leader, some of whose features went into Pierre in *War and Peace*.
Bashilov, Mikhail Sergeyevich
Cousin of Lev Tolstoy's wife, artist and first illustrator of *War and Peace*.
Bazdeyev, Joseph Alexeyevich
Masonic leader who converts Pierre in *War and Peace*, modeled by Tolstoy on the historical Mason O. A. Pozdeyev.
Behrs, Andrey Yevstafyevich, Dr.
Lev Tolstoy's father-in-law.
Behrs, Sofya Andreyevna, "Sonya"
Maiden name of Lev Tolstoy's wife.
Behrs, Tatyana Andreyevna, "Tanya"
Younger sister of Lev Tolstoy's wife and model for Natasha in *War and Peace*.
Behrs, Yelizaveta Andreyevna, "Liza"
Older sister of Lev Tolstoy's wife, thought to have modeled for Vera Rostov in *War and Peace*.
Benckendorff, Count A. Kh.
Head of Nicholas I's Third Department of domestic political spies.
Bestuzhev, Alexander
Decembrist, joint editor with Ryleyev of *The Polar Star*.
Bestuzhev, Staff Captain M. A.
Decembrist.
Bestuzhev-Riumin, Mikhail P.
One of the five Decembrists hung by Tsar Nicholas I.
Bezukhov, Count Kiril Vladimirovich
Father of Pierre Bezukhov in *War and Peace*.
Bezukhov, Count Pierre Kirilovich
Protagonist of *War and Peace*.
Bolkonsky, Prince Andrey Nikolayevich
Close friend of Pierre Bezukhov and fiancé of Natasha Rostov in *War and Peace*.
Bolkonsky, Princess Marya Nikolayevna
Prince Andrey's sister, with Natasha Rostov a major heroine in *War and Peace*.
Bolkonsky, Prince Nikolay Andreyevich
Prince Andrey and Princess Marya's father in *War and Peace*,

former Russian army Commander-in-Chief, as was Lev Tolstoy's maternal grandfather.

Bolkonsky, Prince Nikolay Andreyevich
Prince Andrey's son, who in the "Epilogue" to *War and Peace* becomes a devoted disciple of his father's friend, the Decembrist leader Pierre Bezukhov.

Borovkov, A. D.
Decembrist.

Botkin, Vasily Petrovich
Critic, friend of Lev Tolstoy.

Bourienne, Mademoiselle
Flirtatious companion to Princess Marya Bolkonsky in *War and Peace*.

Caulaincourt, Ambassador Armand de
French Ambassador to the court of Alexander I who appears in *War and Peace*.

d'Anthès, Lieutenant Georges
Attempted seducer of Alexander Pushkin's wife and killer of the great poet.

Davout, Marshal Louis Nicholas
French Napoleonic general who appears in *War and Peace*.

Dmitrievna, Marya (Akhrosimova)
Friend of the Rostov family who rescues Natasha from Anatole Kuragin in *War and Peace*.

Dolgorukov, Prince Peter
Writer of anonymous letters that helped precipitate Alexander Pushkin's fatal duel with Lieutenant d'Anthès.

Dolokhov
Sadistic rake, first to cuckold his friend and benefactor Pierre Bezukhov in *War and Peace*.

Dostoyevsky, Fyodor Mikhailovich
Russian novelist who was arrested as one of the Petrashevtsy.

Drubetskaya, Princess Anna Mikhailovna
Impoverished aristocrat who sees to it that Pierre Bezukhov receives his inheritance, mother of Boris Drubetskoy in *War and Peace*.

Drubetskoy, Prince Boris
Childhood sweetheart of Natasha Rostov, later careerist and one of the lovers of Pierre's wife Helene, then husband of the heiress Julie Karagin in *War and Peace*.

Dyakov, Dmitry Alexyevich
Friend and neighbor of Lev Tolstoy.

Enissienne, Mademoiselle
Frenchwoman with whom Lev Tolstoy's mother had a romantic friendship, later wife of Prince Mikhail Volkonsky.

Ergolskaya, Tatyana Alexandrovna
Lev Tolstoy's beloved "Auntie" who brought him and his brothers up after his mother died. Model for life story of Sofya Alexandrovna, "Sonya" in *War and Peace*.

Fet, Afanasy Afanasyevich
Russian poet, friend of Lev Tolstoy and Ivan Turgenev.

Fiquelmont, Countess
Memoirist of the Russian court during the reign of Nicholas I.

Garshin, E.
Russian critic.

Gerassimova, Marya, "Crazy Ivanushka"
The nun who became godmother to Lev Tolstoy's sister Marya and who appears in *War and Peace*.

Glebov, Colonel P. N.
Observer of Lev Tolstoy in the thick of the fighting at Sevastopol.

Goncharov, Natalya Nikolayevna
Maiden name of Alexander Pushkin's wife, model for Helene Kuragin in *War and Peace*, Pierre's first wife.

Herzen, Alexander Ivanyich
Russian writer, liberal thinker, in exile most of his life; one of the models for Pierre Bezukhov in *War and Peace*.

Islavin, Konstantin Alexandrovich, "Kostya," "Kostenka"
Youngest illegitimate son of Islenyev, close friend of Lev Tolstoy and later model for Anatole Kuragin in *War and Peace*.

Islavin, Lyubov Alexandrovna
Illegitimate daughter of Islenyev, childhood sweetheart of Lev Tolstoy, later his mother-in-law.

Islenyev, Alexander Mikhailovich
Friend of Lev Tolstoy's father, model for Prince Vasily Kuragin in *War and Peace*.

Kakhovsky, Pavel G.
One of the five Decembrists hung by Nicholas I.

Karagin, Julie
Friend and correspondent of the Princess Marya Bolkonsky, later heiress and wife of Boris Drubetskoy in *War and Peace*.

Karataev, Platon
 In *War and Peace* the serf-soldier and fellow prisoner of the French with Pierre, from whose folk wisdom Pierre learns to come to terms with life.

Katkov, Mikhail Nikiforovich
 Editor of the *Russian Herald* in which *War and Peace* was first published.

Kisselov, Sergey Dmitrievich
 Friend of Alexander Pushkin.

Kleen, Viscount Victor-Hector de
 Swedish lover of Lev Tolstoy's sister Marya, after her separation from her husband, and father of her illegitimate child.

Korenitsky, Captain-Lieutenant
 Lev Tolstoy's commander in the Crimean War, whom Tolstoy rescued from a threatened court-martial.

Küchelbecker, V. K.
 Friend of Alexander Pushkin, poet and Decembrist sentenced to hard labor by the Emperor Nicholas I.

Kuragin, Prince Anatole Vasilyevich
 The handsome "stallion" who compromises Natasha in *War and Peace*.

Kuragin, Princess Helene Vasilyevna
 The depraved beauty Pierre is trapped into marrying.

Kuragin, Prince Vasily Sergeyevich
 The relation of Pierre Bezukhov who first tries to cheat Pierre out of his inheritance and then traps him into marrying his daughter.

Kuzminsky, Alexander, "Sasha"
 Later on, the husband of Lev Tolstoy's sister-in-law Tatyana Andreyevna Behrs.

Lambert, Countess
 Friend of Ivan Turgenev.

Lanskoy, Major Peter Petrovich
 Widower who was married to Alexander Pushkin's widow when she became pregnant from her affair with the Emperor Nicholas I.

Lanskoy, Count Sergey Stepanovich
 Minister of the Interior to whom Lev Tolstoy submitted his plan for reorganization of the army.

Lunin, Mikhail Sergeyevich
 Prominent Decembrist, part of whose story went into Pierre Bezukhov in *War and Peace*.

Lyubochka (Irtenyev)
    The little girl in Tolstoy's early novel *Boyhood*, modeled on his
    sister Marya.
Muravieva, Alexandra
    Decembrist wife who carried Pushkin's poem celebrating them to
    his imprisoned Decembrist friends in Siberia.
Muraviev-Apostol, Sergey I.
    One of the five Decembrists hung by Nicholas I.
Naryshkin, Dmitry Lvovich
    Cuckold husband of Alexander I's long-term mistress.
Naryshkina, Marya Antonovna
    Mistress of Alexander I who appears with him in *War and Peace*.
Nashchokina, Vera
    Wife of Alexander Pushkin's friend Nashchokin.
Nekrasov, Nikolay Alexyevich
    Russian writer, friend of Ivan Turgenev.
Nelidova
    The Emperor Nicholas I's mistress after Alexander Pushkin's
    widow.
Odoyevsky, Prince Alexander I.
    Poet, Decembrist condemned to hard labor.
Ogarev, Marya Lvovna (née Rosavlev)
    Nikolay Ogarev's first wife, whose adulteries and successful grasp
    of a large part of his fortune went into Tolstoy's portrayal of
    Pierre's first wife in *War and Peace*.
Ogarev, Nikolay Platonovich
    Lifelong friend and associate of Alexander Herzen and later of
    Mikhail Bakunin, whom Lev Tolstoy knew from childhood.
Ogarev, Platon
    Close friend of Lev Tolstoy's father, himself father of the revolu-
    tionary Nikolay Platonovich Ogarev.
Perfilyev, Vasily Stepanovich, "Vasenka"
    Friend of Lev Tolstoy and husband of Tolstoy's cousin Praskovya
    Fyodorovna Tolstoy.
Perovsky, V. A.
    His story of being captured by the French in the Battle of Borodino
    went into the story of Pierre's capture in *War and Peace*.
Pestel, Colonel Pavel Ivanovich
    Leader of the southern societies, one of the five Decembrists hung
    by Nicholas I.

Petrashevsky, M. V.
    Idealist arrested with his friends in 1849 whose story went into
    Pierre's imprisonment in *War and Peace*.
Pletnev, Peter Alexandrovich
    Friend of Alexander Pushkin.
Poggio, Alexander Viktorovich
    Italian-origin Decembrist, lifelong comrade in prison and exile and
    final liberation of Lev Tolstoy's cousin Sergey Volkonsky.
Pokrovskoye
    Estate of Lev Tolstoy's brother-in-law, Count Valerian Tolstoy.
Potëmkin, General
    Liberal commander of the Semenovsky Guards, deposed by the
    Grand Dukes Nicholas and Mikhail.
Pushchin, Ivan I.
    Close friend of Alexander Pushkin, Decembrist sentenced to hard
    labor.
Pushchin, Mikhail I.
    Brother of Alexander Pushkin's friend Ivan Pushchin, later a friend of
    Lev Tolstoy, who persuaded him to write his memories of Pushkin.
Pushkin, Alexander
    Great Russian poet, friend of the Decembrists, whose story inspired
    that of Pierre in *War and Peace*.
Rostova
    Russian feminine of Rostov.
Rostov, Count Ilya Andreyevich
    Father of Natasha, Nikolay, Petya, and Vera Rostov in *War and Peace*.
Rostov, Countess Natalya Ilyinishna, "Natasha."
    Main heroine of *War and Peace*.
Rostov, Count Nikolay Ilyinich
    Natasha's older brother, who ultimately marries the Princess Marya
    Bolkonsky in *War and Peace*.
Rostov, Count Peter Ilyinich, "Petya"
    Natasha's younger brother in *War and Peace*.
Rostov, Countess Vera Ilyinishna
    Natasha's older sister, who marries Berg in *War and Peace*.
Ryleyev, Kondratin Fyodorovich
    Poet, one of the five Decembrists hung by Nicholas I.
Samarin, Yury Fyodorovich
    Friend of Lev Tolstoy, part model for Prince Andrey's cool and
    flexible mind in *War and Peace*.

Sand, George
     French woman novelist, liberal thinker.
Scheffer, Ary
     French portrait painter, lover of Pauline Viardot.
Scherer, Anna Pavlovna
     St. Petersburg society lady in *War and Peace*.
Schwarz, Colonel G. C.
     Commander whose cruelty brought about the revolt of the Semen-
     ovsky Guards, spoken of in the "Epilogue" to *War and Peace*.
Shishkina, Marya, "Masha"
     Gypsy singer, who after bearing him four children married Lev
     Tolstoy's brother Sergey.
Smirnova, Alexandra Yosipovna
     Née Alexandra Rossetti, memoirist who knew Alexander Pushkin
     and his wife.
Sologub, Count Vladimir Alexandrovich
     Memoirist whom Lev Tolstoy knew well.
"Sonya" (Sofya Alexandrovna)
     The orphaned relative of the Rostovs, who loves Nikolay Rostov as
     Lev Tolstoy's Aunt Tatyana Alexandrovna had loved his father.
Spasskoye
     Estate of Count Ivan Sergeyevich Turgenev.
Speransky, Mikhail Mikhailovich
     Powerful politician under Alexander I, later exiled, then recalled by
     Nicholas I to arrange the trial of the Decembrists. He appears in
     War and Peace.
Stankevich, Nikolay
     Philosopher, friend of Turgenev and Bakunin, much admired as a
     person and for his theory of history by Lev Tolstoy.
Steingel, Baron Vladimir Ivanovich
     Decembrist.
Stendhal (Henri Beyle)
     Novelist whose *Charterhouse of Parma* gave Tolstoy insight into the
     realities of warfare.
Strakhov, Nikolay Nikolayevich
     Russian critic, friend of Lev Tolstoy who did much of the cutting
     of *War and Peace* for its second edition.
Stroganov, Countess
     Memoirist of the Russian court during the reign of Nicholas I.
Tolstaya
     Russian feminine of Tolstoy.

Tolstoy, Countess Alexandra A., "Babushka"
    Lev Tolstoy's beloved cousin, high in court society at St. Petersburg.
Tolstoy, Countess Alexandra Ilyinishna, "Aunt Aline"
    Lev Tolstoy's paternal aunt, later Countess Osten-Saken, who filled the Tolstoy estate with pilgrims and religious devotees.
Tolstoy, Avdotya Maximovna
    Widow of Lev Tolstoy's cousin "The American," Count Fyodor Tolstoy.
Tolstoy, Count Dmitry Nikolayevich
    Lev Tolstoy's brother, first to die of the family consumption.
Tolstoy, Fyodor, "The American"
    Cousin of Lev Tolstoy, friend of Alexander Pushkin, model in part of Dolokhov in *War and Peace*.
Tolstoy, Count Ilya Andreyevich
    Lev Tolstoy's grandfather, model for Count Ilya Andreyevich Rostov in *War and Peace*.
Tolstoy, Count Ilya Ilyinich
    The younger brother who died in childhood of Lev Tolstoy's father.
Tolstoy, Countess Marya Nikolayevna, "Masha," "Mashenka"
    Lev Tolstoy's younger sister, model for the personality of Princess Marya Bolkonsky in *War and Peace*.
Tolstoy, Count Nikolay Ilyinich
    Lev Tolstoy's father, who died when Lev was nine years old.
Tolstoy, Count Nikolay Nikolayevich, "Nikolenka"
    Lev Tolstoy's oldest and best-loved brother.
Tolstoy, Countess Pelageya Ilyinishna
    Lev Tolstoy's aunt, later his legal guardian after the death of his father.
Tolstoy, Praskovya Fyodorovna, "Polenka"
    Daughter of Lev Tolstoy's cousin "The American," Fyodor Tolstoy, later married to Tolstoy's friend Vasily S. Perfilyev.
Tolstoy, Count Sergey Nikolayevich, "Serozha"
    Lev Tolstoy's much-admired second oldest brother.
Tolstoy, Countess Sofya Andreyevna, "Sonya"
    Lev Tolstoy's wife, née Behrs, model for the personality of Sonya in *War and Peace*.
Tolstoy, Count Valerian Petrovich
    The second cousin who married Lev Tolstoy's sister Marya.
Trubetskoy, Prince
    Provisional leader of the Decembrists, condemned to hard labor.

Turgenev, Ivan Sergeyevich
  Older novelist who had a great influence on Lev Tolstoy's development.
Tushin, Captain
  The real hero of the Battle of Schön Grabern in *War and Peace*, who is reprimanded for his pains.
van Heeckeren, Baron Louis Beveriwaert
  Dutch Ambassador, lover of Georges d'Anthès, who helped him in his attempt to seduce Pushkin's wife.
Vasilchikov, General I. V.
  Nicholas I's aide-de-camp, who rounded up the Decembrists.
Vergani, Mademoiselle
  Scheming governess of Valerya Vladimirovna Arsenyeva.
Viardot, Pauline
  Opera singer, great love of Ivan Turgenev.
Viazemsky
  Russian poet, friend of Alexander Pushkin.
Volkonskaya
  Russian feminine of Volkonsky.
Volkonsky, Prince Alexander A., "Sasha"
  Lev Tolstoy's cousin, who contributed a part of the character of Prince Andrey in *War and Peace*.
Volkonsky, Prince Alexander Sergeyevich
  Brother of Lev Tolstoy's grandfather and father of Princess Varvara Alexandrovna Volkonskaya.
Volkonsky, Prince Gregory
  Father of Lev Tolstoy's Decembrist cousin Sergey Volkonsky.
Volkonsky, Princess Louisa Ivanovna
  Wife of Lev Tolstoy's cousin Sasha, model for Prince Andrey's wife in *War and Peace*.
Volkonsky, Princess Marya
  Née Raevskaya, wife of Lev Tolstoy's Decembrist cousin Sergey Gregoryevich Volkonsky.
Volkonsky, Princess Marya Nikolayevna
  Maiden name of Lev Tolstoy's mother, whose life story went into the Princess Marya Bolkonsky in *War and Peace*.
Volkonsky, Prince Mikhail Alexandrovich
  Cousin of Lev Tolstoy's mother who married her French friend Mademoiselle Enissienne.
Volkonsky, Prince Nikolay Gregoryevich
  The Decembrist Prince Sergey's younger brother, hero at Austerlitz

who appears in *War and Peace*; named Repnín to prevent the extinction of his mother's illustrious family name.

Volkonsky, Prince Nikolay Sergeyevich
Tolstoy's maternal grandfather, model for Prince Nikolay Andreyevich Bolkonsky in *War and Peace*, and in part for his son Prince Andrey.

Volkonsky, Prince Sergey Gregoryevich
Lev Tolstoy's Decembrist cousin, Napoleonic war hero, one of the fifteen surviving Decembrists freed with the amnesty of 1856; inspiration in part of Pierre Bezukhov in *War and Peace*.

Volkonsky, Princess Sofya
Mother of Lev Tolstoy's cousins Sergey Volkonsky and Nikolay Repnin, Mistress of the Robes to the Dowager Empress Marya Fyodorovna (mother of the emperors Alexander I and Nicholas I).

Volkonsky, Princess Varvara Alexandrovna
First cousin of Lev Tolstoy's mother from whom he learned much of her as a girl and of his grandfather.

Volkova, M. A.
Letter-writer of Napoleonic times from whom Tolstoy took his first hint for Prince Andrey in *War and Peace*.

Yasnaya Polyana
The estate Lev Tolstoy inherited from his grandfather.

Yazikov, S. I.
Lev Tolstoy's godfather.

Notes

1. The Birth of *Death in Venice*

page 7:

"ALMOST CONTINUALLY." "ONE OF US!" Letter to Heinrich Mann, August 4, 1910, in Nigel Hamilton, *The Brothers Mann* (London: Secker & Warburg, 1978), 142.

"BROTHER-AND-SISTERLY BOND." "SUPERIOR TO THE." Thomas Mann, *A Sketch of My Life*, trans. H. D. Lowe-Porter (Paris: Harrison, 1930), 38.

"WHAT A BLOW." Letter to Paul Ehrenberg, August 12, 1910, in *Letters of Thomas Mann 1889–1955*, selected and translated by Richard and Clara Winston, 2 vols. (London: Secker & Warburg, 1970), 1:57.

"TO COME TO SOME TERMS." Letter to Paul Ehrenberg, September 3, 1910 (ibid., 1:58).

page 8:

"JE T'AIME." Mann, *A Sketch of My Life*, 37. See also Richard Winston, *Thomas Mann: The Making of an Artist 1875–1911* (New York: Knopf, 1981), 252.

CARLA HAD BEEN A FRAGILE. Mann, *A Sketch of My Life*, 35.

JULIA, WOULD DO SO. Ibid., 39.

"SCURRILOUS NAME." Ibid., 35–36.

"A WHOLE REGIMENT." "FOR A COMPANY." Letter to Paul Ehrenberg, August 12, 1910 (*Letters of Thomas Mann*, 1:57).

DETAILS OF HER DYING. Mann, *A Sketch of My Life*, 37.

page 9:

"IN SAD DISORDER." Letter to Paul Ehrenberg, September 3, 1910 (*Letters of Thomas Mann*, 1:58). Mann was staying at Tölz on the Isar. He also tells Ehrenberg that he must go to Munich for a prize jury conference and will "take in the Mahler symphony as well."

KLAUS HAD BEEN STUDYING. *Gustav Mahler–Richard Strauss: Correspondence 1888–1911*, trans. Edmund Jephcott (Chicago: Chicago University Press, 1984), 141. See also Klaus Pringsheim, "Erinnerungen an Gustav Mahler," *Neue Zürcher Zeitung*, in *Mahler: A Documentary Study*, ed. Kurt Blaukopf (London: Thames & Hudson, 1976), 242n.

KLAUS SAID THAT. *Mahler: A Documentary Study*, ed. Blaukopf, 244.

"BETTER, MORE BEAUTIFUL." Kurt Blaukopf, *Gustav Mahler*, trans. Inge Goodwin (London: Lane, 1973), 142.

MAHLER CAME TO MUNICH. From the *Munich Chronicle*, September 12, 1910, in *Mahler: A Documentary Study*, ed. Blaukopf, 267. It was the premiere performance.

"TRY TO IMAGINE." Letter to Willem Mengelberg, August 18(?), 1906, *Selected Letters of Gustav Mahler*, ed. Knud Martner, trans. Eithne Wilkins and Ernst Kaiser (London: Faber & Faber, 1979), 294.

"DEVOURINGLY INTENSE." Hamilton, *The Brothers Mann*, 147.

"THE IMPRESSION OF BEING." Katia Mann, *Unwritten Memories*, ed. Elisabeth Plessen and Michael Mann, trans. Hunter Hannum and Hildegarde Hannum (London: Deutsch, 1975), 65.

"A POOR EXCHANGE." Blaukopf, *Gustav Mahler*, 232.

MANN FOLLOWED THE VIENNA NEWSPAPER. Letter to Wolfgang Born, March 18, 1921 (*Letters of Thomas Mann*, 1:110).

"NO, NOT PAIN." In a letter to René Schickele, July 25, 1935 (ibid., 235), Mann recalled this in compassion for Schickele's suffering. Mann would have learned from the Vienna newspapers that Mahler was suffering from a streptococcus infection. His friendship with Bruno Walter began a year after he had finished *Death in Venice*. Mann's clear remembrance in 1935 of what Bruno Walter had told him shows how profoundly he felt for Mahler. Bruno Walter himself, when he came to write *Theme and Variations* (London: Hamilton, 1947), had forgotten all about it, remembering instead only that Mahler had a defective heart and assuming his death came of that.

"ALL ACTUALITY IS DEADLY EARNEST." Mann, *A Sketch of My Life*, 38.

page 10:

"I REGARD MY LIFE WORK." Letter to Irita Van Doren, August 28, 1951 (*Letters of Thomas Mann*, 2:628).

"OF THE AGED GOETHE." Letter to Carl Maria Weber, July 4, 1920 (ibid., 1:103–4).

"TRAGEDY OF SUPREME." Letter to Elisabeth Zimmer, September 6, 1915 (ibid., 1:76).

"PASSION AS CONFUSION." Letter to Carl Maria Weber, July 4, 1920 (ibid., 1:103).

"GOETHE'S DESIRE FOR ORDER." Letter to B. Fucik, April 15, 1932 (ibid., 1:185).

"THE DIONYSIAN SPIRIT." Letter to Carl Maria Weber, July 4, 1920 (ibid., 1:102–3).

HE READ THE BOOK. Ibid., 1:103.

"A PERSONAL LYRICAL TRAVEL EXPERIENCE." Ibid.

page 11:

SOME OF THEIR CHILDREN. The Manns might have brought the older children, because their original idea seems to have been to stay the entire time at the beach at Brioni. Recalling the trip in *Unwritten Memories*, 62, Katia Mann speaks of Heinrich as being "also in our party," which suggest more people than Katia and Thomas Mann alone. Then the nuisance that they found in the Brioni hotel at having to arise two minutes after they had sat down, and again at the end of the meal, whenever the mother of the Archduke Karl of Austria entered and left the dining room would have been considerably greater with several small children. The point certainly cannot be decided, and it is of interest only in gauging how far the reality differed from the story. Of course, the major difference is that the Manns were in Venice for only a week, with no time for anyone's character to disintegrate, whereas Aschenbach stays on for weeks in the diseased city, keeping its evil secret.

"LOVED FOR DEEP AND COMPLEX." Letter to Karl Kerényi, August 4, 1934 (*Letters of Thomas Mann*, 1:223).

"LÜBECK'S SOUTHERN SISTER." Winston, *Thomas Mann: The Making of an Artist*, 4. Winston is referring to Mann's essay of 1926, "Lübeck as a Way of Life and Thought."

MARKETPLACE AT LÜBECK. Thomas Mann, *Diaries 1918–1939* (New York: Abrams, 1982), 119. When Mann returned to Lübeck on September 17, 1921, he noted "the architecture of the marketplace: Lübeck and Venice."

"IN SPIRIT I AM WITH YOU." Letter to Erika and Klaus Mann, May 25, 1932 (*Letters of Thomas Mann*, 1:187).

page 12:

"UNDENIABLE PROOFS." "AN OLD MAN." Winston, *Thomas Mann*, 268–69. Winston's information on Count Moes comes from Peter de Mendelssohn, *Der Zauberer* (Frankfurt: Fischer, 1975), 873.

"A VERY STRANGE THING." Hamilton, *The Brothers Mann*, 148.

"BELOW MIDDLE HEIGHT." *Death in Venice,* in Thomas Mann, *Stories of Three Decades,* trans. H. T. Lowe-Porter (New York: Knopf, 1948), 387.

"LESS THAN AVERAGE HEIGHT." Natalie Bauer-Lechner, *Recollections of Gustav Mahler,* ed. Peter Franklin, trans. Dika Newlin (London: Faber Music, 1980), 83.

"LEAN, FIDGETY, SHORT." Walter, *Theme and Variations,* 83.

"THE NOSE-PIECE" OF ASCHENBACH'S. *Death in Venice,* 387.

"STERN AND FORBIDDING." Oskar Fried, *Musikblätter des Anbruch,* 1:16–17 (in *Mahler: A Documentary Study,* ed. Blaukopf, 240).

"IMPERIOUS IS HIS HOOKED NOSE." *Recollections of Gustav Mahler,* 84.

"STRONG NOSE." "LARGE MOUTH WITH." Romain Rolland, "Musique française et musique allemande," *Musiciens d'aujourd'hui* (Paris, 1908), in *Mahler: A Documentary Study,* ed. Blaukopf, 241.

"FURROWED AND AGED." *Recollections of Gustav Mahler,* 83.

page 13:

"STRETCHED OUT." So Alfred Roller described Mahler at Maiernigg. *Mahler: A Documentary Study,* ed. Blaukopf, 237.

"HALF-AND-HALF A MUSICIAN." Letter to Theodore W. Adorno, December 30, 1945 (*Letters of Thomas Mann,* 1:495).

"RUDE COUNTRY HOUSE." *Death in Venice,* 381.

"A DISTASTE FOR LUXURY." Bauer-Lechner, *Recollections of Gustav-Mahler,* 167.

"WORK HUT." Karen Monson, *Alma Mahler: Muse to Genius* (London: Collins, 1984), 58.

"ON PAIN OF DEATH." Blaukopf, *Gustav Mahler,* 125.

"TO ACHIEVEMENT." "DURCHHALTEN." "LONELINESS." *Death in Venice,* 383, 387.

"THE LISTS TO FIGHT." Letter to Friedrich Lohr, November 28, 1885 (*Selected Letters of Gustav Mahler,* ed. Martner, 1:93).

"SET MY AIMS HIGH." "PLEDGED ALL I." Egon Gartenberg, *Mahler: The Man and His Music* (London: Cassell, 1978), 148. So Mahler said in his farewell letter to the staff at the Vienna Court Opera, offering his self-driving in explanation of why he had felt "I could ask others to exert their full powers."

"TERRIBLE SUFFERINGS." Bauer-Lechner, *Recollections of Gustav Mahler,* 38.

"WRESTLING WITH GOD." Ibid., 76.

"HIS DEDICATED SERIOUSNESS." Ibid., 107.

"WHOSE ENTIRE APPEARANCE BESPEAKS." Gartenberg, *Mahler,* 107. Mendes was describing Mahler at the Paris World Exhibition in the *Neues Wiener Tagblatt,* June 22, 1900.

page 14:

"I AM AN ASCETIC." Letter to Kurt Martens, March 28, 1906 (*Letters of Thomas Mann,* 1:50).

"ONE CANNOT SERVE." Ibid.

"FOR THE EASILY SATISFIED." Letter to Katia Pringsheim [late August 1904] (ibid., 42).

"I HAVE ALWAYS LIKED." Letter to Agnes Meyer, February 9, 1955 (ibid., 2:677).

"THE CLEAREST FEELING." Mann, *A Sketch of My Life*, 42.

"BY THE INHERENT SYMBOLISM." Ibid., 41.

" 'WANDERER' AT THE NORTHERN." Ibid., 42.

"LONG, WHITE, GLISTENING." *Death in Venice*, 379.

"CURLED BACK HIS LIPS." Ibid., 393.

"GRINNING." "STRONG WHITE TEETH." Ibid., 425.

"TWO PRONOUNCED PERPENDICULAR." Ibid., 379. In the ballad singer, they are "two deep wrinkles of defiance" (425).

"NAKED-LOOKING" OR "BALD." Ibid., 424, 379.

page 15:

"COFFIN." "VISIONS OF DEATH." Ibid., 392.

"BOLD." "DOMINEERING." "RUTHLESS." Ibid., 379.

"OVERBEARING." "DESPOTIC." Ibid., 393–94.

"LAWLESS, SILENT ADVENTURES." Ibid., 392.

"UPRIGHT CLERK" IN COOK'S. Mann, *A Sketch of My Life*, 42. It is Katia Mann in *Unwritten Memories* who specifies "Cook's" (63).

"TROPICAL MARSHLAND." "REEKING SKY." *Death in Venice*, 380.

MEDICAL PATHOLOGY BOOKS. For instance, Dr. August Hirsch, *Handbook of Geographical and Historical Pathology*, vol. 1: *Acute Infective Diseases*, trans. Charles Creighton, M.D. (London: New Sydenham Society, 1883), 431.

"THE HOT, MOIST SWAMPS." *Death in Venice*, 427.

SO MANN TELLS US. In *Death in Venice*, Mann tells us that the cholera victim "suffocates in a few hours" (428). In *A Sketch of My Life*, Mann says of Carla's death: "Dark spots on the hands and face showed that death by suffocation—after a brief delay—must have ensued very suddenly" (37).

BLUISH-BLACK DISCOLORATION. In *Death in Venice*, 428, Mann speaks of the "horrible vibrions," meaning the discolored areas, and of the "blackened corpses" of the victims—the bacteria of cholera being of the genus *Vibrio*, for their comma shape.

"HOARSE CRIES." Ibid.

page 16:

"YOUNG-OLD MAN." Ibid., 391.

"AN ARTIFICIAL ACCENTUATION." *A Sketch of My Life*, 36.

"ROUGE AND COSMETICS." In his later novel, *Doctor Faustus* (London:

Secker & Warburg, 1951), where he portrayed Carla as Clarissa Rodde, Mann specified this "mistaken self-dramatization" (381).

"THAT EMOTIONAL TENDENCY." "WISH TO DISAVOW." "I AM A FAMILY FOUNDER." Letter to Carl Maria Weber, July 4, 1920 (*Letters of Thomas Mann*, 1:102–5).

page 17:

"PROTESTANT, PURITAN ('BOURGEOIS')." Ibid., 103.

"UNBOURGEOIS INTELLECTUALLY SENSUAL." "ETERNAL TENSION." "PROBLEM OF BEAUTY." Ibid., 105.

"THE UNREAL, ILLUSIONARY." Entry dated April 25, 1934 (Mann, *Diaries*, 207).

"EXTRAORDINARY AND DAEMONIC." *Tonio Kröger*, in *Stories of Three Decades*, 108.

"IT IS DEATH WHOM YOU PROCLAIM." *Fiorenza*, in *Stories of Three Decades*, 271.

page 18:

"CLOISTER-LIKE PLAINNESS." "PEDAGOGIC SEVERITY." *Death in Venice*, 397.

"SELF-RESPECTING DIGNITY." Ibid., 398.

"THE STERN, STARK." Ibid., 385.

"THE NOBLEST MOMENT OF." Ibid., 396.

"RAVISHMENT OVER A." Ibid., 400.

"WHAT DISCIPLINE, WHAT." Ibid., 411.

"MARBLE MASS OF LANGUAGE." Ibid., 412.

"FATHER'S." Ibid., 403.

"PURE AND GODLIKE SERENITY." Ibid., 396.

"NOTHINGNESS." Ibid., 401.

"VIRGINALLY PURE." "MYTHOLOGIES." Ibid., 403. In the sight of the boy emerging from the sea, Mann was referring primarily to the birth of Venus, in the birth of beauty. Although he surrounded Tadzio with an aura of many myths, he was careful not to identify him with a particular one until the finale of the story.

SINGULAR TWILIGHT GREY EYES. Lowe-Porter's translation is "strange, twilit grey eyes." Perhaps hers is poetic, but it blurs the symbolic meaning of "eigentümlich dämmergrauen Augen." Ibid., 398, 433.

"SUMMONER." Ibid., 437.

page 19:

"HERMES PSYCHOPOMPOS." In his letter to Carl Maria Weber, July 4, 1920, Mann said he was alternating the pathological view "with the symbolic motif (Tadzio as Hermes Psychopompos)" (*Letters of Thomas Mann*, 1:103).

"PRIVATE JOKE." Letter to Karl Kerényi, February 20, 1934 (ibid., 1:213).
"RINGLETS," THE GREEK LINE. Ibid.

page 20:

"GROWING SYMPATHY WITH DEATH." Letter to Heinrich Mann, August 11, 1913 (Hamilton, *The Brothers Mann*, 150).

"NEVER BE ABLE TO OBEY." "I DO NOT KNOW." Letter to Kurt Martens, December 30, 1914 (*Letters of Thomas Mann*, 1:72).

"DEATH AS A SEDUCTIVE." "THE VOLUPTUOUSNESS OF DOOM." Letter to Elisabeth Zimmer, September 6, 1915 (ibid., 1:76).

"WHO SUCCUMBS TO LASCIVIOUS." Letter to Wolfgang Born, March 18, 1921 (ibid., 1:110).

"SENSUOUSLY AND INTELLECTUALLY." Letter to Joseph Ponten, February 1925 (Hamilton, *The Brothers Mann*, 209).

"OF A NEW HUMANITY." Ibid.

2. The Real Treasure in *Treasure Island*

page 23:

RAKE IN "MORE COIN." So Stevenson told William Ernest Henley when he began the writing. *The Letters of Robert Louis Stevenson*, ed. Sidney Colvin, 2 vols. (London: Methuen, 1899), 1:219.

"A LOW PENNY PAPER." Dr. Alexander Hay Japp, an authority on Thoreau, visited Stevenson at Braemar to discuss a recent essay on Thoreau that Stevenson had written. Taking off from a map he had drawn for Lloyd Osbourne, Stevenson had just begun a boys' adventure story. Japp suggested that Stevenson might get real money from *Young Folks* for a serialization of it there. David Daiches, *Robert Louis Stevenson and His World* (London: Thames & Hudson, 1973), 55. Stevenson told Henley that Japp thought he would get 100 pounds from that "low penny paper." John Connell, *W. E. Henley* (London: Constable, 1949), 93.

THAT SAME BOY'S ORDERS. In his letter to Henley telling of his plan, Stevenson said: "No women in the story, Lloyd's orders; and who so blithe to obey?" (*Letters of Robert Louis Stevenson*, ed. Colvin, 1:221).

"AWFUL FUN." "INDULGE THE PLEASURE." Ibid.

"VERY SPIRIT OF MY LIFE'S." Robert Louis Stevenson, "A Penny Plain and Two-Pence Coloured," *Memories and Portraits*, in *The Works of Robert Louis Stevenson*, Vailima edition (London: Heinemann, 1922), 12:170.

page 24:

SKELT'S "LONG TOM COFFIN." Ibid., 162.

THREE-FINGERED JACK. Ibid., 161.

"FALLEN IN LOVE." "YOU WILL NEVER." "ANY LEISURE I." Letter to Cosmo

Monkhouse, March 16, 1884 (*Letters of Robert Louis Stevenson*, ed. Colvin, 1:310–11).

"CHRONIC PNEUMONIA." Stevenson had gone to Davos, Switzerland, for the climate, and the doctor there had diagnosed his case—so Fanny Stevenson reported to Colvin—as "chronic pneumonia, with infiltration of the lungs." E. V. Lucas, *The Colvins and Their Friends* (London: Methuen, 1928), 150.

"FIBROIDAL DISEASE OF THE LUNGS." In the spring of 1887, Fanny Stevenson told Colvin that Dr. Balfour "says just what Ruedi always said, that it is fibroidal disease of the lungs, for which there is no cure, only palliation." Ibid., 175.

"BRONCHIECTASIS." David Daiches submitted Stevenson's symptoms to a "modern medical expert," who told him it was "bronchiectasis," a disease that sets in after a childhood case of pneumonia or whooping cough or repeated attacks of bronchitis. Daiches, *Robert Louis Stevenson and His World*, 49–50.

"MY CHILDHOOD WAS IN REALITY." Letter to William Archer, March 29, 1885 (*Letters of Robert Louis Stevenson*, ed. Colvin, 1:359).

"THE CHILDREN OF LOVERS." Letter to Mrs. Sitwell, spring 1875 (Lucas, *The Colvins and Their Friends*, 91).

"OF DESERTION AND LOSS." "FOR THE WANT." Ibid.

"ANY KIND OF DANGER." Sidney Colvin, *Memories and Notes of Persons and Places* (London: Arnold, 1921), 125.

"I WAS MADE FOR A CONTEST." Jerome Hamilton Buckley, *William Ernest Henley: A Study in the "Counter-Decadence" of the Nineties* (Princeton: Princeton University Press, 1945), 57.

"BRIGHT FACE OF DANGER." Robert Louis Stevenson, "Lantern-Bearers," *Random Memories and Other Essays*, in *Works of Robert Louis Stevenson*, 12:267.

page 25:

"MY HORROR OF THE HORRIBLE." He said this when he was deliberately facing the horror of disease, this time outside himself, but dangerous to him, among the lepers at Molokai Island. Letter of May 1889 to Fanny Stevenson (*Letters of Robert Louis Stevenson*, ed. Colvin, 2:154).

DYING OF GALLOPING CONSUMPTION. In the novel he is "in a decline" which, to a Victorian, meant galloping consumption. Robert Louis Stevenson, *Treasure Island*, ed. M. R. Ridley (London: Dent, 1962), 8 (ch. 1).

"MORTAL SICKNESS." Ibid., 18 (chap. 3).

"TWO FINGERS OF THE LEFT." Ibid., 10 (chap. 2).

"HORRIBLE, SOFT-SPOKEN, EYELESS." Ibid., 18 (chap. 3).

"BLACK SPOT." Ibid., 16 (chap. 3).

"SEAFARING MAN WITH ONE LEG." Ibid., 6 (chap. 1).

"SURF ROARED ALONG THE COVE." Ibid., 6–7 (chap. 1).

HENLEY HIMSELF HAD SUCCEEDED. In a letter to Edmund Gosse, May 20, 1883, Stevenson declared that Henley was his "unpaid agent—an admirable arrangement for me, and one that has rather more than doubled my income on the spot" (*Letters of Robert Louis Stevenson*, ed. Colvin, 1:268).

page 26:

"IT WAS THE SIGHT." Letter to William Ernest Henley, May 1883 (ibid., 1:270).

"THE DRAWING OF A CHARACTER." Letter to Sidney Colvin, February 1885 (ibid., 1:350).

"ONE CLASS OF QUALITIES." Robert Louis Stevenson, "A Humble Remonstrance," *Memories and Portraits*, 12:216.

"PSYCHICAL SURGERY." "HIS FINER QUALITIES." Robert Louis Stevenson, "My First Book," which explains the origin of *Treasure Island*. Quoted in Ridley's "Introduction" to *Treasure Island*, vi.

" 'TWAS A BLESSED HOUR FOR ALL OF US." W. E. Henley to R. L. Stevenson (Connell, in *W. E. Henley*, 114).

page 27:

"LONG LESLIE STEPHEN." "LONG HE WAS ALIKE." Colvin, *Memories and Notes of Persons and Places*, 171–72.

"MISERABLE CRIPPLE." Letter of February 1875, from Leslie Stephen to his wife. Frederic William Maitland, *The Life and Letters of Leslie Stephen* (London: Duckworth, 1906), 250.

"COLVIN'S FRIEND." "AND TOLD HIM ALL." Ibid.

"BLACK WINTER AFTERNOON." Letter from R. L. Stevenson to Mrs. Sitwell, February 1875 (*Letters of Robert Louis Stevenson*, ed. Colvin, 1:87).

"LONG LESLIE STEPHEN, IN HIS VELVET." Letter from R. L. Stevenson to W. E. Henley, September 19, 1883 (ibid., 1:280).

"GAS FLARED AND CRACKLED." Letter from R. L. Stevenson to Mrs. Sitwell, February 1875 (ibid., 1:87).

BRINGING BOOKS AND HIS FRIENDS WITH MORE. Stevenson brought Charles Baxter, and Baxter, as Henley joyously recalled, came to him with big yellow volumes of Balzac in the "transformed back-kitchen where I lay." Connell, *W. E. Henley*, 109.

THAT MRS. FLEMING JENKIN. Buckley, *William Ernest Henley*, 54.

page 28:

HIS YOUNGER SISTER ANNA. Kennedy Williamson, *W. E. Henley: A Memoir* (London: Shaylor, 1930), 42, 66.

"VIKING CHIEF." Buckley, *William Ernest Henley,* 149.

"HEARTBREAKING IN A MAN." Letter from George Bernard Shaw to Kennedy Williamson (Williamson, *W. E. Henley: A Memoir,* 200).

"OUT OF PURE PITY." Stevenson, *Treasure Island,* 35 (chap. 7).

"VERY TALL AND STRONG." "WONDERFUL DEXTERITY." Ibid., 38 (chap. 8).

PORTOBELLO, THIRTY YARDS FROM THE FIRTH. So W. E. Henley told Harry N. in a letter of May 18, 1875 (Connell, *W. E. Henley,* 76).

"A BUSINESS TO CARRY HIM DOWN." Letter to Mrs. Sitwell, April 1875 (*Letters of Robert Louis Stevenson,* ed. Colvin, 1:94).

IN THE BOOK, LONG JOHN SILVER. Stevenson, *Treasure Island,* 48 (chap. 10).

HENLEY TRANSFERRED TO LONDON. Henley became editor of the *London Magazine* in 1878. Later he edited in turn such periodicals as *The Magazine of Art, The National Observer,* and *The Scots Observer.*

HAD HAD "GOOD SCHOOLING." Stevenson, *Treasure Island,* 47 (chap. 10). By the age of eighteen (1867) Henley had passed the entrance examination for Oxford, but with no money and one leg slated for amputation Oxford was out of the question. Buckley, *William Ernest Henley,* 40.

"MAKE ALLOWANCES." "LET US REMEMBER." Letter of Charles Baxter to R. L. Stevenson, April 5, 1888, in *RLS: Stevenson's Letters to Charles Baxter,* ed. Delancy Ferguson and Marshall Waingrow (London: Oxford University Press, 1956), 203. In this letter, eight words have been deleted (after "companionship") from the original, probably by Baxter and probably because they were too specific about the kind of people Henley associated with. The text of the letter has "euphuism," but Baxter clearly meant "euphemism," so even if this was his error, I have substituted the word he meant.

pages 28–29:

COFFEEHOUSE KEEPER NAMED HARRY. The name is given as Harry N. in Connell, *W. E. Henley,* 39, apparently because Connell was refused permission to give the full name. Probably the name was something like "Nichols" or "Nicholson," since Henley would refer to him as "Old Nick" or "the Great Nick"—combining his real name with his devilish propensities.

page 29:

SENT HIM THE SMALL DOLES. See, for instance, Henley's letter of April 6, 1873, asking Harry to send him a few shillings (ibid., 44).

"AND YOU KNOW WHAT THAT MEANS." Ibid., 39.

"OVER WALLS, TO THE END." Ibid., 45.

"I AM GOING INTO GOOD SOCIETY." Letter to Harry, May 18, 1875 (ibid., 76).

HE HAD TAKEN SIR WALTER SCOTT. Scott tells of the supervisor of lighthouses (Stevenson's grandfather) who took him to the Shetland Islands, but not by name, in his notes to *The Pirate*, the novel based on what he learned from that trip.

page 30:

"A STRONGHOLD IN MY GRANDFATHER'S ESTIMATION." "The Northern Lights," *Records of a Family of Engineers*, in *Works of Robert Louis Stevenson*, 12:458.

"COURT AND PLEASE." "HYPOCRITICAL SKILL." "AFTER DINNER FOR." Ibid.

page 31:

CAPTAIN JOHNSON'S *GENERAL HISTORY OF THE PIRATES*. In a letter to Sidney Colvin, July 1884, Stevenson said that *Treasure Island* came in part out of "the great Captain Johnson's *History of Notorious Pirates*" (*Letters of Robert Louis Stevenson*, ed. Colvin, 1:321). I have used Captain Charles Johnson (pseudonym for Daniel Defoe), *A General History of the Pirates*, ed. Philip Gosse, 2 vols. (London: Sainsbury, 1927).

"BE HANGED UP A-SUN-DRYING." Ibid., 2:24.

"HANGED LIKE A DOG." Stevenson, *Treasure Island*, 50 (chap. 11).

"DRYING IN THE SUN AT EXECUTION DOCK." Ibid., 52 (chap. 11).

MAROONING THEM ON DESERT ISLANDS. Johnson, *A General History of the Pirates*, 2:18.

NAME OF THIS CHARACTER, BEN. In a list of white men in the high land of Sierraleon, Johnson puts "At Rio Pungo, Benjamin Gun." Ibid., 2:34.

THE IDEA FROM *ROBINSON CRUSOE*. Stevenson, "My First Book," in Ridley's "Introduction" to *Treasure Island*, vi.

CHARLES KINGSLEY'S *AT LAST*. Stevenson told Sidney Colvin in July 1884: "*T.I.* came out of Kingsley's *At Last*, where I got the Dead Man's Chest—and that was the seed" (*Letters of Robert Louis Stevenson*, ed. Colvin, 1:321).

"RUM ISLAND." "THE DEAD MAN'S CHEST." Charles Kingsley, *At Last: A Christmas in the West Indies* (London: Macmillan, 1889), 11.

"THE SEED" OF HIS STORY. Letter to Sidney Colvin, July 1884 (*Letters of Robert Louis Stevenson*, ed. Colvin, 1:321).

page 32:

THE SEA CHEST OF A DEAD PIRATE. The idea of finding something wonderful in a chest may have been sparked by Stevenson's memories of one of Skelt's Juvenile Drama librettos he owned, called *The Old Oak Chest*. Stevenson, "A Penny Plain and Two-Pence Coloured," in *Memories and Portraits*, 161.

CAPSTAN CHANTY STEVENSON DESIGNED. Speaking of the chorus of his song, "Yo-ho-ho, and a bottle of rum!" Stevenson informed Henley:

"At the third Ho you heave at the capstan bars." *Letters of Robert Louis Stevenson*, ed. Colvin, 1:220.

"THE DEAD MAN'S CHEST" SHOULD BE CAPITALIZED. Not a word in *Treasure Island* leads one to understand that these words are the name of an island. Only someone who has read Kingsley would know it. Possibly Stevenson thought of "The Dead Man's Chest" as the name of his island of buried treasure—although there is no internal or external evidence that he did. Yet all the pirates know the exact longitude and latitude of the island they are headed for, as Captain Smollett realizes at once, although no one has told them, so they could easily have known its name as well. Stevenson, *Treasure Island*, 43–44 (chap. 9).

"SAD AND DESOLATE." "BLUE SEA LEAPING." Kingsley, *At Last*, 28.

"UTTERLY PESTILENTIAL." "SICKLY SMELL." "GAY AND GREEN." Ibid., 121–22, 166.

"THAT ABOMINABLE ANCHORAGE." "THE NASTY STENCH." "FEVER AND DYSENTERY." Stevenson, *Treasure Island* 72 (chap. 16).

page 33:

"IT WAS A TOSS-UP." "A GALLOPING CONSUMPTION." "COLD SWEATS, PROSTRATING." Letter from Stevenson to Edmund Gosse, April 16, 1880 (Daiches, *Robert Louis Stevenson and His World*, 49).

AN INDIGENOUS AMERICAN RATTLESNAKE. Stevenson, *Treasure Island*, 63 (chap. 14). The rattlesnakes on the island fit into the deadly character of the entire ambient.

THE IDEA FOR SUCH A TREE. Stevenson, "My First Book," in Ridley's "Introduction" to *Treasure Island*, vi.

"RED COLUMN AS BIG AS A COTTAGE." Stevenson, *Treasure Island*, 151 (chap. 32).

"CHIC." "THE SCENERY IS." Letter to Sidney Colvin, July 1884 (*Letters of Robert Louis Stevenson*, ed. Colvin, 1:321).

"A STRONG DASH" OF WALTER SAVAGE LANDOR. Letter to W. E. Henley (ibid., 1:221).

A "PROPER CHANCE" TO BE SEEN. "The Persons of the Tale," *Fables*, in *Works of Robert Louis Stevenson*, 25:187.

page 34:

THE COXSWAIN ISRAEL HANDS. Stevenson probably arrived at his name from references in Johnson's *General History of the Pirates* to a pirate named "Israel Hynde" (2:56) or "Israel Hind" (2:65).

STILL LOOKS "VERY SICK." Stevenson, *Treasure Island*, 114 (chap. 25).

"SHEEP BEFORE THIS BUTCHER." Ibid., 120 (chap. 26).

"HOT BLOOD." "BACK AND CHEST." Ibid., 122 (chap. 27).

"LIKE A MONKEY FOR CLEVERNESS." Ibid., 45 (chap. 9).

"LONG JOHN'S EARRINGS." Ibid., 47 (chap. 10).

"WITH THE SPEED." "AGILE AS A MONKEY." Ibid., 65 (chap. 14).

"NEARLY BURNT ALIVE IN HIS BED." Williamson, *W. E. Henley*, 155.

"TILL HE GOT HOLD OF." Stevenson, *Treasure Island*, 92 (chap. 20).

"SILVER SUDDENLY SPRANG UP." Ibid., 136 (chap. 29). Stevenson shows how entirely he put himself into the character along with his friend Henley at this point, for Sidney Colvin recalled as typical of Stevenson "the lissom swiftness of his movements." *Memories and Notes of Persons and Places*, 100.

page 35:

"LEND HIM A HAND." Stevenson, *Treasure Island*, 146 (chap. 31).

"AS MUCH LOVED BY ALL." Williamson, *W. E. Henley*, 22.

AS ONLY "GREAT CAPTAINS" CALL FORTH. So H. D. Lowry said of Henley (ibid., 250).

"HE TERRIFIED US ALSO." William Butler Yeats, *Autobiographies: The Trembling of the Veil* (London: Macmillan, 1926), 157–58.

"ACCEPT HIM AS OUR JUDGE." Ibid., 158.

"BURLY" IN AN ESSAY. *RLS: Stevenson's Letters to Charles Baxter*, ed. Ferguson and Waingrow, 102n.

"BOISTEROUS AND PIRATIC." "LOUD, COPIOUS, INTOLERANT." "ROAR YOU DOWN." "Talk and Talkers," *Memories and Portraits*, 12:122–23.

"THE CREW RESPECTED." Stevenson, *Treasure Island*, 47 (chap. 10).

"SMART AS PAINT." Ibid., 40 (chap. 8).

"SMART AS PAINT." Ibid., 50 (chap. 11).

"WITH A VEHEMENCE THAT SHOOK." Ibid., 135 (chap. 29).

SEES HIM AS "A LION." Ibid., 139–40 (chap. 30).

"BARBECUE FOR EVER!" Ibid., 136 (chap. 29).

page 36:

"FRESH LIGHT TO HIS PIPE." Ibid., 132 (chap. 28).

"PIPE DON'T DRAW." Ibid., 134 (chap. 29).

"SLAPPING TABLES WITH HIS." Ibid., 40 (chap. 8).

"OLD GIANT." "BY CLUTCHING AN AGATE." Connell, *W. E. Henley*, 280–81.

"FLINGING HIMSELF ABOUT AND." Williamson, *W. E. Henley*, 189.

DINNERS FOR HIS FRIENDS AT SOLFERINO'S. Buckley, *William Ernest Henley*, 152. Connell says that Henley "liked good food and good drink" (*W. E. Henley*, 143).

"LIVED EASY." "ATE DAINTY ALL MY DAYS." Stevenson, *Treasure Island*, 51 (chap. 11).

"SILVER TRUSTED ME." Ibid., 141 (chap. 30).

"ALREADY DOUBLY A TRAITOR." Ibid., 144 (chap. 31).

HIS "HEART" IS "SORE." Ibid., 137 (chap. 29).

"BEAMING WITH GOOD NATURE." Ibid., 138 (chap. 30).

"DEADLY LOOK." "CUT EVERY HONEST THROAT." Ibid., 151 (chap. 32).

page 37:

"TOO BLASPHEMOUSLY GIVEN TOWARDS CALIFORNIA." Letter of Henley to Sidney Colvin, January 2, 1880 (Lucas, *The Colvins and Their Friends*, 117).

"SO MUCH THE BETTER; IF WITH HER." Letter of Sidney Colvin to Charles Baxter (Daiches, *Robert Louis Stevenson and His World*, 49).

DOCKED AT LIVERPOOL. Ibid., 52.

"YOU COULD PUT YOUR THUMB." Letter of Sidney Colvin to W. E. Henley, August 1880 (Lucas, *The Colvins and Their Friends*, 127).

"AT PEACE." "WHETHER YOU AND I." Ibid., 128.

"HOW DEAR A HOPE." Letter to Mrs. Sitwell, Spring 1875 (ibid., 91).

DEDICATED HIS *CHILD'S GARDEN OF VERSES*. Daiches, *Robert Louis Stevenson and His World*, 10.

"IF EVER I AM HUNG." "CRUSHED AND EXHAUSTED." "HIGH INDIGNATION." Letter of Sidney Colvin to W. E. Henley, November 30, 1884 (Lucas, *The Colvins and Their Friends*, 160).

HENRY JAMES HAD BEEN. Henry James had written Sidney Colvin immediately after his three-day visit, telling of the "ponderous presence" of the Thomas Stevensons and wondering that they could not see "how they take it out of him" (ibid., 168).

"IF LOUIS DIES OF THIS." Fanny Stevenson to Mrs. Sitwell (ibid., 160).

"MY BACK IS BROKEN." "TO LIFT LOUIS." Fanny Stevenson to Sidney Colvin, 1885 (ibid., 161).

HIS WIFE TO BE TRUE AS STEEL. This paraphrases part of a line in Stevenson's poem "My Wife," which tells all he owes her (ibid., 266).

page 38:

"DYNAMITE EXPLOSION," AS FANNY CALLED HIM. Fanny Stevenson to Charles Baxter, June 1883 (*RLS: Stevenson's Letters to Charles Baxter*, ed. Ferguson and Waingrow, 118).

"FOR ALL HIS CRIPPLED BODILY." From a note written by Sidney Colvin shortly before his death to future biographers of Stevenson (Lucas, *The Colvins and Their Friends*, 106).

"A VERY LITTLE OF THAT BRINGS ON." Letter of Fanny Stevenson to Sidney Colvin, summer 1881 (ibid., 153).

"RESENTED." "SOWED THE FIRST SEEDS." Colvin, *Memories and Notes of Persons and Places*, 142.

ABOVE SARANAC LAKE IN THE. Stevenson needed to be in the United States, for his work was in great demand by American magazines.

"KATHERINE EVEN WHILE SHE CONSENTED." Letter of Stevenson to Charles

Baxter, April 16, 1888 (*RLS: Stevenson's Letters to Charles Baxter*, ed. Ferguson and Waingrow, 212).

"I READ 'THE NIXIE' WITH CONSIDERABLE AMAZEMENT." Connell, *W. E. Henley*, 113–14.

pages 38–39:

"SUPPOSE THAT I AM INSANE." Letter of Stevenson to Charles Baxter, April 16, 1888 (*RLS: Stevenson's Letters to Charles Baxter*, ed. Ferguson and Waingrow, 210).

page 39:

"REMEMBER HOW VERY RARELY." Connell, *W. E. Henley*, 115–16.

"HEART-BREAKING." "OF A PIECE OF." Ibid., 118.

"IT IS YOUR MISTAKE." Ibid.

"I KNEW LONG AGO HOW." Stevenson to Charles Baxter, March 23, 1888 (Connell, *W. E. Henley*, 119–20).

"MAKE HIM CLOSE HIS MOUTH." Ibid., 120.

"YOUR HONESTY WERE NOT SO WARFARING." Ibid., 100.

THICK AS THIEVES. With Henley and Stevenson's cousins at Shepherd's Bush was usually Henley's brother Teddy, whom Stevenson, in a moment of wrath, once called a "drunken whoreson bugger." Letter of December 30, 1887 (*RLS: Stevenson's Letters to Charles Baxter*, 183).

"THERE IS NOT ONE OF THAT." Letter of March 23, 1888 (Connell, *W. E. Henley*, 119).

page 40:

"CORRIDOR'D, AND STEWED, AND." Letter of January 31, 1892 (*RLS: Stevenson's Letters to Charles Baxter*, ed. Ferguson and Waingrow, 294).

THAT WHOLE "CLIQUE." "THEY HAVE SPRUNG." Letter of Stevenson to Charles Baxter, March 23, 1888 (Connell, *W. E. Henley*, 120–21).

"TOO MUCH HOLE-AND-CORNERING." Letter of November 1891 (*RLS: Stevenson's Letters to Charles Baxter*, ed. Ferguson and Waingrow, 289).

"NETTLED AND WORRIED FOR YEARS." Letter of August 15, 1891 (ibid., 283).

"WEARY OF IT ALL—WEARY." Letter of March 23, 1888 (ibid., 194).

"CARE FOR HENLEY." "ALL HIS FINE SPIRIT." Letter of March 24, 1888 (ibid., 198).

"LORD, MAN, I CAN'T HELP." Connell, *W. E. Henley*, 126.

"WILLINGNESS TO SEETHE UP." Letter of April 16, 1888 (*RLS: Stevenson's Letters to Charles Baxter*, ed. Ferguson and Waingrow, 211).

"MAKES A DAMNED HOLE." Letter of June 20, 1891 (ibid., 281).

HOW HE WAS GOING TO END IT. He was so far at first from seeing a resolution that would come out of the conflict between his characters that he thought he might just have a volcano erupt. *Letters of Robert Louis Stevenson*, ed. Colvin, 1:221.

"THE SAME BLAND, POLITE." Stevenson, *Treasure Island*, 157 (chap. 33).
"I THINK WE WERE ALL." Ibid., 161 (chap. 34).

page 41:

"THAT FORMIDABLE SEAFARING MAN." Ibid.

"I SHALL HAVE TO GET YOU TO." Connell, *W. E. Henley*, 120.

"TAK' THE CREDIT O'T." Letter of November 10, 1888 (*RLS: Stevenson's Letters to Charles Baxter*, ed. Ferguson and Waingrow, 238).

"TIME HAS NOT DIMINISHED." Letter of February 8, 1889 (ibid., 241).

"I CANNOT DESCRIBE THE SENSE." Letter of November 1891 (ibid., 289).

"BIG PRESENCE AND HIS WELCOME." Letter of March 11, 1891 (ibid., 277).

HIS LOYAL WIFE, WHO IS A "WOMAN OF COLOUR." Stevenson, *Treasure Island*, 36 (chap. 7). Stevenson's choice of a "woman of colour" for Long John Silver's happy ending came consciously as an exotic touch, but possibly he was so deeply in Silver at this point that he gave him a wife like his own, for Fanny Stevenson has been described by Sidney Colvin as "dark-complexioned" (*Memories and Notes of Persons and Places*, 130), so dark that on seeing her for the first time he spoke of her "little determined brown face" (Lucas, *The Colvins and Their Friends*, 128). Stevenson felt it correct to give Silver a happy ending, but he paid lip service to conventional morality by suggesting that he had small chance of comfort in another world. *Treasure Island*, 161 (chap. 34).

"DARK AND BLOODY SOJOURN." Stevenson, *Treasure Island*, 160 (chap. 34).

"THAT ACCURSED ISLAND." Ibid., 161 (chap. 34).

"UPON HIS DEATH-BED." J. C. Furnas, *Voyage to Windward: The Life of Robert Louis Stevenson* (London: Faber & Faber, 1952), 181. Of course, Yeats's grandfather was probably attracted by Stevenson's sea expertise, but the satisfaction on his deathbed certainly came out of the triumph the book gives over the fear of death.

3. FitzOmar: Live Eagle

The Life

page 46:

THE WEALTHIEST COMMONER. Although a "commoner," Mary Frances FitzGerald was descended from the Earls of Kildare, as her husband was from the Barons of Loughmoe. "Biographical Profiles," *The Letters of Edward FitzGerald*, ed. Alfred McKinley Terhune and Annabelle Burdick Terhune, 4 vols. (Princeton: Princeton University Press, 1980), 1:13–14. Hereafter referred to as *Letters*.

"EXTREME DISCIPLINE AND." Alfred McKinley Terhune, *Life of Edward*

FitzGerald: Translator of the Rubáiyát of Omar Khayyám (London: Oxford University Press, 1947), 7–8. Hereafter referred to as *Life.*

"AND WE CHILDREN WERE NOT." See his letter to Fanny Kemble [February 27, 1872] (*Letters*, 3:331). FitzGerald capitalized important nouns. In quoting him, both in letters and verse, I have changed to modern usage, for he is never either quaint or old-fashioned in language, and his spirit comes through better for a modern reader, with no attention called to form. I have also made changes in his mechanics, such as italicizing book titles, which he never does.

"LIKE THAT IN——." Ibid.

"NOTORIOUSLY MORAL." "MY MOTHER READ." To Stephen Spring Rice, September 29, 1862 (*Letters*, 2:457).

FITZGERALD SENT HIS LACKEY. *Life*, 25.

"WRETCHED POLICY." "TO SUCCUMB TO." To John Allen, January 29, [1830] (*Letters*, 1:79).

"I CARED MUCH FOR." To Stephen Spring Rice, July 27, 1863 (*Letters*, 2:488).

OPERA DANCER HE KEPT. *Life*, 6.

page 47:

GOLD DESSERT PLATES. Ibid. In a letter to Anna Biddell [February 28, 1878], FitzGerald declared that what Fanny Kemble referred to as "grand" family gold plate was actually "silver-gilt" (*Letters*, 4:105).

"STATE OF INNOCENCE." "INCONVENIENCES." *Letters*, 493n.

FOUR BLACK HORSES. Thackeray says only that she arrived in "great state, four in hand." (From a letter owned by Mrs. Richard B. Fuller, in *Life*, 7.) The matched black horses and her coachman, Greathurst, are spoken of in a letter FitzGerald wrote to George Crabbe of Merton, October 22, 1849 (*Letters*, 1:650). This was the poet's grandson. In the *Letters*, his father, the poet's son, is referred to as George Crabbe of Bredfield, and he as George Crabbe of Merton until his father's death.

"AN ARMY OF FLUNKIES." *Life*, 7.

"MY MOTHER WANTS." To John Allen, November 12, 1831 (*Letters*, 1:111).

"HATEFULLEST OF ALL." To Bernard Barton, December 24, 1841 (*Letters*, 1:293).

"ROARING UNSOPHISTICATED OCEAN." To Bernard Barton, December 29, 1844 (*Letters*, 1:469–70).

"FOR WANT OF ROOM." To W. H. Thompson, December 15, [1880] (*Letters*, 4:379). As to the resemblance to the Duke of Wellington, FitzGerald speaks of it in letters to Anna Biddell, March 13, [1880], and to Fanny Kemble, March 26, [1880] (*Letters*, 4:299, 304).

"WE GET ON VERY." To W. K. Browne [April 1843] (*Letters*, 1:388).

HIS SISTERS WOULD RUSH. See To Bernard Barton, January [16], 1842 (*Letters*,

1:299), telling of how his sister Lusia, learning that her betrothed was
dead of fever on the Niger River in Africa, "fell upon" her father's
bosom.

"LITTLE EDWARD." "BY HIS UNFAILING." A recall of the letter comes from
Sarah F. Spedding, who had seen it the year before (*Letters*, 1:411n).

"ALMOST OBLITERATED." "OLD MAGIC LANTERN." To Fanny Kemble [February 27, 1872] (*Letters*, 3:331).

page 48:

"LIEUTENANT-COLONEL IN." "Biographical Profiles," *Letters*, 1:14.

"FITZ." "WHEN HE LEFT ME." Letter of W. B. Donne to J. W. Blakesley
[Autumn 1838] (*Letters*, 1:493n).

"WRETCHED NEWS." "UPON AN ERRAND." To E. B. Cowell, June 13, 1851
(*Letters*, 2:32).

"MY FATHER PROPOSES." To Frederick Tennyson, February 6, 1842 (*Letters*, 1:305).

"THEATRICALIZING." So FitzGerald spoke of it to W. B. Donne, October
25, 1833 (*Letters*, 1:139).

"DEAR OLD HAYMARKET." To Fanny Kemble, December 6, [1880] (*Letters*, 4:377).

"GRANDEUR." So he spoke of it to W. F. Pollock on June 16, [1872]
(*Letters*, 3:355).

"EXCEPT MY MOTHER." To Fanny Kemble, November 17, 1874 (*Letters*, 3:528).

JOB WITH SCISSORS. *Letters*, 3:529.

page 49:

"MY DEAR FELLOW!" To Bernard Barton, February 19, 1842 (*Letters*, 1:307).

"BETTER IDOLS THAN LOVE OF." To E. B. Cowell, September 22, 1848
(*Letters*, 1:617).

"GOT ALL SORTS OF." To John Allen [May 21, 1830] (*Letters*, 1:87–88).

"A LITTLE ABSURD LODGING." To W. F. Pollock, February 11, 1875 (*Letters*, 3:550).

"TALENT FOR DULLNESS." To Frederick Tennyson, December 8, 1844 (*Letters*, 1:465).

"SMOOTH SAILING." "NO VELVET WAISTCOAT." Ibid., 466–67.

"ONE OF THOSE FEW." From Alfred Tennyson to Edward FitzGerald,
November 12, [1846] (*Letters*, 1:548).

page 50:

BERNARD BARTON'S SMALL PENSION. In a letter of December 2, 1848,
FitzGerald told Barton that he had almost forgot to send him his

"weekly dole" in the rush of setting out for his mother at Brighton (*Letters*, 1:624).

ARTIST G. J. ROWE. *Letters*, 3:333n.

COMMISSIONING SAMUEL LAURENCE. The letters show that FitzGerald had Laurence do oil sketches of John Allen, James Spedding, Alfred Tennyson, William Makepeace Thackeray, William Kenworthy Browne, Bernard Barton, "Posh" Fletcher, etc. See all the letters to Laurence.

PERRY NURSEY AND MORRIS MOORE. For Nursey, see "Biographical Profiles," *Letters*, 1:55–56. For Moore, see To Richard Monckton Milnes, August 9, 1843, and To Frederick Tennyson, December 10, 1843 (*Letters*, 1:392, 409).

"SITUATION." "TO WRITE ANOTHER *ILIAD*." To Bernard Barton [January 17, 1845] (*Letters*, 1:475).

"US LITTLE ONES." *Letters*, 1:411n.

WITH FITZGERALD AT THEIR. This was a recollection of Mary S. Crowfoot of Beccles. Ibid.

"IN DELIGHTFUL SPIRITS." Letter of Mrs. Alfred Tennyson to Elizabeth Cowell, August 3, [1854] (*Letters*, 2:132).

"PERSISTS IN THINKING I." To W. M. Thackeray [January 1847] (*Letters*, 1:555).

"PRINCE OF QUIETISTS." "HALF THE SELF-SACRIFICE." Letter of James Spedding to W. B. Donne, April 1835 (*Letters*, 1:161).

"DELIGHTED TO GET OUT." "AMAZED TO SEE." To Bernard Barton, January 11, 1845 (*Letters*, 1:472).

"SPORT A GENTLE EPICURISM." To Frederick Tennyson, December 8, 1844 (*Letters*, 1:466).

page 51:

"RELIGIOUS WANDERINGS AND." To John Allen [April 21, 1830] (*Letters*, 1:82).

"BELIEF AND DISBELIEF." To John Allen [May 21, 1830] (*Letters*, 1:88).

HIS OLDEST BROTHER, JOHN. In this genetically dangerous first-cousin marriage, it seems that John as well as Andalusia had psychotic episodes.

"EXETER HALL WAR-CRY." To Thomas Carlyle, September 20, 1847 (*Letters*, 1:580).

"I MAY TRULY SAY." To John Allen [May 21, 1830] (*Letters*, 1:88).

"COMMANDS OF OUR SAVIOUR." To John Allen [January 31, 1830] (*Letters*, 1:80).

"ONE MIRACLE TOOK PLACE." To W. M. Thackeray, October 10, 1831 (*Letters*, 1:103).

"BARE SCIENCE." "GREATER EPIC THAN." To E. B. Cowell [July 24, 1847] (*Letters*, 1:566).

"BEASTS AND STRANGE CREATURES." To E. B. Cowell [July 30, 1847] (*Letters*, 1:569).

"FUNDED VIRTUES OF." "HEBREW RAGS." To Thomas Carlyle, September 20, 1847 (*Letters*, 1:580).

"I MISLAID THIS SHEET." To W. F. Pollock [May 1–3, 1842] (*Letters*, 1:320).

"I ALWAYS PUT ON." To Frederick Tennyson, December 10, 1843 (*Letters*, 1:408).

page 52:

"WHERE EVERY ONE SAT." To Frederick Tennyson, December 8, 1844 (*Letters*, 1:466).

"WHERE A GOOD LITTLE MAN." To Frederick Tennyson [October 24, 1853] (*Letters*, 2:113).

"M—RR—D." "WHEN ARE YOU." To W. H. Thompson, March 26, 1841 (*Letters*, 1:275).

"PLAIN, SENSIBLE GIRL." To W. M. Thackeray, July 29, 1835 (*Letters*, 1:172–73).

"YOUNG DAMSEL." "MORE THAN EVER." To John Allen, February 4, 1836 (*Letters*, 1:179).

"FAMOUS GIRL (NOW 30)." To Thomas Carlyle, March 20, 1844 (*Letters*, 1:429).

page 53:

"WRAP MYSELF ROUND." To John Allen, January 10, 1837 (*Letters*, 1:190).

"MORE LIKE LOVES." To John Allen, September 9, [1834] (*Letters*, 1:153).

"WITH A LITTLE *CHALK*." To Mrs. Charles Allen, August 15, 1857 (*Letters*, 2:296).

"YOU DON'T KNOW." To W. M. Thackeray, September 1, 1837 (*Letters*, 1:209).

"QUICK TO LOVE AND." To Bernard Barton [April 7, 1844] (*Letters*, 1:430).

"I AM MUCH IN LOVE." To Bernard Barton [June 8, 1838] (*Letters*, 1:213).

"GREAT BLACK DOG." "PLAYING WITH OUR." To John Allen, August 28, [1838] (*Letters*, 1:215).

page 54:

"AN EXERCISE IN PUNCTUATION." W. B. Donne to Bernard Barton, October 29, 1838 (*Letters*, 1:218).

"VENATOR." "ROOKS AND RABBITS." To Bernard Barton [Spring 1839] (*Letters*, 1:225).

"ROW OF SUCH POPLARS." To Bernard Barton, July 24, 1839 (*Letters*, 1:230).

"DEAR OLD BEDFORDSHIRE." To W. F. Pollock, August 14, [1839] (*Letters*, 1:231).

"WITH A BOOK AND." To Frederick Tennyson, June 7, 1840 (*Letters*, 1:250). In this case the book was probably a sketchbook.

"BEST OF GOOD FELLOWS." To W. H. Thompson, September 4, 1840 (*Letters*, 1:258).

"SCREW OF A FATHER." To Bernard Barton [November 1840] (*Letters*, 1:262).

"MR. BROWNE THE ELDER." To Bernard Barton, March 2, 1842 (*Letters*, 1:311).

page 55:

"MOST SPLENDID CARVED FRAME." To Bernard Barton [March 1843] (*Letters*, 1:386). When Browne died, FitzGerald spoke of his house "all hung with the pictures we had bought together for twenty years!" To George Crabbe, March 29, 1859 (*Letters*, 2:329), after his father's death when he no longer needs to be set off from him.

"WHISKERED MAN." "MAN OF BUSINESS." To John Allen, August 29, 1842 (*Letters*, 1:336).

"THAT THEY COULD NOT." To Bernard Barton [April 7, 1844] (*Letters*, 1:430).

"NOW MY OLD SUMMER." To John Allen [c. July 16, 1844] (*Letters*, 1:447).

"WIFE'S HATRED OF THE." To Frederick Tennyson, May 24, 1844 (*Letters*, 1:442).

"MY ROD AND LINE." To Frederick Tennyson, December 8, 1844 (*Letters*, 1:467).

"VERY GOOD, QUIET." To John Allen, August 27, 1845 (*Letters*, 1:508). Mrs. Browne's parents had bought Hester Thrale Piozzi's home thirty-five years before, and FitzGerald was delighted to have in his room some of the furniture that had been in Dr. Johnson's room there.

"GOOD ALDERMAN BROWNE." To Bernard Barton, September 19, 1846 (*Letters*, 1:541).

"CAPTAIN BROWNE." To E. B. Cowell, January 3, 1856, and January 10, 1856 (*Letters*, 2:191, 194).

"FARMER, MAGISTRATE, MILITIA OFFICER." To Mrs. Charles Allen, August 15, 1857 (*Letters*, 2:296).

OLD GERMAN MELODY. To Fanny Kemble, October 7, [1879] (*Letters*, 4:264). In this letter, FitzGerald recalls John Kemble, Fanny Kemble's brother, singing the melody at Cambridge, which afterward FitzGerald had linked, he told her, to some verses for "one I loved."

"KNOWST THOU AN ISLE?" The words to the song are printed in *Life*, 151. E. B. Cowell wrote Aldis Wright in 1887 that his wife Elizabeth thought the vale in the verse referred to Bramford, their village, which did have a winding river (*Life*, 252n). Clearly, she believed she was the "Beloved" of the song. I believe that the references to the poplars beside the river, the references to the island's brave sons defending her liberties, and the clear association between the "Beloved" and England, which FitzGerald had explicitly stated of Browne when he saw "the better virtues and characteristics of Englishmen" in him (*Letters*, 1:209), make it clear that

Browne, not Elizabeth Cowell, was the "one I loved" for whom he wrote the song.

"SUCH POPLARS AS ONLY." To Bernard Barton, July 24, 1839 (*Letters*, 1:230).

SOLO OR IN DUET. George Crabbe, the poet's grandson, recalled that when FitzGerald came to visit his father he would usually come with "concerted pieces" that he had arranged for the family to sing with him in "four parts," for singing was a delight FitzGerald liked to share with all his friends. I assume that he did with his most loved friend Browne. William Causton, organist, pianist, and music teacher at Woodbridge, helped him with the song. Terhune says Causton "set" the poem to music, but it was already set to John Kemble's German melody, so I believe that he probably wrote a piano accompaniment for it. To George Crabbe of Merton [February 27, 1851] (*Letters*, 2:20, 20n).

PICNICKING IN ITS MEADOWS. Although FitzGerald and Browne took their tea in pothouses before Browne's marriage, they picnicked once Browne was assured of a good basket. See, for instance, their dining beneath the "ruins of a noble old place at Amthill." To Bernard Barton, September 19, 1846 (*Letters*, 1:542).

The Catastrophe

"STRONG INWARD CALL." To Bernard Barton, February 21, 1842 (*Letters*, 1:308).

page 56:

"DROWNED OUT." To Thomas Carlyle [September 2, 1843] (*Letters*, 1:398).

"POOR FATHER'S AFFAIRS." To W. B. Donne [mid-June 1848] (*Letters*, 1:609).

"LITERALLY INIQUITOUS TERMS." To Frederick Tennyson, December 7, 1849 (*Letters*, 1:657).

SEPARATION FROM HIS WIFE. Probably FitzGerald senior had tried to borrow money from his wife to pay for pumping out the water, and she had refused to throw good money after bad, bringing their already strained relations to a crisis.

"POOR OLD SEDLEY." To Frederick Tennyson, June 8, 1852 (*Letters*, 2:57).

"GENEROUS, WORTHY, SIMPLE-HEARTED." "MISS ABOUT TO." To Samuel Laurence [June 20, 1847] (*Letters*, 1:562).

page 57:

WEIGHED 14 STONE. To W. F. Pollock, September 17, [16], 1842 (*Letters*, 1:339).

HER GRANDMOTHER HAVING HAD. Lucy Barton's mother had died in childbirth, so she was raised by her grandmother. "Biographical Profiles," *Letters*, 1:22.

BIBLE STORIES FOR CHILDREN. Ibid., 23.

"ALL UNKNOWN TO ME." To W. B. Donne from Bernard Barton, March 29, 1847 (*Letters*, 1:556).

"BECAUSE IT AMUSED." To W. B. Donne, March 9, 1849 (*Letters*, 1:632).

"VERY SLENDERLY PROVIDED." To R. M. Milnes [c. May 15, 1849] (*Letters*, 1:637).

"TO GIVE THEM LOGIC." "DIFFUSE AND WEARY." To W. B. Donne [c. March 15, 1849] (*Letters*, 1:633).

"BOTHERED AND BEWILDERED." To John Allen, August 15, 1849 (*Letters*, 1:648).

"KIND OF ELDER NURSERY." To John Allen, December 13, 1849 (*Letters*, 1:659).

page 58:

"OUT OF ALL RISK." To W. B. Donne [January 17, 1850] (*Letters*, 1:661).

TRY EARNESTLY TO PERSUADE. Afterward FitzGerald took all the blame for his horrible marriage and said that Lucy Barton had little to blame herself for except believing she knew better than what "I had over and over again told her was the truth *before* marriage." To Mrs. W. K. Browne, July 11, 1865 (*Letters*, 2:556).

BROUGHT UP AS A MERCHANT. FitzGerald described Cowell in a letter to George Borrow, August 3, 1853 (*Letters*, 2:96).

"YOU ARE A HAPPY MAN." To E. B. Cowell [October 4, 1845] (*Letters*, 1:512).

"MAKES ME SPOONILY LIKE." To E. B. Cowell, March 12, 1850 (*Letters*, 1:664).

page 59:

"POOR FLAME WHEN SITTING." To Frederick Tennyson, April 17, 1850 (*Letters*, 1:667).

"CHINA-ROSE" COMPLEXION. To Mrs. Charles Allen, August 15, 1857, and October 26, [1859] (*Letters*, 2:295, 345).

ANNE ALLEN DIED. *Letters*, 1:143n.

"WORSE THAN WASTE." To Mrs. Charles Allen, August 15, 1857 (*Letters*, 2:295).

"HAPPY VALLEY." To E. B. Cowell, April 9, 1851 (*Letters*, 2:26).

"SOLITARY HOME OF HOUSEHOLD." To Mrs. Cowell, March 24, 1851 (*Letters*, 2:25). In this phrase, FitzGerald was probably quoting one of Mrs. Cowell's poems.

"LAVENDER GOWN." To E. B. Cowell, April 9, 1851 (*Letters*, 2:26). In a letter to Mrs. Cowell [c. November 20, 1851] (*Letters*, 2:42), FitzGerald asks her to wear her purple silk gown to a party with Thackeray at Oxford because he so loves lilacs and shades of purple.

"HOPE AND DREAM." "ROUSING UP HIS." From Mrs. Cowell to George Kitchin, November 1850 (*Letters*, 1:686–87). Actually, in the years to come, it would be FitzGerald who helped Cowell get his chair in oriental literature at Cambridge through his old friend W. H. Thompson, then Master of Trinity College.

page 60:
"SCRIPTURE BE ALTOGETHER." From Mrs. Cowell to George Kitchin [November 10, 1850] (*Letters*, 1:688).
"EITHER ONE." "ELDERLY KNIGHT." To Mrs. E. B. Cowell [February 13, 1851] (*Letters*, 2:11).
"HAPPY IN EGYPT." "OLD LAND OF." To E. B. Cowell, March 14, 1851 (*Letters*, 2:23).
"DOING IT SLAVISHLY." To Mrs. E. B. Cowell [September 23, 1853] (*Letters*, 2:105).
A WET SUNDAY. H. F. Stewart, the Dean of Trinity College, Cambridge, asked Cowell about how he got FitzGerald to learn Persian and this was his answer (*Life*, 170).
"DELIGHTFUL." "LOVE." To E. B. Cowell, January 5, 1854 (*Letters*, 2:118).
"IDIOMATIC SAXON *WORDS*." To Mrs. E. B. Cowell, January 24, 1854 (*Letters*, 2:119). FitzGerald's Sádí is Sádí of Shiraz and the poem is "The Gulistán" (Rose Garden).
JOHN SELDEN SAID. To E. B. Cowell, May 7, 1855 (*Letters*, 2:164).
"PREJUDICES AND ASSOCIATIONS." To E. B. Cowell, January 10, 1856 (*Letters*, 2:194).

page 61:
"VIGOROUS LANGUAGE." To E. B. Cowell [April 7, 1856] (*Letters*, 2:221).
"THRIFT, THRIFT, HORATIO!" To E. B. Cowell, August 31, [1854] (*Letters*, 2:137).
"THE SHORTER THE BETTER." To E. B. Cowell [March 3, 1851] (*Letters*, 2:23).
"*GROWING* SPONTANEOUSLY." To Mrs. E. B. Cowell, February 17, 1851 (*Letters*, 2:14).
"FOR ALL TENDERNESS." To E. B. Cowell, May 7, 1855 (*Letters*, 2:164).
"THE WINE, MY FRIENDS." "DRUNK." To E. B. Cowell, August 31, [1854] (*Letters*, 2:136–37). FitzGerald just suggests cutting "the" and "my."
AFTER AN INITIAL CRY. To E. B. Cowell [c. May 12, 1854] (*Letters*, 2:129).
"TACT TO DISH UP." To E. B. Cowell, January 10, 1855 (*Letters*, 2:153).

page 62:
"HANG REALLY HEAVY." To E. B. Cowell [January 12, 1856] (*Letters*, 2:194).
"WHEN SHALL WE THREE." To E. B. Cowell [April 4, 1856] (*Letters*, 2:218).

After his marriage, FitzGerald told Cowell his wife was sick of his singing that old glee, which he kept repeating, especially the stanza about sighing in foreign countries. To E. B. Cowell, March [4]–20, [1857] (*Letters*, 2:260).

"HAPPY RECORD." "FELLOWSHIP IN STUDY." To E. B. Cowell [April 4, 1856] (*Letters*, 2:219).

GREEN MALACHITE BROOCH. To Mrs. E. B. Cowell [June 6, 1856] (*Letters*, 2:230). He assured her that malachite was so inexpensive that doors and windows were made of it in Russia, for he wanted to spare her any "delicacy" about accepting it.

A DRY "REMAINDER BISCUIT." To Alfred Tennyson [July 15, 1856] (*Letters*, 2:234). The "remainder biscuit" is a quote of Shakespeare's *As You Like It*, act 2, scene 7, which FitzGerald knew virtually by heart.

FOR BETTER OR FOR. To Alfred Tennyson [c. March 15, 1856] (*Letters*, 2:211). He uses the words from the marriage service out of his apprehension over the marriage then being arranged.

"SORT OF TERROR." To George Crabbe of Bredfield, June 19, 1856 (*Letters*, 2:232).

ONE LAST DESPERATE EFFORT. "Biographical Profiles," *Letters*, 1:23–24.

"SANGUINER THAN MY." To John Allen [October 1856] (*Letters*, 2:238).

"DOUBTFUL EXPERIMENT." To Stephen Spring Rice [October 21, 1856] (*Letters*, 2:239).

"TAIL-LESS"—"A PRETTY." Ibid., 240.

page 63:

"MORTALLY" HATED WEDDING. To W. B. Donne, June 23, 1851 (*Letters*, 2:33).

HER RELATIVES WERE SHOCKED. "UGH! CONGEALED BRIDESMAID!" Most of the information on the wedding seems to have come from F. R. Barton, *Life*, 195.

"FOR FEAR OF UTTERLY." To E. B. Cowell, January 22, 1857 (*Letters*, 2:245).

GLAMOUR OF OPERAS. FitzGerald confided to Frederick Spalding the difficulties of his marriage, and Spalding wrote them into his diary on May 4, 1868. One of them was his wife's putting pressure on him to accompany her to the opera in formal dress, with very much the same social aims as his mother had had, as attested by the diary and also a letter to Mrs. Charles Allen, August 15, 1857 (*Letters*, 2:296). In it he praises his nieces not only for their concern to help the poor but also for having no desire for the opera or for the "fine folks and fine dresses there." Clearly he was comparing the nieces he loved to have near him with the wife he found impossible to live with.

"LARGE FIELD TO WORK ON." To E. B. Cowell, January 22, 1857 (*Letters*, 2:245).

"GIVEN TO PROFUSION." "EMPLOY HERSELF." To George Crabbe of Merton, January 1, 1857 (*Letters*, 2:243).

INTO THE WILD BEASTS. W. B. Donne to Fanny Kemble, January 20, 1857 (*Letters*, 2:244).

"VERY MUCH THE WORSE." *Life*, 199.

page 64:

FITZGERALD DRANK SO MUCH. Letter of W. B. Donne to Fanny Kemble (*Life*, 201). Donne probably heard the story directly from FitzGerald, for in the same letter he was quoting FitzGerald as "improperly" saying that since his marriage, his nieces had been his "chief comfort."

"NEW CHANNELS." To E. B. Cowell, January 22, 1857 (*Letters*, 2:245).

"SHE WAS BROUGHT UP." To Mrs. W. K. Browne, July 11, 1865 (*Letters*, 2:556).

"SHE RUSHED OVER THE." To Marietta Nursey [December 1866] *Letters*, 2:617).

"MY DEAR FITZ." Frederick Spalding's diary, May 4, 1868 (*Life*, 195). The kicking may sound more violent to modern ears than Victorian. At the time, it was a cliché for curing a person of foolishness.

page 65:

"ALL FRIENDLY KINDNESS." To Anna Ling, November 8, [1857] (*Letters*, 2:304).

FITZGERALD SETTLED THE INCOME. "Biographical Profiles," *Letters*, 1:24.

"POOR SOUL." To George Crabbe of Merton, September 19, 1857 (*Letters*, 2:299).

"HEAD NURSE." "WONDER AT MY CRUEL." To George Crabbe, May 26, [1858] (*Letters*, 2:316). (Called so in the *Letters* after his father's death.)

"OLDER, DULLER, SICKER." To Anna Ling, February 20, 1858 (*Letters*, 2:310). FitzGerald uses "dull" in the Victorian meaning "depressed."

"SETTLED" IN THE CHURCHYARD. To Anna Ling, February 24, [1858] (*Letters*, 2:312).

The Work

"OUSELEY MANUSCRIPT." A great impetus had been given to Persian studies by the books of the two Ouseley brothers. Sir Gore Ouseley had gone to Persia as British Ambassador, taking his brother Sir William Ouseley with him as his private secretary. Sir William, it seems, brought back the manuscript of the *Rubáiyát* of Omar Khayyám, transcribed at Shiraz in 1460, and presented it to Oxford University (No. 140, Bodleian Library).

CURIOUS OLD "EPICUREAN TETRASTICHS." To Alfred Tennyson [July 15, 1856] (*Letters*, 2:234). The Persian rubái (tetrastich) is similar to the English quatrain, appearing in the Persian script as two lines falling into two halves, each half line of 13 syllables, so that the quatrain of 10 syllables per line used by FitzGerald gives him a rubái full 12 syllables shorter than the Persian, which therefore cannot hold as complex a treatment. A modern translation—really a translation, not an original poem like FitzGerald's—such as that by Arthur J. Arberry takes two pentameter four-line stanzas to convey a Persian rubái. See Arthur J. Arberry, "Introduction," *Omar Khayyám: A New Version Based upon Recent Discoveries* (London: Murray, 1952), 33–45.

"RING LIKE TRUE METAL." To E. B. Cowell, March 20, [1857] (*Letters*, 2:262).

"DAINTY." "STARTLING UP." To E. B. Cowell, June 5, 1857 (*Letters*, 2:273). FitzGerald's first choice of "monkish" (medieval) Latin for Omar shows his diffidence at presenting a free-thinker like Omar to other than a restricted gentleman's audience (excluding by the language both women and the hoi polloi).

"OMAR BREATHES A SORT." Ibid. FitzGerald knew that Cowell would have wanted him to turn to Anglican Christianity for consolation and would feel sorry that he had found it in skeptical Omar.

page 66:

MORE THAN 500 VERSES. FitzGerald uses the round number in telling George Borrow of the Calcutta manuscript. To George Borrow, July 6, 1857 (*Letters*, 2:291). Edward Heron-Allen lists 510 rubáiyát in the Calcutta manuscript. See his *Rubáiyát of Omar Khayyám with Their Original Persian Sources, Literally Translated* (London: Quaritch, 1899), xv. Heron-Allen has his own system of accents with circumflexes; I have conventionalized it.

JUNE 14, 1857. The transcript Cowell made for FitzGerald is now at Trinity College Library, Cambridge. FitzGerald's note says it was given to him by "dear EBC in Calcutta" and reached him at Gorlestone on June 14, 1857 (*Letters*, 2:276n).

IT ABOUNDED IN VERSES. To George Borrow [June 24, 1857] (*Letters*, 2:284).

"OMAR-LIKE SORROW." To E. B. Cowell, July 1, 1857 (*Letters*, 2:281).

"AS IN PERSIA." To E. B. Cowell, July 14, 1857 (*Letters*, 2:289).

"WITH DAWN PRETTY SOBER." To Bernard Quaritch, March 31, [1872] (*Letters*, 3:339).

EMPTY GLASS TURNED DOWN. This is one of FitzGerald's incomparable touches—quite apart from Omar—because the turned-down cup or glass, whatever the beverage, has been the signal the world over for "I've had enough."

page 67:

"ALAS, THAT SPRING." I quote always from FitzGerald's first 1859 edition of the *Rubáiyát*, except where I specify another. It had 75 rubái (quatrains), and the above quote is from quatrain 72. My reference is always to the Golden Treasury edition, which prints all four of FitzGerald's lifetime editions. *Rubáiyát of Omar Khayyám: The Astronomer-Poet of Persia* (London: Macmillan, 1899), 69–94. This edition maintains FitzGerald's original anonymity.

"LIFE'S LIQUOR." 1859 *Rubáiyát*, quatrain 2.

"WELL OF LIFE." 1859 *Rubáiyát*, quatrain 34.

EMPTY GLASS AND DEATH. 1859 *Rubáiyát*, quatrain 75.

SPEAKER . . . IS OMAR KHAYYÁM. English scholars of Persian never ask the question of whether Omar Khayyám, astronomer-mathematician, was actually the author of all or even most of the epigrams. Yet the question certainly needs to be asked. For one thing, the epigrams were preserved in oral tradition as well as in manuscript and thus variant forms of one epigram—and there appear to be such—probably come about through oral transmission. Also, epigrams in the general style of Omar's could easily have gotten into the collections that have survived. Because the epigrams were a tradition in Persian poetry (both as to form and as to subject matter), they may all have been attributed to Omar Khayyám more as indicating a genre than a person. FitzGerald noticed at once that in the Calcutta manuscript the opening tetrastich could not have been Omar's, but must have been put in as preface "by way of *exorcism* against him" by a true believer. (To E. B. Cowell, June 19, 1857 [*Letters*, 2:275].) Also, FitzGerald noticed that the first three quatrains of the Ouseley manuscript were not in their alphabetical order but put there as a sort of apology for the "unorthodox poetry" to follow, just as in the Calcutta manuscript the first quatrain had appeared as a "malediction" on Omar, not a verse by Omar. (To E. B. Cowell, July 13, [1857] [*Letters*, 2:288].)

"E. FITZOMAR." FitzGerald signed himself thus in a letter to Anna Biddell, September 15, 1876, *Letters*, 3:704, after telling her that Leslie Stephen, in mourning for his wife, Thackeray's youngest daughter, said he had found consolation in FitzGerald's *Rubáiyát of Omar Khayyám*.

HIS READINGS OF LUCRETIUS. During 1848, FitzGerald was reading Lucretius in the Latin, and even made and sent to Cowell a "free translation" of one of the fine passages [c. May 1, 1848] (*Letters*, 1:601–3). Another passage he translated was not "very Christian reading," so he was careful not to send Cowell that one. (To E. B. Cowell, August 5, 1848 [*Letters*, 1:612].) Right in the midst of generating his *Rubáiyát*, FitzGerald told Cowell that he thought of Omar along with Anacreon as one of the "lighter shadows" among the shades that Lucretius presided over "so grimly." FitzGerald always realized that Omar's message was not at all new—only he had *dared* to say it, as Lucretius had dared. (To Mowbray Donne, December 31, 1867 [*Letters*, 3:75].) FitzGerald was even interested in translations of Lucretius into English. He bought one by Thomas Creech and later became very enthusiastic over one by H. A. J. Munro. (To E. B. Cowell, April 9, 1851 [*Letters*, 2:26].)

"PRINCE OF QUIETISTS." James Spedding to W. B. Donne, April 1835 (*Letters*, 1:161).

"GENTLE EPICURISM." To Frederick Tennyson, December 8, 1844 (*Letters*, 1:466).

LUCRETIUS FOR "COMFORT." To Frederick Tennyson, December 31, 1850 (*Letters*, 1:695). Although FitzGerald thought the theory of matter as made of "atoms" dry reading, he found so much great poetry in Lucretius that he liked him best of all the Latin poets. Lucretius was, he believed, the "true sublime satirist of poor man," reaching to something deeper than his vices, and with compassion, not anger. Among the *Letters*, see To E. B. Cowell, June 5, [1848], 1:613; To C. E. Norton, February 14, 1878, 4:96; and To E. B. Cowell, August 31, [1864], 2:529–30.

"MESS." "SAD EPICUREAN." To W. M. Thackeray, November 15, 1852 (*Letters*, 2:75).

"GREAT FELLOW FEELING." To Bernard Quaritch [early August 1867] (*Letters*, 3:40).

"MORE AKIN." To E. B. Cowell, December 8, 1857 (*Letters*, 2:305).

page 68:

"WE WALK IN DIFFERENT." To John Allen [October 1856] (*Letters*, 2:238).

"GREAT ARGUMENT." 1859 *Rubáiyát*, quatrain 27.

"CAME LIKE WATER." 1859 *Rubáiyát*, quatrain 28.

"POOR LITTLE PERSIAN EPICUREAN." To George Crabbe of Bredfield, May 29, 1857 (*Letters*, 2:277).

"OLD PARSON CRABBE." To George Borrow, July 6, 1857 (*Letters*, 2:291).

"LOVELIEST AND BEST." 1859 *Rubáiyát*, quatrain 21.

THE HEADS, THE LIPS. Ibid., and also quatrains 18, 19, 22, 35, 36, etc.

"POOR OLD OMAR." See, for instance, To George Borrow [June 24, 1857], and To E. B. Cowell, April 27, [1859] (*Letters*, 2:284, 334). Sometimes FitzGerald calls him just "poor Omar" and sometimes just "old Omar." See To Bernard Quaritch [early August 1867], and To E. B. Cowell, March 20, [1857] (*Letters*, 3:40, 2:262).

page 69:

"POOR OLD SEDLEY." To Frederick Tennyson, June 8, 1852 (*Letters*, 2:57).

"TO BURY POOR OLD." To W. M. Thackeray, April 13, 1852 (*Letters*, 2:51).

"OLDER" AND "SICKER." To Anna Ling, February 20, 1858 (*Letters*, 2:310).

LIKELY TO BE "SETTLED." To Anna Ling, February 24, [1858] (*Letters*, 2:312).

"POOR INDOLENT OLD FITZ." To W. H. Thompson [June 1866] (*Letters*, 2:587).

FIVE CONSECUTIVE QUATRAINS. 1859 *Rubáiyát*, quatrains 12–16.

"HUSBANDED THE GOLDEN." Ibid., quatrain 14.

QUATRAINS ON THE RUINED SPLENDORS. Ibid., quatrains 5, 8, 9, 17.

HÁTIM TAI. Ibid., quatrain 9.

"THAT GREAT HUNTER." Ibid., quatrain 17.

LOVE IS MENTIONED IRONICALLY. See, for instance, the tetrastich from the Cambridge manuscript as translated by Arthur J. Arberry, *Omar Khayyám*, verse 69, p. 71. In this verse, the irony lies in the fact that the "darling" for whom the speaker suffers is himself suffering for love of someone else, so he, who should have been the cure for the disease of love, is just another victim.

pages 69–70:

TRANSITORY SENSUAL DELIGHT. See Arberry's *Omar Khayyám*, verse 41, p. 62, about the happiness of being with a darling as lovely as the moon, if only the night could be long and lingering instead of speeding by, as it is bound to do.

page 70:

USED OUT OF "DECORUM." FitzGerald cites Lady Duff Gordon's view, as expressed in her *Letters from Egypt*, edited by her mother, Sarah Austin (London, 1865) in To E. B. Cowell, September 5, 1865 (*Letters*, 2:560).

ABOUT HENRI BEYLE (STENDHAL). To C. E. Norton, February 1, 1877 (*Letters*, 4:6), and To W. A. Wright [October 1876] (*Letters*, 3:713).

"THOU," "WE," "MY BELOVED." 1859 *Rubáiyát*, quatrains 11, 19, 20, 73, 74.

page 71:

SCHOLARS HAVE MADE STUDIES. Edward Heron-Allen made the first major study of how much of FitzGerald's *Rubáiyát* was translation in *Edward FitzGerald's Rubáiyát of Omar Khayyám*. Using all the quatrains in FitzGerald's four versions, Heron-Allen declared that 49 are "faithful and beautiful paraphrases" of tetrastichs in either or both the Ouseley and the Calcutta manuscripts; 44 can be traced to more than one tetrastich and therefore can be called "composite"; 2 are from quatrains that FitzGerald found in a publication of the Persian text with a French prose translation of J. B. Nicolas (Paris: Imprimerie Impériale, 1867); 2 reflect only the spirit of the originals; 2 can be traced to the "influence" of the "Mantik ut-tair" of Attár; 2 show the influence of Odes of Háfiz; and 3, suppressed after the first and second editions, cannot be attributed to any Persian source. Heron-Allen—who remained marvelously blind to all the differences from his originals in the overall structure and meaning of FitzGerald's poem, as well as all the ways he transformed images suggested by his originals—summed up his findings this way: "A translation pure and simple it is *not*, but a translation in the most artistic sense of the term it undoubtedly is" (xi, xii, xiv). Heron-Allen clearly saw himself as vindicating FitzGerald. He saw the poem as a translation by definition, so it could only be a good or bad one. It never occurred to him that it might be a great original poem inspired by but distinct from the Persian.

"HERE WITH A LOAF." 1859 *Rubáiyát*, quatrain 11.

"IF A HAND SHOULD." I have made this translation by studying the translations of Heron-Allen (*FitzGerald's Rubáiyát*, 23) and Arberry (*Omar Khayyám*, 22).

PARTS OF THE BODY. Arberry points out that parts of the body are named in the Persian (*Omar Khayyám*, 23). From his suggestion that there are "obscene echoes" in them, I have concluded that the wit of the Persian lies in their relevance to the sexual aim of the picnic. From the translations, I have also concluded that a part of the wit lies in the parallel tenderness of the fine white bread and the prime cut of mutton to the boy sweetheart.

"BOUGH" WOULD NOT BE. Ibid., 23.

page 72:

THACKERAY'S HORROR IF. To W. M. Thackeray, July 29, 1835 (*Letters*, 1:173).

VOLUMES OF POETRY. Heartbroken at Browne's dying, FitzGerald had noticed in his house all the shelves of books with "EFG to WKB" written in them. (To George Crabbe, March 29, 1859 [*Letters*, 2:329].) That many of the books were poetry can be assumed from FitzGerald's great love for that medium.

"KNOWST THOU AN ISLE?" *Life*, 151.

"SANS TEETH, SANS EYES." *As You Like It*, act 2, scene 7. That FitzGerald had this scene (perhaps the entire play) virtually by heart is shown by his quotation from this same scene about the "remainder biscuit" in To Alfred Tennyson [July 15, 1856] (*Letters*, 2:234).

"SANS WINE, SANS SONG." 1859 *Rubáiyát*, quatrain 23.

"LYING ON THE BANKS." To W. F. Pollock, August 14, [1839] (*Letters*, 1:231).

"FLEDGES THE RIVER'S LIP." 1859 *Rubáiyát*, quatrain 19.

"ALONG THE RIVER BRINK." Ibid., quatrain 48.

"AND WILDERNESS IS." Ibid., quatrain 11.

QUOTED PETRARCH'S SONNET. To E. B. Cowell, March 12, 1850 (*Letters*, 1:664–65). FitzGerald gives the line in Petrarch as "Che solean fare in terra un paradiso."

THE FUNGI, THE DISMAL SERMONS. To Frederick Tennyson, December 10, 1843, and December 8, 1844 (*Letters*, 1:408, 466).

pages 72–73:

"POOR BEDFORD LAD." "HE AND I WERE." To Stephen Spring Rice, December 24, 1859 (*Letters*, 2:351).

page 73:

"W. BROWNE IS TOO." To Mrs. E. B. Cowell, August 21, 1860 (*Letters*, 2:371).

"POOR OLD OMAR." "KIND OF CONSOLATION." To E. B. Cowell, April 27, [1859] (*Letters*, 2:334).

"YOU KNOW, MY FRIENDS." 1859 *Rubáiyát*, quatrain 40.

"LEARNING AND FAITH." Heron-Allen, *FitzGerald's Rubáiyát*, 87.

"REASON AND FAITH." Arberry, *Omar Khayyám*, verses 63, 69.

page 74:

PEN . . . WRITES "UNHALTINGLY." Heron-Allen, *FitzGerald's Rubáiyát*, 107.

"THE MOVING FINGER WRITES." 1859 *Rubáiyát*, quatrain 51.

"OH, THOU, WHO MAN." Ibid., quatrain 58.

"MAKING OMAR WORSE THAN." FitzGerald repeats the accusation in answering E. B. Cowell, December 17, [1867] (*Letters*, 3:68).

COWELL TOLD ALDIS WRIGHT. See "Note by the Editor" in the Golden Treasury *Rubáiyát*, 111.

pages 74–75:

"LITERALLY." "MASHED UP TWO." To E. B. Cowell, December 17, [1867] (*Letters*, 3:68).

page 75:

"*POTTER* TETRASTICHS." To E. B. Cowell, June 19, 1857 (*Letters*, 2:275).

IN ALL ANCIENT LITERATURE. See FitzGerald's notes for his final edition of the *Rubáiyát*, note to quatrain 87, p. 66.

"KÚZA-NÁMA." 1859 *Rubáiyát*, quatrains 59–66. For its translation, "Book of Pots," see *Letters*, 3:67n. In later editions, FitzGerald cut the inner title so as not to confuse readers.

"SORRY SCHEME OF THINGS." 1859 *Rubáiyát*, quatrain 73.

Aftermath

page 76:

"MY 'GO' (SUCH AS IT WAS)." To E. B. Cowell, September 3, 1858 (*Letters*, 2:318).

HE HAD DRUNK OF REAL CREATION. By 1859, FitzGerald was back to translations, first with two plays of Calderón and then with the *Agamemnon* of Aeschylus. They were, of course, free translations, and FitzGerald even told E. B. Cowell on November 13, [1863] (*Letters*, 3:110), that his version of the *Agamemnon* was more a "perversion," for he had found it hard to make the play live with any strict adherence to what was left of the text.

HAD GIVEN JOHN PARKER. To E. B. Cowell, September 3, 1858 (*Letters*, 2:318).

"LESS WICKED." "NO WICKEDNESS CAN." To W. H. Thompson, December 9, 1861 (*Letters*, 2:419).

ON JULY 10, 1861. The copy with its inscription is now in the Morgan Library. *Letters*, 2:417n.

WHEN FITZGERALD LEARNED OF IT. To E. B. Cowell, January 18, 18[72] (*Letters*, 3:320–21n).

page 77:

"OLD OMAR." "THE WORKS OF." To Bernard Quaritch, August 24, [1872] (*Letters*, 3:371).

READ ANYTHING "SO GLORIOUS." From John Ruskin, September 2, 1863 (*Letters*, 3:416). Burne-Jones's copy had been given to him by Swinburne (*Letters*, 3:414).

"WHY HE'S NO MORE REVEREND." *Letters*, 3:414.

"SUDDEN FIT OF FANCY." To Thomas Carlyle [April 15, 1873] (*Letters*, 3:417).

"PEACEABLE, AFFECTIONATE, AND." Thomas Carlyle to C. E. Norton, April 18, 1873 (*Letters*, 3:418).

"ANONYMOUS AUTHOR." "ALL THE MERIT." *Life*, 209.

BECAME "INTOXICATED," SHE SAID. This is a quote from a letter of Sarah Wister to Aldis Wright, May 22, 1905 (*Letters*, 3:257). Sarah Wister was a daughter of Fanny Kemble, FitzGerald's old friend, and on later visits to her mother in England, she tried to find out who the anonymous author was. At that time her mother did not know.

"BEAUTIES OF OMAR." Horace Howard Furness to Bernard Quaritch, November 21, 1870 (*Letters*, 3:253).

"THEY ARE A VERY ODD." To Mrs. E. B. Cowell [December 21, 1875] (*Letters*, 3:637). The oddness, for FitzGerald, lay in their fighting England but overrating (in his case, he thought) its authors.

page 78:

> FOUR LIFETIME EDITIONS. First edition: 75 quatrains, 250 copies, March 1859. Second edition: 110 quatrains, 200 copies, St. Valentine's Day 1868. Third edition: 101 quatrains, ? copies, August 23, 1872. Fourth edition: 101 quatrains, 1,000 copies, August 2, 1879. The third edition must have been considerably *over* 250 copies, for FitzGerald told Quaritch at the time that he hoped they had not overestimated their "transatlantic friends." (To Bernard Quaritch, August 24, [1872] [*Letters,* 3:371].)
>
> "LEAVE WELL ALONE." "MORE HARM THAN." To E. B. Cowell, December 2, 1867, and [November 1867] (*Letters,* 3:65, 60).
>
> "OF TOO MUCH IMPORTANCE." To E. B. Cowell, March 25, [1872] (*Letters,* 3:335).
>
> HE WOULD COMPROMISE. To Bernard Quaritch, March 31, [1872] (*Letters,* 3:338–39).
>
> "I ADMIRED IT." "YOU STOLE A BIT." Alfred Tennyson to Edward FitzGerald [late March 1872] (*Letters,* 3:337). Tennyson spells it "Gardner's."
>
> "RANKLES IN POOR ALFRED'S." To Mrs. Alfred Tennyson [late March 1872] (*Letters,* 3:338).
>
> "ONE MOMENT IN ANNIHILATION'S." 1859 *Rubáiyát,* quatrain 38.
>
> "SHORES OF NOTHING." "The Gardener's Daughter," lines 15–17. *Tennyson: Representative Poems,* ed. Samuel C. Chew (New York: Odyssey Press, 1941), 179.

pages 78–79:

> "CONFUSION." "MUCH FINER." Alfred Tennyson to Edward FitzGerald, April 11, 1872 (*Letters,* 3:345).

page 79:

> IN HIS "IMMORTAL WORK." To Mrs. Alfred Tennyson [December 1872] (*Letters,* 3:389).
>
> "A MOMENT'S HALT." Fourth edition: *Rubáiyát of Omar Khayyám of Naishápúr,* quatrain 48, Golden Treasury *Rubáiyát.*
>
> "AWAKE! FOR MORNING." 1859 *Rubáiyát,* quatrain 1.
>
> SIGNAL AMONG NOMADIC TRIBES. FitzGerald had become familiar with the practice from translating *Salámán and Absál* and liked its flavor of desert life. To E. B. Cowell, June 29, [1857] (*Letters,* 2:280–81).
>
> "WAKE! FOR THE SUN." Fourth edition *Rubáiyát,* quatrain 1.

page 80:

> "A LITTLE WAY / TO FLY." 1859 *Rubáiyát,* quatrain 7.
>
> "A LITTLE WAY / TO FLUTTER." Fourth edition *Rubáiyát,* quatrain 7.
>
> "IN FLOWING PURPLE." Ibid., quatrain 33.

"MASTER." "SECRET PRESENCE." "THEY CHANGE AND." Ibid., quatrains 50, 51.

"WHY, IF THE SOUL." Ibid., quatrain 44.

EXPUNGED FROM HIS FINAL. Heron-Allen, *FitzGerald's Rubáiyát*, xii. These three were in the first and second editions, and then suppressed.

"MOON OF MY DELIGHT." 1859 *Rubáiyát*, quatrain 74. Compare fourth edition *Rubáiyát*, quatrain 100.

"A BOOK OF VERSES." Fourth edition *Rubáiyát*, quatrain 7.

page 81:

"SAD" AND "GENTLE." These were FitzGerald's own words for his Epicureanism. See to Frederick Tennyson, December 8, 1844, and to W. M. Thackeray, November 15, 1852 (*Letters*, 1:466, 2:75).

"MOST INGENIOUSLY TESSELATED." To E. B. Cowell, November 2, 1858 (*Letters*, 2:323).

"IT BEING INDEED, QUITE." To Bernard Quaritch, December 18, 1875 (*Letters*, 3:634).

"THINGS TAKEN—I MUST NOT." The critic was Thomas Sergeant Perry, who reviewed for *The Nation* and *The Atlantic Monthly*. (To T. S. Perry, November 23, 1875 [*Letters*, 3:622].)

NO DIFFERENCE BETWEEN HIS OMAR. He saw no difference in the quality of his work, but he did know that Omar awakened greater interest. As he told T. S. Perry, "For his *subject* must interest all us poor mortal men, right or wrong." Ibid.

"AT ALL COST, A THING." To E. B. Cowell, April 27, [1859] (*Letters*, 2:335).

page 83:

COLERIDGE COULD NOT HAVE WRITTEN *THE RIME*. I had originally thought of including Coleridge's *Rime of the Ancient Mariner* as one of the works to be analyzed in this study. But the more I read into him the more I discovered that he had the kind of memory that rearranges the past perpetually according to his feelings at the moment. Thus he does not provide sufficiently trustworthy evidence for this kind of analysis. One of the very stimulating books I read on Coleridge was Norman Fruman's *Coleridge: The Damaged Archangel* (London: Allen & Unwin, 1972). Afterward I had a valuable exchange of ideas with Professor Fruman by letter. I was glad to learn that he had come in the years since writing his penetrating study to my own opinion (although on different grounds) that applying Freud's Oedipus complex to Coleridge is a mistake. Coleridge's real attachment was to his father, and his ambivalence was directed at his mother. As for Coleridge's problems in sexual identity, they are attested to frequently in the nightmares he recorded in his

diaries, and a number of scholars besides Fruman have been aware
of them.

E. M. FORSTER LOST HIS CREATIVE PUSH. Forster himself confessed himself
"balked as a novelist" as he struggled with *Passage to India* and Virginia
Woolf reported (on March 12, 1922) that Forster was depressed on
returning from India "without a novel, and with no power to write one."
Philip N. Furbank, *E. M. Forster: A Life*, 2 vols. (London: Secker &
Warburg, 1978), 2:105.

4. War and Mir

A Who's Who of names in Chapter 4 is in the Appendix.

page 85:

"THE LIFE HE KNOWS." Quoted in Aylmer Maude, *The Life of Tolstoy: First
Fifty Years* (London: Constable, 1908), 1:431. Hereafter, Maude, *Life
of Tolstoy*.

RECORDED IN A MASS OF MEMOIRS. Tolstoy said he had not "invented" the
speeches, but quoted them from materials that had accumulated to "form
a whole library." Ibid., 1:427.

BOTH OF WHOM HAD DIED. Tolstoy's maternal grandfather Nikolay Sergeye-
vich Volkonsky died on February 3, 1821. *Leo Tolstoy: His Life and
Work*, Autobiographical Memoirs, Letters, and Biographical Material
Compiled by Paul Birukoff and Revised by Leo Tolstoy, 2 vols. (Lon-
don: Heinemann, 1906), 1:12–13 (hereafter, Birukoff, *Leo Tolstoy*).
Tolstoy's paternal grandfather, Ilya Andreyevich Tolstoy, died in 1820.
Maude, *Life of Tolstoy*, 1:5.

NOT BEEN QUITE TWO YEARS OLD. Tolstoy was born on August 28, 1828
(Maude, *Life of Tolstoy*, 1:9). His mother died five months after his sister
Marya Nikolayevna Tolstoy was born on March 2, 1830. See Reginald
Frank Christian, *Tolstoy's Letters*, 2 vols. (London: Athlone Press,
1978), 1:53.

page 92:

"PAINFULLY TORN FROM MY INSIDE." Letter to A. A. Fet, May 10, 1869
(Christian, *Tolstoy's Letters*, 1:221).

"THE REMAINS OF AN ORGY." Letter to A. A. Tolstaya, beginning of
February 1873 (ibid., 1:257).

Rostovs and Tolstoys

SEE INSTANTLY THE CAREFREE PRODIGALITY. In an early draft of the book,
Tolstoy called the Count "Prostoy," which in Russian means "simple."

Reginald Frank Christian, *Tolstoy's "War and Peace": A Study* (Oxford: Clarendon Press, 1962), 84. Tolstoy saw his Tolstoy grandfather as "simple" in the best sense of the word, describing him as "a man of limited intelligence, gentle in manner, merry, and not only generous, but carelessly extravagant, and above all trustful." Birukoff, *Leo Tolstoy,* 1:6.

NO ONE WAS MORE INFLUENTIAL. It was Auntie Tatyana Ergolskaya who first suggested to Tolstoy that he ought to write and who first interested him in history. See his letters to her of November 12, 1851, and May 30–June 3, 1852 (Christian, *Tolstoy's Letters,* 1:23, 26).

"WITH HER CRISP BLACK CURLING HAIR." Birukoff, *Leo Tolstoy,* 1:41. I have changed the British translation "plait" to "braid."

page 93:

"SHORT, STOUT, BLACK-HAIRED." "I SIMPLY LOVED." Maude, *Life of Tolstoy,* 1:13; Birukoff, *Leo Tolstoy,* 1:41.

"CARESSINGLY TOUCHED ME." "PASSIONATELY TENDER LOVE." Birukoff, *Leo Tolstoy,* 1:41.

"THE SPIRITUAL DELIGHT OF LOVE." "HER WHOLE BEING." Ibid., 1:43.

"THE TWO PEOPLE I LOVE." Letter to T. A. Ergolskaya, January 6, 1852 (Christian, *Tolstoy's Letters,* 1:20). Christian transcribes her name as "Yergolskaya."

"I LIVED WITH HER ALL." Letter to A. A. Tolstaya, June 23, 1874 (ibid., 1:271).

THE DAGUERREOTYPES OF TANYA. Tolstoy asked Mikhail Sergeyevich Bashilov, "Can't you model Natasha on Tanichka Behrs?" Letter to Bashilov, December 8, 1866 (ibid., 1:209).

TANYA HERSELF WROTE RECOLLECTIONS. When, late in life, Tanya wrote her reminiscences (T. A. Kuzminsky, *Tolstoy as I Knew Him*), she saw herself so much as Natasha that she seems to have recollected as part of her life episodes that took place only in the novel. She believed that she had been the victim of a decision like that of old Prince Bolkonsky—in her case made by Tolstoy—that she must not be married to Sergey Tolstoy for a year. Christian, *Tolstoy's "War and Peace,"* 622. But Tolstoy believed in no delays. He proposed to Sonya on September 16, 1862, and set the marriage for September 23, only a week later. In the novel, he shows the delay as destructive. Also, Tanya believed Natasha's seduction by Anatole Kuragin was modeled on a flirtation of her early years with a young man named Anatole Shostak. Cynthia Asquith, *Married to Tolstoy* (London: Hutchinson, 1960), 61.

TOLSTOY'S OLDEST SISTER-IN-LAW, "LIZA." In one plan for the novel, Tolstoy actually called the Vera-character "Lisa" (Christian, *Tolstoy's "War and Peace,"* 1:85; Christian is citing a Soviet article by E. E. Zaidenshnur). Vera is a composite character, for she is given a penchant for saying exactly what will be most disagreeable to her listeners. Tolstoy thought Liza dull, virtuous, and cold, but not at all malicious.

HER OWN GIRLISH COMRADERIE. Tanya Behrs said only that some aspects of the Countess Rostova recalled her mother (ibid., 1:84). Probably only the affectionate intimacy was similar, and the rest of the character is Tolstoy's grandmother, a much older and more unbending woman. Lyubov Behrs had been married at sixteen, and so she could be girlish with her daughters.

EVEN THE YOUTHFUL PETYA ROSTOV. Petya is mentioned more often than the other brothers in Tolstoy's letters.

page 94:

"GIRLS, I'M GOING TO TELL YOU." Christian, *Tolstoy's "War and Peace,"* 84.

SIX ILLEGITIMATE CHILDREN CALLED "ISLAVIN." In Russia it was illegal to call illegitimate children by their father's family name. In this case, their mother was a noblewoman, but she had been unhappily married earlier and could not marry Islenyev until well after her children had been born when her husband finally died.

A PUSH FROM A TERRACE. S. A. Behrs, Sofya Tolstaya's younger brother said in his *Reminiscences of L. N. Tolstoy* that his mother would tell Lev, laughing, "Evidently you pushed me off the terrace in my childhood that you might marry my daughter afterwards." Birukoff, *Leo Tolstoy,* 1:76.

"WHAT DELIGHTFUL, MERRY LITTLE GIRLS." I have put together this translation from two others, selecting the "merry" from Maude (*Life of Tolstoy,* 1:149) and "delightful" from Anne Edwards (*Sonya: The Life of Countess Tolstoy* [London: Hodder & Stoughton, 1981], 466n).

page 95:

HE MARRIED THE OLDER GIRL. Right after marriage, he wrote A. A. Tolstaya on September 28, 1862, "I've lived to the age of thirty-four and I didn't know it was possible to be so much in love and so happy" (Christian, *Tolstoy's Letters,* 1:169).

"PRETTY HALF-GROWN KITTEN." Leo Tolstoy, *War and Peace,* trans. Louise and Aylmer Maude, ed. George Gibian (New York: Norton Critical Edition, 1966), 41. Hereafter, *War and Peace,* trans. Maude.

"AS A KITTEN SHOULD." Ibid., 70.

"MELTING" DARK EYES. Leo Tolstoy, *War and Peace,* trans. Ann Dunnigan (New York: Signet Classic, 1968), 71. In this case, Maude's translation has "with a tender look in her eyes" (41). In some passages Maude's translation seems better, and in others Dunnigan's. Best of all, of course, would be Tolstoy's Russian. Hereafter, *War and Peace,* trans. Dunnigan.

"BLACK" BEHRS. "WHITE" BEHRS. Letter to Sofya Tolstaya, December 7, 1864 (Christian, *Tolstoy's Letters,* 1:90).

"L[IZA] B[EHRS] TEMPTS ME." Edwards, *Sonya: The Life of Countess Tolstoy*, 52.

INDIFFERENT TO "INTELLECTUAL INTERESTS." Letter to Sofya Tolstaya, December 7, 1864 (Christian, *Tolstoy's Letters*, 1:90).

"THEY CAN, BUT THEY DON'T." Ibid.

"I THINK NOT, AND YET—YES." *War and Peace*, trans. Dunnigan, 662. Maude (606) has "She does not deign to be clever."

page 96:

"MY JEALOUSY BROKE OUT." Asquith, *Married to Tolstoy*, 51.

"I BELIEVE I SHALL KILL." Henri Troyat, *Tolstoy*, trans. Nancy Amphoux (London: Allen, 1968), 258.

"WHOLE LIFE, HIS THOUGHTS." Asquith, *Married to Tolstoy*, 51.

"PASSIONATELY ANGRY LOOK." "TORTURE ME AND." *War and Peace*, trans. Dunnigan, 72, 74.

ONE NEW YEAR. Birukoff, *Leo Tolstoy*, 1:50. In Russia, Christmas is purely a religious holiday. Masquerades and gifts are for celebrating the New Year.

"JOYFUL POETIC PERIOD OF CHILDHOOD." So Tolstoy spoke of it in his "Reminiscences" (Birukoff, *Leo Tolstoy*, 1:xxiv).

"HOW CHARMING LITTLE GIRLS ARE." "PURE POETRY." "FEEDING THEM." Letter to A. A. Tolstaya, January 18–23, 1865 (Christian, *Tolstoy's Letters*, 1:192).

"WONDERFULLY SWEET NATURE." Letter to Tatyana Behrs, October 1?, 1862 (ibid., 1:170).

"YOUR SWEET, WILD, ENERGETIC NATURE." Letter to Tatyana Behrs, January 1–3, 1864 (ibid., 1:183).

"LITTLE VOLCANO." *War and Peace*, trans. Maude, 43. Dunnigan (73) has "a little spitfire," which is more idiomatic but trails connotations of ill-temper that are not appropriate to Natasha.

CALLS HER THE "COSSACK." *War and Peace*, trans. Maude, 63.

"RINGING FIT OF LAUGHTER." Ibid., 40.

pages 96–97:

"BRIGHT AND HAPPY LIFE." "WHAT IS SHE." *War and Peace*, trans. Maude, 460.

page 97:

"STRIKINGLY POETIC, CHARMING GIRL." Ibid., 511.

"BRIMMING OVER WITH MYSTIC FORCES." Ibid., 858.

"FRANKNESS OF SOUL." "INNER, SPIRITUAL FORCE." Ibid., 867.

HOW "RESOLUTE" SHE WAS. Birukoff, *Leo Tolstoy*, 1:41.

"I WILL DO IT." "YOU WILL NOT." Ibid., 1:40.

"THE SCAR OF A BURN." Ibid.

"I BURNED MY ARM." *War and Peace*, trans. Maude, 323.

"STALLION" OF A MAN. In a letter to Mikhail Sergeyevich Bashilov, April 4, 1866, Tolstoy asked him to make the character Anatole Kuragin "bigger and also fuller-chested," because he would "play in future the important role of a handsome, sensuous, and coarse stallion." Christian, *Tolstoy's Letters*, 1:204.

"HANDSOME APPEARANCE, HIS SINGING." Maude, *Life of Tolstoy*, 1:20.

SAW HIMSELF AS UGLY. Tolstoy would tear himself apart in his diary as "ugly, awkward, uncleanly," as well as "rude, intolerant, and as bashful as a child." Birukoff, *Leo Tolstoy*, 1:170.

"ALTOGETHER HIMSELF, HANDSOME." Ibid., 1:54.

page 98:

HER EXTRAORDINARY CONTRALTO VOICE. A. A. Fet spoke in his *Reminiscences* of Tanya Behrs's "beautiful contralto voice" (ibid., 1:357). References to Tanya's singing appear throughout Tolstoy's letters.

BACK IN 1851, SERGEY HAD CONTRACTED. In a letter to Sergey Nikolayevich Tolstoy, December 23, 1851, Lev tells him of their sister Masha's kindly reaction to his liaison, so it appears to have been just under way at that time. Christian, *Tolstoy's Letters*, 1:15.

"TANYA, MY DEAR FRIEND." Letter to Tatyana Behrs, March 20–April 3, 1863 (ibid., 1:176).

"MANY FRIENDS WHO LOVE YOU." "CONTROL OF YOURSELF." Letter to Tatyana Behrs, January 1–3, 1864 (ibid., 1:183).

"IT WILL BE NO." Ibid., 184.

SHE SWALLOWED A POISONOUS. Edwards, *Sonya: The Life of Countess Tolstoy*, 139.

"TANYA CRIES DAY AFTER DAY." "AFTER ALL THE COMMOTION." Letter to Sofya Tolstaya, November 27, 1864 (Christian, *Tolstoy's Letters*, 1:186–87).

page 99:

"SASHA," ALEXANDER KUZMINSKY. Tanya Behrs married him in 1867 when she was twenty-one years old. Ibid., 1:169.

"NOW, THIS MINUTE!" *War and Peace*, trans. Maude, 570.

"WHERE AM I TO GO?" Ibid., 571.

"SOBBING SO VIOLENTLY." Ibid., 576.

"TANYA ASSURED US THAT." Letter to Sofya Tolstaya, December 7, 1864 (Christian, *Tolstoy's Letters*, 1:189).

"I HATE YOU." *War and Peace*, trans. Maude, 641.

"ENEMY IS THE TWENTY EXTRA." Letter to Tatyana Behrs, January 1–3, 1864 (Christian, *Tolstoy's Letters*, 1:183).

Bolkonskys and Volkonskys

page 100:

SEEN SO MUCH AS A PICTURE. NO RECOLLECTION. So Tolstoy himself said, Birukoff, *Leo Tolstoy,* 1:17.

"SO ELEVATED, PURE, AND." Ibid., 1:21.

HE SAID, WAS "BEAUTIFUL." Ibid., 1:17.

"CRAZY IVANUSHKA." The male disguise would have been adopted to protect her chastity.

MARYA GERASSIMOVA STAYED. Ibid., 1:63.

SHOT HER POINT BLANK. While Aunt Aline was recovering from the shot, her husband—still at large—asked to see her tongue, took hold of it, and attempted to cut it out, thus convincing everyone of his lunacy. Maude, *Life of Tolstoy,* 1:29.

"SHE NEVER HAD ANY MONEY." Ibid.

page 101:

LONG CONVERSATIONS WITH PILGRIMS. A letter of N. N. Strakov to Danilevsky, June 1878, says that Lev Tolstoy at Yasnaya Polyana "walks to the high road (a quarter of a mile from his house), and there at once finds men and women pilgrims. With them he starts conversation, and if he chances upon good specimens and is himself in good form, he hears wonderful tales." Maude, *Life of Tolstoy,* 2:8.

TOLSTOY ERASES THE "CRAZY." *War and Peace,* trans. Maude, 424.

PRINCESS VARVARA ALEXANDROVNA VOLKONSKAYA. "DEAR OLD LADY." Birukoff, *Leo Tolstoy,* 1:14–15, 246.

SEVERAL WEEKS AT HER ESTATE. Maude, *Life of Tolstoy,* 1:174, places the visit in January 1858.

"ONE OF THE PURE, BRIGHT." Birukoff, *Leo Tolstoy,* 1:15.

SIMPLICITY AND HONESTY. Tolstoy speaks of the "truthfulness and simple tone" of his mother's expressions, compared with the "inflated" language of her contemporaries. Ibid., 1:19.

WHICH ENDED IN DISILLUSIONMENT. Tolstoy printed one of his mother's letters telling of two girls living with her in whom she says she sees as in a mirror "the exalted and romantic friendship which had animated and troubled my life during several years." The letter has no date, but in it she speaks of her "ripe years," so it probably dates from after her marriage. Tolstoy speaks of having "several of her letters to my father and aunts." Birukoff, *Leo Tolstoy,* 1:18, 20.

pages 101–2:

TO REFRAIN FROM PASSING JUDGMENT. Tolstoy says in his "Reminiscences" that his mother and brother "never condemned anyone." Ibid., 1:18.

page 102:

STORY SIMILAR TO HIS MOTHER'S. Two disparate sources put together make
it clear that the Princess Bolkonsky's shocking experience of losing her
suitor Anatole to Mlle. Bourienne came of a similar experience of his
mother with Mlle. Enissienne. In his "Reminiscences," telling of the
"passionate friendship," Tolstoy says it was "terminated by a disillusionment. Mlle. Enissienne married a cousin of my mother's, Prince Mikhail
Volkonsky, the grandfather of the present-day writer of that name."
Birukoff, *Leo Tolstoy*, 1:20.

In A. N. Wilson, *Tolstoy* (London: Penguin, 1989), 14, the author
reports from material in the Russian biographical study of Tolstoy by N.
N. Gusev that when Tolstoy's mother was left a spinster of thirty-one at
her father's death, she suggested to the family, apropos of the inheritance, that "she might marry a cousin, Prince Mikhail Alexandrovich
Volkonsky." Wilson continues: "Nothing came of this idea. Prince
Mikhail got married to someone else in Moscow that April, and Princess
Marya attended the ceremony. There she met a less eligible bachelor,
Prince Nikolay Ilyich Tolstoy, five years her junior, and the two families
immediately entered into discussions with their lawyers." From this it
seems likely that Prince Mikhail Volkonsky came as a suitor to Tolstoy's
mother, saw and preferred her companion Mlle. Enissienne, and, not
being in need of the Volkonsky money, married the woman of his choice.
Tolstoy appears to have been working with the truth in this episode.

GAVE THE PRINCESS A BROTHER. Most biographers recognize Tolstoy's
mother in Princess Marya, but none recognizes his sister. As a result,
one of them (A. N. Wilson, *Tolstoy*, 22) jumps to the Freudian conclusion
that out of "classical" Oedipus rivalry Tolstoy has turned his parents
into brother and sister to remove his mother from his father's bed. To
arrive at this interpretation, Wilson has to assume, erroneously, that
Prince Andrey is modeled on Tolstoy's father. Tolstoy himself made it
very clear that it was Nikolay Rostov who was modeled on his father.

"SMALL." "RICKETS HER LEGS ARE STILL CROOKED." Lev Tolstoy, *Childhood—Boyhood—Youth* (Moscow: Foreign Language Publishing House,
n.d.), *Boyhood*, 204–5.

"BEGUN TO WEAR DRESSES." *Youth*, ibid., 236.

"TEARFUL LYUBOCHKA." "HER CROOKED LEGS." Ibid., 393.

"THAT'S WHAT THE PIGEON-TOED." Letter to Sergey Nikolayevich Tolstoy,
December 23, 1851 (Christian, *Tolstoy's Letters*, 1:15).

"BAD." "LOCAL ASSEMBLY ROOMS." "I CAN'T HELP." Letter to Sergey
Nikolayevich Tolstoy, July 20, 1853 (ibid., 1:37).

page 103:

"THIN FACE AND WEAK, UNCOMELY BODY." *War and Peace*, trans. Dunnigan,
127. Maude (94) has a "weak, ungraceful figure," which conflicts with

the fact that the Princess Bolkonsky is sometimes both graceful and dignified.

"LARGE, DEEP AND LUMINOUS." "SO BEAUTIFUL THAT." *War and Peace*, trans. Maude, 94–95.

"SAME CRYBABY AS EVER." "THROUGH HER TEARS." Ibid., 100.

"LARGE MOIST EYES." David Magarshack. *Turgenev: A Life* (London: Faber & Faber, 1954), 152. Russian specialists prefer the spelling "Magarshak," but English-language publishers have decided that "Magarshack" seems more natural to English speakers.

RESPECTED THE RELIGIOUS FEELING. Tolstoy said of "the poor simple unlettered folk" that, whatever their superstitions, they were "at least a necessary part of their lives" and that these people had "a real faith." Maude, *Life of Tolstoy*, 1:407.

ENTERED A CONVENT. Marya Nikolayevna Tolstaya became a nun in the Convent of Shamordin founded by Father Ambrose very close to the Optina Monastery. Maude, *Life of Tolstoy*, 2:411. There are pictures of her in her black habit with her brother Lev at Yasnaya Polyana in Wilson's *Tolstoy*, one between pages 290 and 291 and the other between pages 386 and 387.

"SICKLY." "UNATTRACTIVE MARTYRLIKE EXPRESSION." *War and Peace*, trans. Maude, 94, 236.

"MASHA, WHO IS WONDERFULLY." Entry of June 20, 1852, *The Diaries of Leo Tolstoy 1847–1852*, trans. C. J. Hogarth and A. Sirnis (London: Dent, 1917), 173. This quotation is not in *Tolstoy's Diaries*, ed. and trans. Reginald Frank Christian, 2 vols. (London: Athlone Press, 1985). All editions of the diaries are selections, so they do not have the same entries.

page 104:

"AN ENCHANTING WOMAN." Leonard Schapiro, *Turgenev: His Life and Times* (Oxford: Oxford University Press, 1978), 111.

"ONE OF THE MOST ATTRACTIVE." Letter to P. V. Annenkov, November 1, 1854 (Magarshack, *Turgenev*, 152–53).

AND THE "TURGENEVO PRIEST." BEING "25 VERSTS." Letter to N. A. Nekrasov, November 10, 1854 (October 29, 1854), *Turgenev Letters*, ed. and trans. David Lowe, 2 vols. (Ann Arbor, Mich.: Ardis, 1983), 1:82.

YASNAYA POLYANA, ONLY 10 VERSTS. So Turgenev said in a letter to I. F. Minitsky, May 12, 1853, reporting that *Childhood* was by "a certain Count L. N. Tolstoy—he lives 10 versts from Turgenevo—but he's in the Caucasus now" (ibid., 1:74).

SOLD THE BEAUTIFUL MANSION. In a letter to his Aunt Tatyana Ergolskaya, October 17–18, 1854, Tolstoy sends thanks to Valerian for selling the house. A note tells us that the main building was sold for 5,000 paper rubles (then worth only about 3,000 in metal) to be dismantled and reerected elsewhere. Christian, *Tolstoy's Letters*, 1:43.

AT POKROVSKOYE, TURGENEV HUNTED. Schapiro, *Turgenev*, 111.

"IF NOT EVERYTHING, THEN ALMOST." Magarshack, *Turgenev*, 31. That it would have taken Turgenev so many months to discover that Masha's hands were not beautiful makes one wonder if he was using this defect for less mentionable ones. But he may have meant what he said, for Pauline Viardot had very beautiful hands, and Turgenev himself had "beautiful hands, des mains soignées, large manly hands," according to Constantine Leontiev, quoted in Nicolas Berdyaev, *Leontiev* (London: Centenary Press, 1940), 18.

"PAINTING THE TOWN RED." Letter to A. A. Fet, December 1855 (Magarshack, *Turgenev*, 155).

page 105:
"YOU HAVE QUITE A BROTHER." Letter to M. N. and V. P. Tolstoy, December 8/20, 1855 (*Turgenev Letters*, ed. Lowe, 1:100).

"INFURIATED EVERYONE." Letter of Turgenev to V. P. Botkin, February 8, 1856 (ibid., 1:102).

"TIED TO THE HANGMAN'S CART." D. V. Gregorovich reported in *Literary Reminiscences* that this is what Tolstoy said at the dinner. Birukoff, *Leo Tolstoy*, 1:199.

ACTUALLY TOLSTOY HAD ADMIRED. In his diary entry of August 27, 1854, Tolstoy says he has been reading "an admirable novel by George Sand." *The Private Diary of Leo Tolstoy 1853–1857*, trans. Louise Maude and Aylmer Maude (London: Heinemann, 1927), 98.

"MORE COMFORTABLE TO KEEP." Letter to L. N. Tolstoy, November 16/18, 1856 (*Turgenev Letters*, ed. Lowe, 1:114).

"SAD AND HAS LOST WEIGHT." Letter to D. Ya. Kolbasin, May 21 / June 2, 1856 (ibid., 1:104).

"ILL ALL THE TIME." Letter to L. N. Tolstoy, November 16/18, 1856 (ibid., 1:114).

"COUNT IS FLOURISHING." Letter to D. Ya. Kolbasin, May 21 / June 2, 1856 (ibid., 1:104).

"I WAS STILL DREAMING." Letter to M. N. Tolstaya, January 6, 1857 (new style) (ibid., 1:118).

A TURN FOR THE "BETTER." Both Druzhinin and Botkin reported to Turgenev an almost incredible change in Tolstoy. Magarshack, *Turgenev*, 170.

"BLISSFUL POETIC TEARS." "INTOXICATED BY THE." Entry of January 4, 1857, *The Private Diary of Leo Tolstoy 1853–1857*, trans. Maude, 192.

page 106:
"FREE OF YOUR OWN VIEWS." Letter to L. N. Tolstoy, January 3/15, 1857 (*Turgenev Letters*, ed. Lowe, 1:121).

MUCH BETTER, MUCH "SMARTER." Letter to V. P. Botkin, February 17 / March 1, 1857 (ibid., 1:124). A. N. Wilson (*Tolstoy*, 145) says that in the spring of 1857 "Nekrasov and Turgenev took Tolstoy to Paris," citing N. N. Gusev as his source. A glance at Turgenev's letters makes it clear that Turgenev had been in Paris all winter, and Tolstoy arrived there about February 10.

HE HAD ONCE FIERCELY REJECTED. According to G. P. Danilevsky (*Historical Review*, March 1886, 529), during the winter of 1855 he met Tolstoy at the house of a woman who was reading aloud a new work of Herzen. At first shyly, then "boldly and hotly," Tolstoy attacked Herzen with such effect that the family dropped Herzen at once. Birukoff, *Leo Tolstoy*, 1:199–200.

"VERY HAPPY AND HE ASKS ME." Letter to A. I. Herzen, February 21 / March 5, 1857 (*Turgenev Letters*, ed. Lowe, 1:126). *N.B.*, for "Nota Bene," was much used in the nineteenth century.

"VAIN AND SHALLOW." "KIND AND TERRIBLY WEAK." "BELIEVE IN ANYTHING." "NICE, BUT HE IS SIMPLY TIRED." Entries of February 17, 24, 25, and 27, 1857, *The Private Diary of Leo Tolstoy 1853–1857*, trans. Maude, 199, 201, 202.

"I AM VERY FOND." Entry of April 8, 1857 (ibid., 207).

"SENIOR SULTANA IN HIS HAREM." Christian, *Tolstoy's Letters*, 1:53.

REPORTING TO V. P. BOTKIN. In a letter to V. P. Botkin, July 17/29, 1857, Turgenev tells him that Tolstoy had asked him to send 500 francs, but Turgenev went to Tolstoy instead, in hopes of getting him to go on with him to Fecamp. In a second letter to Botkin, July 23 / August 4, 1857, Turgenev gives the details of Tolstoy's condition and of the letter he received from his sister Masha. *Turgenev Letters*, ed. Lowe, 1:133–34.

page 107:

"MASHA TOLD US ABOUT TURGENEV." *The Private Diary of Leo Tolstoy 1853–1857*, trans. Maude, 238.

"EGOTISTIC, SPOILT, AND NARROW." Entry of September 2, 1857 (ibid., 243).

"TO GET ON WITH MASHENKA." Entry of October 12, 1857 (ibid., 248).

"TURGENEV IS BEHAVING BADLY." Entry of September 4, 1858 (Schapiro, *Turgenev*, 144). Christian, Tolstoy's Diaries, translates "The pig" as "He's a bad lot."

MASHA WAS CONSUMPTIVE. In an entry of November 10, 1857, Tolstoy speaks of a dinner at Fet's where they had a "sad conversation about Mashenka's consumption" (*The Private Diary of Leo Tolstoy 1853–1857*, trans. Maude, 251).

HER HUSBAND VALERIAN, WHO DIED. Troyat, *Tolstoy*, 282.

"DIGNITY AND GRACE." *War and Peace*, trans. Maude, 1053.

SENSE OF HIMSELF AS UGLY. In a diary entry of July 7, 1854, Tolstoy says: "I am ugly, awkward, untidy, and socially uneducated." *The Private Diary of Leo Tolstoy 1853–1857*, trans. Maude, 82.

page 108:

DMITRY HAD SUCCUMBED FIRST. In his diary for January 9 and 10, 1856, Tolstoy writes: "My brother Dmitry is dying." It has been thought that when Tolstoy adds "Masha and Tatyana Alexandrovna are nursing him" he meant Auntie Tatyana and the prostitute Masha with whom Dmitry had been living. But Tolstoy must have meant his sister Masha here, because he goes on to say, "I again dislike Valerian." Valerian would not have been there without his wife. Ibid., 142.

The prostitute Masha was also there and had been nursing him before his family arrived, for in his "Reminiscences" Tolstoy recalled: "Poor pock-marked Masha, whom he had rescued, wearing a kerchief round her head, was with him and nursed him." Birukoff, *Leo Tolstoy,* 1:212.

LEV HIMSELF HAD NIGHTMARES. In an entry of his diary on August 24, 1860, Tolstoy wrote: "Feared all day for my chest." Christian, *Tolstoy's Diaries,* 1:158.

"NIKOLENKA'S DEATH IS THE MOST." Derrick Leon, *Tolstoy: His Life and Work* (London: Routledge, 1944), 95. See also Christian, *Tolstoy's Diaries,* 1:158.

"THE KEY POINT OF THE WHOLE." In a letter to P. I. Bartenev, November 1, 1867, to whom he was sending the proofs, Tolstoy tells him he has just finished the end of the third volume, which had been very difficult, being "the key point of the whole novel." This part presents the story of Natasha's infatuation with Anatole Kuragin. Christian, *Tolstoy's Letters,* 1:216.

Prince Andrey

page 109:

"PRINCE ANDREY HAS DECIDED." Christian, *Tolstoy's "War and Peace,"* 80.

"A BRILLIANT YOUNG MAN." Letter of May 3, 1865 (Christian, *Tolstoy's Letters,* 1:194). In this same letter, Tolstoy says: "I began my novel with the Battle of Austerlitz," which, having been placed ahead, would now be "described later" in the book.

"TOOK PITY ON HIM." Ibid.

"VERY HANDSOME YOUNG MAN." *War and Peace,* trans. Maude, 14.

"TOO TALL." "TOO BIG AND COARSE." Letter to M. S. Bashilov, December 8, 1866 (Christian, *Tolstoy's Letters,* 1:208).

"A CLEVER AND TALENTED." So Tolstoy said of him. Birukoff, *Leo Tolstoy,* 1:19.

"THAT LITTLE OFFICER WHO GIVES." *War and Peace,* trans. Maude, 24.

"A KIND OF INTELLECTUAL PRIDE." Ibid., 109.

"ONLY PRAISES OF MY GRANDFATHER'S." Birukoff, *Leo Tolstoy*, 1:13.

RESEMBLANCE OF THE WIFE. Christian, *Tolstoy's Letters*, 1:194.

"ANDREY BOLKONSKY IS NOBODY." Letter to Louisa Ivanovna Volkonskaya, May 3, 1865 (ibid., 1:194).

page 110:

"MORE SUPERCILIOUSLY LANGUID." Letter to Mikhail Sergeyevich Bashilov, April 4, 1866 (ibid., 1:203).

"I DISLIKE ALL THE MORE." Letter to A. A. Fet, Janaury 23, 1865 (ibid., 1:193).

"TEDIOUS, MONOTONOUS, MERELY UN HOMME." Letter to A. A. Fet, November 7, 1866 (ibid., 1:208).

"COLD, FLEXIBLE, AND TRAINED." Entry of May 23, 1856, *The Private Diary of Leo Tolstoy 1853–1857*, trans. Maude, 153.

"A PERSON OF INDEPENDENT MIND." "I HAVE LOVED." Letter to Yury Fyodorovich Samarin, January 10, 1867 (Christian, *Tolstoy's Letters*, 1:210).

"IDIOTS." "LACKEYS." So Prince Andrey speaks of being confined to St. Petersburg drawing rooms "side by side with a court lackey and an idiot!" *War and Peace*, trans. Maude, 28.

"YOU ARE CLOSER TO ME." Letter to Yury Fyodorovich Samarin, January 10, 1867 (Christian, *Tolstoy's Letters*, 1:210).

"WHAT CRITICISMS, JUDGMENTS, OR." Letter to Nikolay Strakhov, May 5, 1875, ibid., 1:279–80.

page 111:

"ANY KIND OF EMOTION SEEMED FALSE." From a quote of Turgenev in E. Garshin's reminiscences, Birukoff, *Leo Tolstoy*, 1:200.

AT THE TIME OF THEIR GREAT QUARREL. It came on June 25, 1861. Christian, *Tolstoy's Diaries*, 1:162.

TOLSTOY'S "PENETRATING GLANCE." "WITH TWO OR THREE." "TO THE VERGE." Ibid.

"HANDLING DIRTY, STINKING RAGS." This is a quote from A. A. Fet's reminiscences (ibid., 1:300). Birukoff's translation is "a richly dressed girl who manipulates dirty ill-smelling rags." *Leo Tolstoy*, 1:300.

"BEHAVED DISGUSTINGLY AFTER DINNER." "I SAID UNPLEASANT." Entries of April 21 and May 5, 1856, *The Private Diary of Leo Tolstoy 1853–1857*, trans. Maude, 146–47.

"AS LOVERS OF MUSIC DO." *War and Peace*, trans. Maude, 100.

TURNS TO HER, "COLDLY IRONIC." Ibid., 114.

"WITH VENOMOUS IRONY." "SO AS NOT TO LAY WASTE." Ibid., 861.

"DISAGREEABLE IRONICAL TONE." "LIKE A STORM." HE "FELL OFF HIS HORSE." Ibid., 260.

"SMALL AND FRAIL." "OF ALL THE MEN." Ibid., 261–62.

page 112:
    READING STENDHAL'S *CHARTERHOUSE OF PARMA*. Tolstoy spoke of Stend-
hal's teaching him "to understand war" in an interview with Professor
Boyer from Paris in the spring of 1901. Birukoff, *Leo Tolstoy*, 1:195.
    COMMANDER CANNOT POSSIBLY KNOW. The commander at the battle of
Schön Grabern is not named, but merely described as "old" and "feeble-
looking." Tolstoy says, "He did not himself know what had happened
during that half-hour." *War and Peace*, trans. Maude, 195.
    "BY NECESSITY, BY ACCIDENT." Ibid., 193.
    "FOR FOUR DAYS AT A TIME." From a letter of Tolstoy to his brother, May
1855 (Maude, *Life of Tolstoy*, 1:110).
    "ACTION OF THAT BATTERY." *War and Peace*, trans. Maude, 212.

page 113:
    KORENITSKY, HAD BEEN BROUGHT. Birukoff, *Leo Tolstoy*, 1:216.
    TOLSTOY HAD ENOUGH INFLUENCE. The Emperor Alexander II had read
Tolstoy's "Sevastopol in December" in the *Contemporary* magazine
and had been profoundly moved by it. Birukoff, *Leo Tolstoy*, 1:179.
Tolstoy wrote in his diary about his sudden prestige at court: "Have
reached a period of real temptation through vanity. I could gain much
in life if I wished to write without conviction." Ernest J. Simmons,
Introduction to Tolstoy's Writings (Chicago: University of Chicago
Press, 1968), 22.
    Tolstoy did not succumb to the temptation. His next part, "Sevastopol
in May" made the horror of that war—the truth of it—too terrible for
the censors to allow, although it had to be published as the Emperor
Alexander was looking forward to it, and so they virtually rewrote it.
One of the editors, Panayev, was so "horror struck" when he saw their
changes that he tried to withdraw the article, but the censors declared
that it *must* appear. The co-editor, Nekrasov, wrote Tolstoy: "The
shocking state to which your article was brought turned my last drop of
blood" (Birukoff, *Leo Tolstoy*, 1:180–81). Tolstoy's indignation at this
censor's trick of erasing the truth of the appalling plight of Russia's army
with its obsolete weapons is shown in his ironic opening of an early draft
of the novel he planned, "The Decembrists," talking of the time when
"the victorious Russian army was returning from Sevastopol which it
had surrendered to the enemy" and "Russia was celebrating the destruction" of its Black Sea fleet. Christian, *Tolstoy's "War and Peace,"* 3. It
was the success of his Sevastopol descriptions at court, even censored
into lies, that gave Tolstoy his influence in defending Korenitsky.

"MORE POWER THAN OTHERS." From a quote of Tolstoy's "How I Came to Believe," Birukoff, *Leo Tolstoy*, 1:104.

MIGHT EASILY "CHOOSE THE FORMER." Entry of July 7, 1854, *The Private Diary of Leo Tolstoy 1853–1857*, trans. Maude, 82.

"TOULON." "BRIDGE OF ARCOLA." *War and Peace*, trans. Maude, 293–94.

"THOSE DEAREST TO ME." "MOMENT OF GLORY." Ibid., 284.

"SHOUTING AND FIGHTING." Ibid., 301.

"YES! ALL IS VANITY." Ibid., 301–2.

"BEYOND THE OUTLINE." "ALL-ABSORBING DEATH." Maude, *Life of Tolstoy*, 2:74–75.

pages 113–14:

AT ALEXANDER I'S ORDER. According to the ukase of Alexander I, the name of the family that had so "gloriously served" Russia was thus "never to be obliterated." Birukoff, *Leo Tolstoy*, 1:16.

page 114:

TOLSTOY'S COUSIN HAD REPLIED. Tolstoy found this account, taken from a letter of Prince Repnín to Mikhailovsky-Danilevsky, in Mikhailovsky-Danilevsky's history of 1805. Ibid., 1:16.

"THE PRAISE OF A GREAT COMMANDER." *War and Peace*, trans. Maude, 313.

"SO MEAN." "HIS PALTRY VANITY." "LOFTY, EQUITABLE." Ibid., 314.

Decembrists

THE 121 DECEMBRISTS. Makhail Zetlin, *The Decembrists*, trans. George Panin (New York: International Universities Press, 1958), 341. Tolstoy gave the date 1856 for his first idea of "The Decembrists" in his unpublished "Foreword" to the first thirty-eight chapters of "1805" (the first published title of *War and Peace*). Reginald Frank Christian, *Tolstoy: A Critical Introduction* (Cambridge: Cambridge University Press, 1969), 100.

WHEN HIS SON REACHED HIM. The Emperor Alexander II sent the young prince the decree of liberation by special messenger. Zetlin, *The Decembrists*, 341.

SERGEY VOLKONSKY WITH HIS WIFE. Christian, *Tolstoy's Diaries*, 1:366 n. 1.

"AN OLD TESTAMENT PROPHET." "ASTONISHING OLD MAN." Wilson, *Tolstoy*, 158.

page 115:

TOLSTOY REACHED PARIS IN FEBRUARY. In a letter to P. V. Annenkov, February 15/27, 1861, from Paris, Turgenev told him: "A few days ago Tolstoy arrived from Italy, not without eccentricities, but pacified and softened. His brother's death had a very strong effect on him." *Turgenev Letters*, ed. Lowe, 1:185.

THE STORY OF THE DECEMBRISTS. Only after their revolt were they called "Decembrists." Actually they were comprised of several secret societies with different names. One of the first was called "The Union of Salvation" or the "Society of True and Faithful Sons of the Fatherland," established in St. Petersburg. Pavel Pestel's society in the south of Russia was called the "Union of Common Weal." Anatole G. Mazour, *The First Russian Revolution 1825: The Decembrist Movement* (Berkeley and Los Angeles: University of California Press, 1937), 66.

THIRTY COLONELS AND FIVE GENERALS. Sidney Monas, *The Third Section: Police and Society in Russia Under Nicholas I* (Cambridge: Harvard University Press, 1961), 54.

DURING RUSSIA'S CAMPAIGNS IN EUROPE. Marc Raeff, *The Decembrist Movement* (Englewood Cliffs, N.J.: Prentice-Hall, 1966), 11, 20, 24, 32. See also the quotations from Mikhail Fonzvin's, Pavel Pestel's, and Alexander Bestuzhev's testimony in answer to the question "How did the revolutionary ideas originate and spread?" Mazour, *The First Russian Revolution 1825*, 55, 273, 278.

"OH, SOVEREIGN, TO ERADICATE." Mazour, *The First Russian Revolution, 1825*, 63, 280. Mazour translates the passage slightly differently in these two citations.

"THE SPIRIT OF THE TIMES." "SHINE AS AN EXAMPLE." From Kakhovsky's testimony to General Levashev, February 24, 1826 (ibid., 274).

"THE ENTIRE CONTEMPORARY GENERATION." W. Bruce Lincoln, *Nicholas I: Emperor and Autocrat of All the Russias* (London: Lane, 1978), 90.

A COUP D'ÉTAT COULD BE EFFECTED. There was some confusion as to whether Constantin, Alexander I's next younger brother or his much younger brother Nicholas was heir to the throne. Constantin had been passed over as successor to the throne because he had married the daughter of a Polish count who was not of royal lineage. By gaining control of one of the conflicting heirs, the Decembrists thought to effect a semi-legal coup through which they hoped to force him to accept a limited monarchy. Mazour, *The First Russian Revolution 1825*, 68.

DECLARED IT HOPELESS. Lincoln, *Nicholas I*, 39.

HE DREW UP THEIR MANIFESTO. Mazour, *The First Russian Revolution 1825*, 283.

KONDRATIN FYODOROVICH RYLEYEV, THE POET. In the hope of sacrificing himself to save his comrades, Ryleyev declared emphatically during the interrogations: "I own myself to have been the principal author of the events of the 14th (26th) December. I might have arrested all action; but I set others the example of a criminal ardour." J. H. Schnitzler, *Secret History of the Court and Government of Russia Under the Emperors Alexander and Nicholas*, 2 vols. (London: Bentley, 1847), 1:218.

"BUT OUR EXAMPLE WILL REMAIN." Lincoln, *Nicholas I*, 39. Lincoln translates as "motherland," but "fatherland" seems the common form in
Russian, or at least in translations from the Russian.

"WE SHALL DIE!" Mazour, *The First Russian Revolution 1825*, 164.

pages 115–16:

STAFF CAPTAIN M. A. BESTUZHEV. Lincoln, *Nicholas I*, 41.

page 116:

HOLES WERE CUT IN THE ICE. Schnitzler, *Secret History of the Court and
Government of Russia*, 1:246.

"DRAINED"—SO IT WAS REPORTED—"OF HIS VERY LIFE-BLOOD." Zetlin, *The
Decembrists*, 206.

FIVE HUNDRED AND SEVENTY-NINE WERE ARRESTED. Lincoln, *Nicholas I*, 80.

CHAINS SO HEAVY. Zetlin, *The Decembrists*, 276, tells us that the five
Decembrists taken to be hung wore such "heavy iron fetters" that they
"could hardly move."

"I CAN'T EXPRESS THE STRANGE, POWERFUL." Letter to Pyotr Nikolayevich
Svistunov, March 14, 1878 (Christian, *Tolstoy's Letters*, 317). Svistunov
was one of a number of Decembrists who attempted suicide while in the
Petrapavlosk fortress. He first threw himself into the Neva and then ate
glass—but he survived.

THE IRONS ACCOMPANIED THE DECEMBRISTS. At the end of 1828, Nicholas I
ordered Leparsky, the commandant of the fortress where the Decembrists were confined, to remove the chains from all of them who deserved
relief. Leparsky, who, as far as he could, had shown much kindness to
these men, removed the chains from all. Monas, *The Third Section*, 78.
The coming of the Decembrists' wives and their letters to their families
did much to bring about amelioration of the prisoners' condition.

SHE THREW HERSELF AT HIS FEET. Zetlin, *The Decembrists*, 290.

CABAL THAT WAS HOSTILE TO HIS LIBERALISM. Mazour, *The First Russian
Revolution 1825*, 26–28. See also Marc Raeff, *Michael Speransky: States-
man of Imperial Russia* (The Hague, 1957).

page 117:

"REORGANIZATION OF THE ARMY." Tolstoy had his first idea for reorganiz-
ing the army on March 2–5, 1855. In a diary entry May 11, 1856, Tolstoy
says he is working to present his plan through A. I. Levshin, Assistant
Minister of the Interior, and on May 17, he has met with the minister
himself, Count Sergey Stepanovich Lanskoy. In Moscow on Christmas
Day 1856, he has dined at Dusseau's with Lanskoy. Later Lanskoy
recommended him as "peace mediator" for Tula after the serfs were

freed. *The Private Diary of Leo Tolstoy 1853–1857*, trans. Maude, 114, 148–49, 151, 189. See also Birukoff, *Leo Tolstoy*, 1:307.

"MAJOR OFFENDER." "PRIVILEGED TREATMENT." Zetlin, *The Decembrists*, 263, 242. The hot tea, which was desperately important for maintaining body heat in those icy, arctic dungeons, was really a necessity, not a luxury.

"THE SEVERITY THAT BEFITS." Ibid., 242.

"AN ABSOLUTE IDIOT." "STOOD BEFORE ME." Monas, *The Third Section*, 57; Zetlin, *The Decembrists*, 237.

ON JULY 13, 1826. Lincoln, *Nicholas I*, 82; Zetlin, *The Decembrists*, 276–77. Besides the 5 hanged and the 121 "most responsible conspirators" sent to hard labor, 134 were found guilty of lesser offenses and punished by loss of rank and redistribution into troops in remote places at dangerous posts. Mazour, *The First Russian Revolution 1825*, 212–13.

"THE DEAD ARE DEAD." "WHEN I THINK." Zetlin, *The Decembrists*, 284. Zetlin has "120 friends."

KEEP THEIR "PATIENCE PROUD." Monas, *The Third Section*, 206.

LAUGHING "IN SPIRIT OVER TSARS." Ernest J. Simmons, *Pushkin* (London: Oxford University Press, 1937), 264–65.

"SHATTERED THE CHILDHOOD SLEEP." Alexander Herzen, *My Past and Thoughts*, as quoted in Martin Malia, *Alexander Herzen and the Birth of Russian Socialism 1812–1855*, Russian Research Center Studies 39 (London: Oxford University Press, 1961), 33.

HE AND NIKOLAY PLATONOVICH OGAREV. Ibid., 50. They were inspired by the oath in Schiller's *Don Carlos*.

VOROBYEV HILLS. Widely translated—erroneously, according to present opinion—as "Sparrow Hills." The former owner of the hills was Vorobyev.

page 118:

"THE POLAR STAR." Ibid., 394. *The Polar Star* can also be translated *The North Star*, and the original symbolism of the title rested on the function of the North Star as a guide to a goal on sea and land.

"A VERY NICE AND GOOD." Letter to A. I. Herzen, September 16, 1859. *Turgenev Letters*, ed. Lowe, 154.

"I AM SEEING A LOT OF TOLSTOY." Troyat, *Tolstoy*, 203. Herzen seems to be going on the reports of Turgenev that he could not be in Tolstoy's company for a day without their quarreling, when he tells Turgenev that he has already quarreled with Tolstoy.

IN THE AUTOCRACY, IN GREEK ORTHODOXY, AND IN RUSSIANISM. Nicholas V. Riasanovsky, *Nicholas I and Official Nationality in Russia 1825–1855* (Berkeley and Los Angeles: University of California Press, 1959), 70–78.

"YOU SAY I DON'T KNOW RUSSIA." Letter to A. I. Herzen, March 14/26, 1861 (Christian, *Tolstoy's Letters*, 1:145).

"YOU CAN'T IMAGINE HOW INTERESTING." Ibid.

HE MOVED HIS BEGINNING BACK. In his unpublished "Foreword" to "1805," Tolstoy tells how he kept moving his book back in time. Christian, *Tolstoy: A Critical Introduction*, 101.

page 119:

"OUR FAILURES AND OUR SHAME." Ibid.

"NEITHER MY TIME NOR CAPACITY." Tolstoy, "Some Words about *War and Peace*" (published in *Russian Archive*, 1868) in *War and Peace*, trans. Maude, 1366.

"LEAD NOT ONE, BUT MANY." "Foreword" to "1805," in Christian, *Tolstoy: A Critical Introduction*, 101.

HAS GROWN UP IN PARIS. Tolstoy makes a point of Pierre's European clipped hair, which he probably took from Pavel Annenkov's description of Herzen's transformation into a Parisian, only reversing it. Herzen had arrived in Paris "wearing long hair," but changed instantly into a "complete gentleman of the Western race, with clipped hair, a dandified beard that quickly assumed the correct outlines, and a jacket of free and elegant cut." Malia, *Alexander Herzen and the Birth of Russian Socialism*, 343. When Pierre first appears fresh from Paris, he has "close-cropped hair." After his marriage, at his wife's command, he has "let his hair grow" in the Russian fashion. *War and Peace*, trans. Maude, 9, 331.

HE WAS CALLED "MONSIEUR SERGE." Zetlin, *The Decembrists*, 58.

EVERYONE CALLS TOLSTOY'S PROTAGONIST. Tolstoy himself as narrator calls him "Monsieur Pierre" and has Anna Scherer, as well as Julie Karagina, do so. *War and Peace*, trans. Maude, 20, 22, 95.

"SUPERIOR INNER ARTLESSNESS." Zetlin, *The Decembrists*, 344.

page 120:

PIERRE'S SOCIAL GAFFES. Some of these are ludicrous, such as picking up the wrong hat at Anna Scherer's soiree, or crossing himself with the hand holding a candle, to the mirth of the youngest Princess at his father's deathbed. In his diary, Tolstoy reproves himself for similar lapses, such as, on March 27, 1851, "lost my stick—absence of mind." *Diaries of Leo Tolstoy 1847–1852*, 72.

"BY HIS KINDLY, SIMPLE." *War and Peace*, trans. Maude, 22.

MISTRESS OF THE ROBES TO. Zetlin, *The Decembrists*, 58.

PRINCE GREGORY VOLKONSKY. He appears in various memoirs of St. Petersburg society. At a ball of the Odoyevskys in November 1833, a younger courtier reported that he had been ravished with the beauty of Alexander Pushkin's wife and that "Prince Gregory Volkonsky came over to me and whispered, 'You would do well not to stare at her too hard.' " Henri Troyat, *Pushkin: A Biography* (London: Gollancz, 1951), 375.

GERMAN FOR "HEARTS." Herzen's mother, Henrietta Wilhelmina Luisa Haag, was a German from Stuttgart, daughter of a civil servant. As she was not Greek Orthodox, Yakovlev could not marry her legally in Russia.

PIERRE SUDDENLY BLUSHES "CRIMSON." *War and Peace*, trans. Maude, 29.

ABLE TO MAKE HIM NOBLE. Herzen's father got him an official position in the dvorianstvo and paid for the promotion of everyone who stood between him and the rank of collegiate assessor, which conferred nobility. When Herzen retired, he had reached the rank of "court councilor." Malia, *Alexander Herzen and the Birth of Russian Socialism*, 201, 278.

page 121:

"HE WANTED TO REST HIS HEAD." Alexander Herzen, *My Past and Thoughts*, trans. Constance Garnett, 2 vols. (London: Chatto & Windus, 1924), 2:308.

"EVERYONE TURNED TO ME." Ibid., 2:309.

"ONE OF HIS ARMS FELL." *War and Peace*, trans. Maude, 87.

SUCH RAPACITY "VERY HORRID." "WITH A KIND." "OBLIGED TO PERFORM." Ibid., 56, 82.

"GAUNT" FIGURE OF THE OLD DECEMBRIST. The elderly Prince Sergey Volkonsky is described by Zetlin, *The Decembrists*, 322, as "tall and gaunt."

"STOUT, HEAVILY BUILT YOUNG MAN." *War and Peace*, trans. Maude, 9.

"ABOVE AVERAGE HEIGHT, BROAD." The text of the Norton Critical Edition of Maude's translation of *War and Peace* has not been reedited and preserves a printer's error never caught in earlier editions, so that Pierre is described as "about average height" instead of "above average height" (22), which conflicts with many later references to his tallness.

"LARGER FEATURES." "TO SUGGEST A GREATER." Letter to Mikhail Sergeyevich Bashilov, December 8 and April 4, 1866 (Christian, *Tolstoy's Letters*, 1:209, 203).

"A THICK-SET POWERFUL FIGURE." A quote from von Meysenbug's *Memoirs* in Edward Hallett Carr, *The Romantic Exiles: A Nineteenth Century Portrait Gallery* (London: Penguin, 1968), 131–32.

pages 121–22:

AGREED TO EXCHANGE PHOTOGRAPHS. In Tolstoy's letter to Alexander Herzen, March 14/26, 1861, he writes: "I enclose the promised photographs for you and Ogarev and look forward to yours in return." Christian, *Tolstoy's Letters*, 1:145.

page 122:

HABIT OF READING STRETCHED OUT. In June 1851, Tolstoy writes in his diary that a person he did not like came in, so he "went on reading where I lay." *Diaries of Leo Tolstoy 1847–1852,* 99.

"I WONDER IF YOU CAN DO." Letter to Mikhail Sergeyevich Bashilov, April 4, 1866 (Christian, *Tolstoy's Letters,* 1:203).

ONE OF BAKUNIN'S YOUNGER BROTHERS. In a June 14, 1855, note to I. I. Panayev, editor-in-chief of the *Contemporary,* Tolstoy says he is interested as much as ever in military articles and in a few days will go to Sevastopol "to spur on Rostovsev and Bakunin and collect their articles" (ibid., 1:51). The oldest Bakunin brother, the great anarchist Mikhail Alexandrovich Bakunin, had been a prisoner ever since he had been captured as a revolutionary in 1848. All five of the other Bakunin brothers—Nikolay, Pavel, Ilya, Alexander, and Alexis—fought in the Crimean War. Edward Hallett Carr, *Michael Bakunin* (London: Macmillan, 1975), 217, 222.

HE SAW HIM OFTEN. When this Bakunin first appeared in Moscow, November 25, 1856, Tolstoy spoke of him as "the unbearable Bakunin," but he went right on seeing him. *The Private Diary of Leo Tolstoy 1853–1857,* trans. Maude, 184, 189, 190, 192.

STANKEVICH'S GERMAN-METAPHYSICAL CIRCLE. Edward J. Brown, *Stankevich and His Moscow Circle 1830–1840* (Stanford, Calif.: Stanford University Press, 1966), 4, 8, 9, etc. In his early years, Turgenev had hoped to take a chair in philosophy at Moscow University, but the study of philosophy was then suppressed by Nicholas I for fear that freethinking would damage belief in the autocracy or in Greek Orthodoxy. Magarshack, *Turgenev,* 58.

BAKUNIN'S GRANDFATHER. "SAMSON." "ENORMOUS STATURE." "MUSCULAR PROWESS, AND HIS UNGOVERNABLE." Carr, *Michael Bakunin,* 3–5. Bakunin's grandfather was Mikhail Vasilyevich Bakunin.

NOT HIS DEMONIC STRENGTH. Ibid., 10. Carr says that although Bakunin was "big-framed, he was not remarkable, like his grandfather and namesake, for exceptional physical strength."

CALL HIM "HERCULES." *War and Peace,* trans. Maude, 32.

HE SHOWS HIMSELF "SO STRONG." Ibid., 35.

pages 122–23:
"HIS FATHER'S NATURE." THE "WHOLE HOUSE." Ibid., 345.

page 123:
"HIS ACTIVITY, HIS LAZINESS." Herzen, *My Past and Thoughts,* 5:140.
"LEONINE HEAD." "HIGH, STOUT, UNCOVERED CHEST." *War and Peace,* trans. Maude, 85.

"SOMETHING CHILDLIKE, SIMPLE." Herzen, *My Past and Thoughts*, 5:140.

TOLSTOY, WHO HAD THE STRENGTH. In his battery at Sevastopol Tolstoy was famous because "lying on the floor" he could take a man "weighing 13 stone," that is, 182 pounds, on his hands, and "lift him up by straightening his arms." Maude, *Life of Tolstoy*, 1:128. As for laziness, Tolstoy wrote in his diary on July 7, 1854, "I am not methodical in my life, and am so lazy that for me idleness has become almost a necessary habit." Birukoff, *Leo Tolstoy*, 1:170.

BREAK WITH THE KURAGINS. *War and Peace*, trans. Maude, 29.

LED ASTRAY BY A FAMILY. The Kuragins include a very ugly and dim-witted son, Hippolyte, but he probably did not come out of the Islavins. Tolstoy speaks of only one of Konstantin's brother's, Mikhail Islavin: "He is difficult because of his shyness." Entry of May 10, 1854, *The Private Diary of Leo Tolstoy 1853–1857*, trans. Maude, 148.

ALTHOUGH HE TRIED TO DIFFERENTIATE. Kuragin has a habit, unique to him, of bending a person's hand down, and his cheeks twitch when he is nervous. *War and Peace*, trans. Maude, 75, 76, 78, 88, 89, etc. In Tolstoy's *Childhood, Boyhood,* and *Youth*, it is Irtenyev's shoulder that twitches (20, 44, 208, 333).

"BALD, SCENTED, AND SHINING." *War and Peace*, trans. Maude, 3.

"BALD HEAD." "DELICIOUSLY PERFUMED." Tolstoy, *Childhood*, 44; *Youth*, 235.

pages 123–24:

"GET THE UPPER HAND." "HAPPINESS AND PLEASURE." "WHETHER HE HAD." Tolstoy, *Childhood*, 44–46.

page 124:

"WHO DELIBERATELY THOUGHT OUT." "WITH APPARENT ABSENT-MINDED-NESS." *War and Peace*, trans. Maude, 217. There are other, less important traits common to both Irtenyev and Prince Vasily Kuragin. Both easily dissolve in tears, both are notorious for "gallantry," both take small quick steps. Compare Tolstoy, *Childhood, Boyhood,* and *Youth*, 44, 45, 207, 208, with *War and Peace*, trans. Maude, 90, 230.

"GOVERNING PASSION," GAMBLING AT CARDS. Irtenyev has two passions, "cards and women." Tolstoy, *Childhood*, 44.

"WHY ARE YOU SO SET." "THE EVIL OF GAMBLING." Birukoff, *Leo Tolstoy*, 1:112.

"SO LOATHSOME TO ME." Letter of December 7, 1864 (Christian, *Tolstoy's Letters*, 1:189).

"KOSTENKA." AN "IDEAL LOVE." "SELF-SACRIFICE." Wilson, *Tolstoy*, 131.

"MY LOVE FOR ISLAVIN." Birukoff, *Leo Tolstoy*, 1:211.

COMPANION IN NIGHTS AMONG THE GYPSIES. See such entries in Tolstoy's

diary as that of May 25, 1856: "Without going to bed went to the Vorobyev Hills with Kostenka. Bathed, drank milk, and slept there in the garden." *The Private Diary of Leo Tolstoy 1853–1857*, trans. Maude, 154. Maude has "Sparrow Hills," an error.
"NOTHING WILL EVER." Ibid.

page 125:

"DRINKING, SMOKING, WASTING." From Tolstoy's *Recollections* (Birukoff, *Leo Tolstoy*, 1:211).

"SEDUCER WAS A DEEPLY IMMORAL." Ibid.

"A LOST SOUL, A DRUNKARD." Entry of June 10, 1893 (Christian, *Tolstoy's Diaries*, 1:323).

HIS OWN "WEAK CHARACTER." *War and Peace*, trans. Maude, 30.

"INDECISION, INCONSEQUENCE, LACK OF STEADFASTNESS." Tolstoy repeats the accusation "lack of character" almost every day starting August 14, 1854, and ending September 20. In the same months a year later, 1855, comes the same repetition of the same words. *The Private Diary of Leo Tolstoy 1853–1857*, trans. Maude, 80, 95–101, 135, 137.

"WANT OF FIRMNESS." Entry of June 4, 1851, *Diaries of Leo Tolstoy 1847–1852*, 105.

"NON-FULFILLMENT OF RESOLUTIONS." *The Private Diary of Leo Tolstoy 1853–1857*, trans. Maude, 137.

"WOMEN, MY DEAR FELLOW." *War and Peace*, trans. Maude, 30.

"RESTRAIN THYSELF FROM WINE." Entry of June 25, 1853 (*The Private Diary of Leo Tolstoy 1853–1857*, trans. Maude, 11).

"SOMEONE IN A PINK DRESS." Entry of April 18, 1851 (*Diaries of Leo Tolstoy 1847–1852*, 76).

"DISGUSTING! GIRLS, SILLY MUSIC." Entry of May 14, 1856 (*The Private Diary of Leo Tolstoy 1853–1857*, trans. Maude, 150).

"NOTORIOUS GAMBLER AND DUELIST." *War and Peace*, trans. Maude, 31.

COUNT FYODOR TOLSTOY—"THE AMERICAN." In Aylmer Maude's notes to the characters in *War and Peace* in the Inner Sanctum edition of his translation (New York: Simon & Schuster, n.d.), 1366, Maude points out that other models from the same period, beside Fyodor Tolstoy, such as R. I. Dorokov, entered into the character.

page 126:

"HANDSOME FACE, BRONZED AND SHAVEN." Lev Tolstoy, "Recollections," in *Recollections and Essays*, Tolstoy Centenary Edition, trans. Aylmer Maude (London: Oxford University Press, 1937), 40.

FYODOR'S WIDOW, AVDOTYA MAXIMOVNA. Diary entries of December 21 and 25, 1850, *Diaries of Leo Tolstoy 1847–1852*, 46. Tolstoy had a special affection for Vaska and Apoloshka, Fyodor Tolstoy's grandchildren. A

note from them made him, he said, "awfully glad, like a lover." Entry
of May 12, 1856, *The Private Diary of Leo Tolstoy 1853–1857*, trans.
Maude, 149.

"EXTRAORDINARY, CRIMINAL, AND ATTRACTIVE." Tolstoy, "Recollections,"
in *Recollections and Essays*, 40. Birukoff translates "criminal" as
"guilty." *Leo Tolstoy*, 1:56.

TOLSTOY, KNOWING THE GONCHAROV FAMILY. See such letters of Pushkin
to his future mother-in-law, Madame Goncharova, as that of May 1,
1829: "I should have written you on my knees with tears of gratitude
when Count Tolstoy brought me your answer, which is not a refusal
since you allow me to hope." Troyat, *Pushkin*, 285.

PUSHKIN HIMSELF HAD BET. Ibid., 97.

Pushkin and Pierre

pages 126–27:

"WITHOUT RAPTURE, WITHOUT CHILDISH." Letter to Nikolay Ivanovich
Krivtsov, February 10, 1831 (*The Letters of Alexander Pushkin*, trans.
J. Thomas Shaw, 3 vols. [Bloomington and Philadelphia: Indiana Univer-
sity Press and University of Pennsylvania Press, 1963], 2:459).

page 127:

GATHERING KNOWLEDGE OF PUSHKIN. On June 3, 1856, he notes having
read Pushkin's *Don Juan:* "Enchanting. Truth and power I had never
expected in Pushkin." On June 9 he is reading a biography of Pushkin
"with pleasure." On January 4, 1857, he has read a "wonderful" article
on Pushkin: "Only now have I understood Pushkin." *The Private Diary
of Leo Tolstoy 1853–1857*, trans. Maude, 158–59, 192.

"DEAR," "CHARMING" PAVEL VASILYEVICH ANNENKOV. Entries of November 25, December 15, 21, 1856 (ibid., 184, 187, 189).

"THE GREAT PUSHKINIAN SPIRIT." Letter of Turgenev to P. V. Annenkov,
October 28, 1852 (*Turgenev Letters*, ed. Lowe, 1:68). Lowe translates
"severe and youthful beauty." I changed it to "austere and youthful."

"DELIGHTFULLY KIND-HEARTED." So Tolstoy spoke of both Mikhail Pushchin and his wife on April 19, 1857, *The Private Diary of Leo Tolstoy
1853–1857*, trans. Maude, 209. From Clarens, Switzerland, Tolstoy
wrote Pavel Vasilyevich Annenkov, April 22 / May 4, 1857: "This
Pushchin is a charming and good-natured man. His and his wife's
kindness to me here is very touching." Christian, *Tolstoy's Letters*, 99.

IVAN HAD BEEN ONE. Alexander Pushkin wrote Anton Antonovich Delvig,
February 20, 1826, on the day the Decembrists were to be sentenced,
"But what about Ivan Pushchin?" and added, "My heart is in my
throat." *The Letters of Alexander Pushkin*, 1:305.

MIKHAIL PUSHCHIN'S REMINISCENCES OF THE POET. Christian, *Tolstoy's Letters*, 1:99.

"RIDICULOUS AND NASTY." Entry of July 31, 1857, *The Private Diary of Leo Tolstoy 1853–1857*, trans. Maude, 234.

"GOD, HOW YOU BORE ME." Troyat, *Pushkin*, 341.

SOLOGUB, WHOM TOLSTOY SAW OFTEN. *The Private Diary of Leo Tolstoy 1853–1857*, trans. Maude, 48, 66.

"SUCH PERFECTION OF CLASSICALLY CORRECT." Simmons, *Pushkin*, 338.

"FOREMOST BEAUTY OF THE TIME." Troyat, *Pushkin*, 375.

page 128:

"I HAVE NEVER SEEN." Ibid. My translation is adapted from those of Troyat, *Pushkin*, 375, and Simmons, *Pushkin*, 373.

"SHE WAS RESERVED TO THE POINT." Troyat, *Pushkin*, 299.

"CERTAINLY SHE ALWAYS SEEMED." Ibid., 413.

"PUSHKIN IS GOING TO MARRY." Ibid., 329.

"THIS WOMAN IS GENERALLY SUPPOSED." Ibid., 429.

"BEAUTIFUL FIGURE AND SHAPELY." *War and Peace*, trans. Maude, 11.

"MARBLE BEAUTY." Ibid., 222.

"WONDERFUL CLASSIC BEAUTY." Ibid., 12.

"HER BEAUTIFUL HEAD." "OVER HER CLASSICALLY." Ibid., 16.

"CAN'T HELENE BE MADE FULLER." Letter to Mikhail Sergeyevich Bashilov, April 4, 1866 (Christian, *Tolstoy's Letters*, 1:203).

"PAPA, WE SHALL BE LATE." *War and Peace*, trans. Maude, 16–17.

"HER BEAUTY." "SILENTLY DIGNIFIED IN." Ibid., 221.

"A BRIEF BUT APPROPRIATE." Ibid., 225.

"AND HOW SHE CARRIES HERSELF!" Ibid., 221.

page 129:

"GLANCING NOW AT HER BEAUTIFUL." Ibid., 12.

"TURGENEV'S OPINION THAT YOU." Letter to A. A. Fet, May 10–20, 1866 (Christian, *Tolstoy's Letters*, 1:205).

REDUCED TO "N N." Simmons, *Pushkin*, 362.

TOLSTOY SPOKE OF HELENE IN A WAY. In Christian, *Tolstoy's Letters*, 1:205, Christian passes over the reference to N N in Tolstoy's letter to Fet with no explanation, although the initials in this context are entirely obscure. Only after I had discovered all the parallels between Pushkin's life and Pierre's and between Pushkin's wife, Natalya Nikolayevna, and Helene, did I see, on returning to this passage, why Tolstoy calls Helene "N N."

I have selected Maude's translation "Helene," rather than Dunnigan's "Ellen," because for an English-speaking reader it preserves the suggestion of the beautiful and adulterous Helen of Troy.

"BEST THING I CAN DO." Entry of June 15, 1856, *The Private Diary of Leo Tolstoy 1853–1857*, trans. Maude, 162.

"VERY CHARMING" BUT "FRIVOLOUS." Entries of June 17 and 18, 1856 (ibid., 162–63).

"DO I LOVE HER SERIOUSLY?" Entry of June 26 (ibid., 164).

"EXTREMELY BADLY EDUCATED." Entry of June 28, 1856 (ibid.).

"A SPLENDID GIRL." "SHE CERTAINLY DOES NOT." Entry of June 30, 1856 (ibid.).

"NICER THAN EVER, BUT." Entry of July 12, 1856 (ibid., 166–67).

page 130:

"MUCH COLD WATER." Entry of July 23, 1856 (ibid., 168).

"SIMPLY STUPID." Entry of July 31, 1856 (ibid., 169).

"CRUELLY AFFECTED AND STUPID." Entry of August 1, 1856 (ibid.).

"NOT STUPID." "REMARKABLY KIND." Entry of August 10, 1856 (ibid., 170).

"SWEET BUT, ALAS, SIMPLY STUPID." Entry of September 25, 1856 (ibid., 173).

"SIMPLE AND NICE." Entry of August 12, 1856 (ibid., 170).

"LIMITED AND INCREDIBLY FUTILE." Entry of September 26, 1856 (ibid., 173).

"INCOMPETENT BOTH IN PRACTICAL." Entry of September 29, 1856 (ibid., 174).

"A DEAR, DEAR GIRL." Entry of October 27, 1856 (ibid., 178).

"TERRIBLY SHALLOW, WITHOUT PRINCIPLE." Entry of October 1, 1856 (ibid., 174).

"MORE THAN INDIFFERENT." "DECEIVE EITHER MYSELF." "I HAVE NOT ONLY." Birukoff, *Leo Tolstoy*, 1:226–27.

"I WAS ALWAYS TELLING YOU." Derrick Leon, *Tolstoy: His Life and Work* (London: Routledge, 1944), 78.

"DECEIVING YOURSELF." "BUT SHE'S STUPID." *War and Peace*, trans. Maude, 342, 223.

"NO, SHE IS NOT STUPID." Ibid., 225.

"DREADFUL ABYSS." "WHAT AM I DOING?" Ibid.

MADEMOISELLE VERGANI HAD ENGINEERED. Tolstoy said of the governess, "Her narrowness frightens me and the constraint of my position angers me." When the affair was all over, he said: "Mlle. Vergani has come. I am beginning to disgust her and she seems to have given me up as a bad job." Entries of October 30, 1856, and September 29, 1857, *The Private Diary of Leo Tolstoy 1853–1857*, trans. Maude, 178, 246.

"SHE HAD HAD HER HAIR." Entry of October 28, 1856 (ibid., 178).

page 131:

"ARRANGED ON THE TOP." *War and Peace*, trans. Maude, 236.

FAR FROM A "DEPRAVED" WOMAN. Ibid., 342.

"LADY WITH SENSUAL EYES." "THOUGHT WITH HORROR." Entry of November 25, 1856, *The Private Diary of Leo Tolstoy 1853–1857*, trans. Maude, 184.

"LANGUID PASSIONATE LOOK." *War and Peace*, trans. Maude, 342.

"THE WORD PROSTITUER." Entry of June 28, 1856, *The Private Diary of Leo Tolstoy 1853–1857*, trans. Maude, 164.

"COARSENESS AND BLUNTNESS." *War and Peace*, trans. Maude, 343.

"TERRIFYING." "AM AFRAID HERS IS." Entry of July 12, 1856, *The Private Diary of Leo Tolstoy 1853–1857*, trans. Maude, 167.

"WANT TO HAVE CHILDREN." *War and Peace*, trans. Maude, 343.

ENROLLED IN THE MINISTRY. Troyat, *Pushkin*, 343. The appointment commenced on November 14, 1831. Magarshack, *Pushkin: A Biography* (London: Chapman & Hall, 1967), 261.

page 132:

"THE DAY BEFORE YESTERDAY." Simmons, *Pushkin*, 362.

"AGREEABLE MOOD IN WHICH." "PITIABLE ROLE AND." Troyat, *Pushkin*, 384.

"ENTERED IN THE DIPLOMATIC." *War and Peace*, trans. Maude, 219.

"SINCE THE INTIMACY." Ibid., 519.

"ENJOYING THE FAVORS." Ibid., 676.

"SPECIAL PROTECTION OF A GRANDEE." Ibid., 931.

CIRCUMLOCUTIONS AND CONFUSIONS. The "royal prince" at first seems Russian, since he has been instrumental in making Pierre a "gentleman of the bedchamber" of the Russian Emperor and he is always at court functions. Then he is defined as a "foreign" royal prince, so that his influence in the matter of the Imperial Bedchamber looks strange. Perhaps translation has furthered the confusion.

During the publication, Tolstoy was acutely aware of the problem of getting through the censorship. He told P. I. Bartenev of the *Russian Herald* on December 6, 1867, apropos of a passage reflecting on the Emperor Alexander I, "Cross out this passage and ones like it, if you find them dangerous as far as the censorship is concerned. I give you carte blanche to cross out everything that seems dangerous. You know better than I do what is allowed and what isn't." Christian, *Tolstoy's Letters*, 1:217.

"GIRLISH IMPRUDENCE." "SHE DANCES AT BALLS." Letter to Pavel Voynovich Nashchokin, January 8 and 10, 1832 (*Letters of Alexander Pushkin*, 2:543).

page 133:

WOULD "HAVE A MISCARRIAGE." Letter to Natalya Nikolayevna Pushkina, December 8, 1831 (ibid., 2:538).

FOUND HER "BECOMING ILL." Letter to Pavel Voynovich Nashchokin, middle of March 1834 (ibid., 3:636).

NATALYA NIKOLAYEVNA'S COURT WARDROBE. Magarshack, *Pushkin*, 261.

"I AM RUSHING ABOUT." Letter of February 2, 1833 (ibid., 265).

"DON'T COQUETTE WITH THE TSAR." Letter of October 11, 1833 (*Letters of Alexander Pushkin*, 3:615 and 615n). The Princess "Lyuba" Lyubov Alexandrovna Khilkova's fiancé was S. D. Bezobrasov.

"LIKE A LITTLE BITCH." Letter of October 30, 1833 (ibid., 3:616–17). I have transposed "Like a little bitch," which reads in the translation, "Male dogs are running after you like a little bitch, with their tails, etc."

"WHERE THERE'S A TROUGH." Ibid., 3:617. Pushkin is using a folk adage here.

"ENTIRE DIPLOMATIC CORPS." Letter to Natalya Nikolayevna Pushkina, c. October 3, 1832 (ibid., 2:561).

A LIST IN ALPHABETICAL. Letter to Natalya Nikolayevna Pushkina, October 21, 1833 (ibid., 3:615 and 615n). The chief pursuer was Nikolay Alexandrovich Ogarev, probably a cousin of Nikolay Platonovich Ogarev, Herzen's friend.

"GRANDEE" AND THE "YOUNG FOREIGN PRINCE." *War and Peace*, trans. Maude, 931.

"MADLY IN LOVE." "FOR I LOVE YOU ALSO." Georges d'Anthès to Baron van Heeckeren, January 20, 1836 (Troyat, *Pushkin*, 427–28).

page 134:

"BECAUSE I REGARD IT." "DIVORCE HER INSTANTLY." Letter to Valerya Vladimirovna Arsenyeva, October 1856 (Leon, *Tolstoy*, 76).

A NEW MISTRESS, NELIDOVA. According to Riasanovsky, *Nicholas I and Official Nationality in Russia*, 20, the interest of Nicholas I in Nelidova began in the autumn of 1841, "but it was several years before she became his mistress." Apparently that was because later that fall he met Natalya Nikolayevna Pushkina in the English shop at St. Petersburg and made her his mistress instead. Troyat, *Pushkin*, 505.

Natalya Nikolayevna certainly believed in physical faithfulness to a husband, although she allowed herself full leeway in flirtation. Pushkin, the Emperor Nicholas, and d'Anthès all testified to her probity in that respect. Probably it was because she was pregnant by the Emperor that the marriage to Lanskoy was arranged, and both she and Nicholas I were agreed to terminate the relationship with the birth of the child. Lanskoy had been a friend of d'Anthès and had been patroling under Idalia Poletika's windows (Troyat, *Pushkin*, 463) while d'Anthès tried to get Natalya to elope with him to France. According to Simmons (*Pushkin*, 433), her marriage to Lanskoy was happy.

THEY ALL LIVED HAPPILY. Van Heeckeren suffered nothing worse than transfer to the more comfortable city of Vienna, and d'Anthès, once he had inherited the money and title, rose to become a senator in the government of Napoleon III. Simmons, *Pushkin*, 430.

page 135:

YOUNG PRINCE PETER DOLGORUKOV. In 1927 the Pushkin specialist Shego-lev had the anonymous letters examined by handwriting experts, and they concluded that Dolgorukov had written them. Troyat, *Pushkin*, 437.

ANONYMOUS CALUMNY AND ATTEMPTED BLACKMAIL. In 1843, Dolgorukov published under a false name in Paris a book besmirching most of the noble families of Russia. He was condemned by a Paris court for attempting to blackmail Prince M. C. Vorontzov. Ibid., 437.

"MOST SERENE ORDER OF CUCKOLDS." To Alexander Pushkin, November 4, 1836 (*Letters of Alexander Pushkin*, 3:821n). On the receipt of this letter, Pushkin tried—hopelessly—to liberate himself from Nicholas's patronage. He had been lent 20,000 on February 28, 1834, to pay for publishing his book on the Pugachev rebellion. He tried on November 6, 1836, to get Count Kankrin, Minister of Finance, to have the treasury take over his small estate in settlement of the money he still owed the state. Magarshack, *Pushkin*, 269, 290. See also Waclaw Lednicki, *Push-kin's Bronze Horseman: The Story of a Masterpiece* (Westport, Conn.: Greenwood Press, 1978), 75.

Pushkin also sent an immediate challenge to van Heeckeren for d'Anthès. Van Heeckeren then concocted a plan meant to save d'Anthès from the danger of a duel, while giving him full access (with no violation of propriety) to the woman he loved. He had d'Anthès propose to and marry Natalya Nikolayevna's older sister Ekaterina. Although Pushkin withdrew the challenge, he did not attend the wedding, which took place in a combined Catholic–Greek Orthodox ceremony on January 10, 1837, and he refused to admit d'Anthès to his house. Only a week or so after the marriage to Ekaterina, d'Anthès was trying to get Natalya Nikolayevna to elope with him. The duel in which he killed Pushkin took place on January 27, 1837. Troyat, *Pushkin*, 456.

A SINECURE OF 40,000 RUBLES. Ibid., 436–37.

"AH, HERE SHE IS." *War and Peace*, trans. Maude, 501.

"GLOOMY AND ABSENT-MINDED." Ibid., 506.

"MORE AND MORE SILENT." The source of this passage, presented in a translation of Troyat's French, is not given, but it seems to have come from a specific report because Troyat places it at an Anichkov Palace ball on December 16, 1834. Troyat, *Pushkin*, 395.

page 136:

    D'ANTHÈS WAS DELIBERATELY GOADING. Madame Smirnov, whom Tolstoy
had known at Baden-Baden, had said of d'Anthès in her reminiscences,
"[He] never ceased pursuing his sister-in-law. He even dropped all
reserve, appearing at times to goad the jealousy of the husband." Troyat,
Pushkin, 459.

    "MORE DARING WITH WOMEN." Ibid., 424.

    "ALL SOCIAL PROPRIETIES." Magarshack, *Pushkin*, 289.

    "HAD SUCH A TERRIBLE LOOK." Troyat, *Pushkin*, 456.

    "HERE'S TO THE HEALTH." *War and Peace*, trans. Maude, 337. Maude found
only the by-no-means idiomatic "Peterkin" to use for the more natural
Russian "Petrusha."

    "TERRIBLE AND MONSTROUS." Ibid., 336.

    DURING A PRIVATE RENDEZVOUS. Natalya Nikolayevna had been called to
her friend Idalia Poletika, not expecting to find d'Anthès there. When
Pushkin confronted her with the letter, she cried on his shoulder and
told him all.

    "HIS LIPS TREMBLED." Troyat, *Pushkin*, 452. Pushkin was proud that his
maternal great-grandfather had been an Abyssinian prince adopted by
Peter the Great. He and his friends liked to attribute his strong emotions
to his African heredity—which Count Sologub does further on in
this quote.

    "WAIT! I FEEL STRONG ENOUGH." They were speaking French, of course,
so the words were "Attendez!" and so on. Magarshack, *Pushkin*, 299.

    ON HIS "LEFT HAND." Ibid.

    "HIS BODY SIDEWAYS." "ACROSS HIS CHEST." Troyat, *Pushkin*, 475.

pages 136–37:

    "NO, IT'S NOT OVER." "LEFT HAND." *War and Peace*, trans. Maude, 340.

page 137:

    "WITH HIS BROAD CHEST." "SIDEWAYS! COVER YOURSELF!" Ibid.

    "DRESSED UP AS A SAVAGE." Letter to B. N. Chicherin, October 28, 1861
(Christian, *Tolstoy's Letters*, 1:151).

    "IT'S STRANGE. I THOUGHT." Troyat, *Pushkin*, 475. Troyat's translation
from the Russian, retranslated into English from the French, came out,
"That is odd." I have changed it to "It's strange."

    "ONE THING I THANK GOD." *War and Peace*, trans. Maude, 415.

    SAVED FROM JOINING THEIR IMMOLATION. Pushkin had not been initiated
into a secret society beforehand because all his friends knew he could
not keep a secret. He had planned to go to St. Petersburg the very
evening of the revolt, and changed his mind at the last minute. If he had

gone, he would have headed straight for Ryleyev's, where he would have found all his friends preparing the rebellion, and he would certainly—so he later told Nicholas I under interrogation—have joined them.

"OPEN HOUSE, ESPECIALLY FOR." Carr, *Michael Bakunin*, 80.

COMPROMISING CONTIGUITY WITH KATKOV. Shocked, Bakunin went about telling everyone. Determinedly blind, Ogarev joined with Katkov against Bakunin in defending his wife's honor.

page 138:

"MESSALINA OF THE GUTTER." Edward Hallett Carr, *The Romantic Exiles: A Nineteenth Century Portrait Gallery* (London: Gollancz, 1933), 178.

EXACTED A CRIPPLINGLY LARGE PART. Ogarev gave Marya Lvovna a bond for 300,000 rubles, secured on his estates, which gave her an income (at 6 percent) of 18,000 rubles a year. Ibid., 168.

GIVE HER "A FORTUNE." "IN GREAT RUSSIA." *War and Peace*, trans. Maude, 345.

GIVING THEM THE LAND. The deadlock for more than a century on emancipating the serfs of Russia was over what proportion of the land should be given them. In the end, when the Emperor Alexander II emancipated them, they were given no land, and thus were freed into economic slavery, becoming an agricultural proletariat rather than a peasantry.

Ogarev had wanted to give the Belo-mut serfs the land, and he felt that all nobility had been removed from the act by the law of repayment. Carr, *The Romantic Exiles*, 161.

OGAREV HAD BEEN SO PRODIGAL. In a letter to Maria Reichel on February 7, 1871, Alexander Herzen's daughter Natalie declared that Ogarev had thrown his fortune—originally ten times greater than theirs—away. She said, "He gave away huge sums to scoundrels who drank, caroused and gambled them away, while he himself was left virtually penniless." Michael Confino, *Daughter of a Revolutionary: Natalie Herzen and the Bakunin-Nechayev Circle*, trans. Hilary Sternberg and Lydia Bott (London: Alcove Press, 1974), 335.

"HIS PURSE WAS ALWAYS." *War and Peace*, trans. Maude, 592.

"FROM WINE—HE HAS DRUNK." Letter of Alexander Herzen to his son Sasha Herzen, July 31, 1869 (Confino, *Daughter of a Revolutionary*, 120).

"DRINKING BECAME MORE AND." *War and Peace*, trans. Maude, 594.

ANOTHER MAJOR NOVEL, *ANNA KARENINA*. In a letter to Nikolay Nikolayevich Strakhov, March 25, 1873, Tolstoy told how he came on the fragment in Pushkin's *The Tales of Belkin* and how it set off characters and events with all the threads becoming "so well and truly tied up that the result was a novel, which I finished in draft form today." Christian, *Tolstoy's Letters*, 1:258.

page 139:

EVEN THE GAFFES THAT APPEAR. Tolstoy's gaffe of making Pierre a Gentleman of the Bedchamber twice over came out of the push in him to
express Pushkin's shameful position at court in Pierre from the moment
he becomes entangled with Helene. Once Tolstoy found that he had put
this in too early to use in his story at this point, he forgot all about it, so
that by the time he needed it he put it in all over again. Tolstoy also got
into trouble by changing the royal prince who put Pierre in that position
to a *foreign* prince, so that his ability to make appointments in the
Russian court becomes very strange. This change was made apparently
because of the danger of making an uncomplimentary reference to
Russian royalty at that time in literature.

Wherever external considerations such as avoidance of censorship
demand alterations in the memory system informing a work, mistakes
can easily come about. When Eugene O'Neill wrote his first version of
the scene in *The Great God Brown* where Billy Brown comes looking
for Dion Anthony at the prostitute's house, he was strongly informed
by his brother Jamie's old New London haunts and placed it in the
parlor of the local brothel. Then, to avoid censorship problems, he gave
the woman her own private cottage. As a result, Brown's seeking Dion
there becomes strange, for instead of being a hangout of Dion, it is a
place he has stumbled upon for the first time, and therefore should not
be known to Brown. See Doris Alexander, *Eugene O'Neill's Creative
Struggle: The Decisive Decade 1924–1933* (University Park: The Pennsylvania State University Press, 1992), 65.

Love, Brotherly and Romantic

OGAREV'S "FRAGMENT" FROM HIS. It was entitled "Caucasian Waters: A
Fragment from My Confession." In 1838 at Pyatigorsk in the Caucasus,
Ogarev had come under the influence of the exiled Decembrist Prince
Odoyevsky and became filled with his religious exaltation, ending up
praying for hours at a time that he too "might receive the crown of
martyrdom for Russian freedom." Carr, *The Romantic Exiles*, 159.

"VERY PROUD." "INSTINCTIVELY DIVINED THE." Letter to Alexander Ivanyich Herzen, March 28 / April 9, 1861 (Christian, *Tolstoy's Letters*,
1:146).

LIKE PUSHKIN HAD JOINED LODGES. Pushkin joined the lodge "Ovid, Number 25" at the beginning of his first exile. Troyat, *Pushkin*, 150.

RYLEYEV, PESTEL, MURAVIEV. Mazour, *The First Russian Revolution 1825*,
51.

THE "UNION OF SALVATION." Ibid., 66.

page 140:

INTRIGUED AND DEPRESSED TOLSTOY. In 1866, Tolstoy told his wife: "What is distressing is that all those Masons were fools." *War and Peace*, trans. Maude, 386n.

"WHAT IS BAD?" Ibid., 378.

"OF WHAT USE AM I?" Letter to A. A. Tolstaya, May 1859 (Leon, *Tolstoy*, 91).

THE HISTORICAL MASONIC LEADER. *War and Peace*, trans. Maude, 384n.

"THE FRATERNITY AND EQUALITY." Ibid., 388.

THE NEBULOUS "IMPORTANT MYSTERY." Ibid., 388–89.

"ALL THAT COULD BE GOT." Ibid., 413.

"FREED FROM BONDS." Ibid., 420.

"STUPENDOUS IDEA." "THE RELIGION OF CHRIST." Entry of March 2–5, 1855, at Belbec (*The Private Diary of Leo Tolstoy 1853–1857*, trans. Maude, 114).

"WE MUST LIVE." *War and Peace*, trans. Maude, 422.

"NEW LIFE" FOR PRINCE ANDREY. Ibid., 423.

page 141:

REFORMS THAT TOLSTOY SUCCEEDED. It was in the summer of 1857 that Tolstoy began efforts at reform. By September 12, 1857, he had most of his peasants on quit-rent, and his chief income came, he said, from "the woods and the meadows for feeding the horses." *The Private Diary of Leo Tolstoy 1853–1857*, trans. Maude, 245.

"AN OLD FROZEN-OUT POTATO." Birukoff, *Leo Tolstoy*, 247. The letter is addressed to "Auntie," his name for Aunt Tatyana Ergolskaya, but Birukoff attributes it to A. A. Tolstaya, who was addressed by Tolstoy as "Babushka."

"AGED, STERN, AND SCORNFUL." "YOUTHFUL THOUGHTS AND HOPES." "QUITE TRANSFIGURED." "SEIZED BY." *War and Peace*, trans. Maude, 459, 462.

"YESTERDAY I TORMENTED MYSELF." Ibid., 520.

FIRST "IRRESISTIBLE" ATTRACTION. In his diary, Tolstoy wrote of Sonya that although she was no different from others "she attracts me irresistibly." Leon, *Tolstoy*, 114.

"I WOULD HAVE DIED." Letter of September 14, 1862 (Christian, *Tolstoy's Letters*, 1:168).

"DON'T PHILOSOPHIZE, DON'T DOUBT." *War and Peace*, trans. Maude, 520.

page 142:

"TO STAB HIS BARE." Ibid., 484.

"FOREIGN PRINCE OF THE BLOOD." "GRANDEE." Ibid., 519, 931.

"PREOCCUPIED, ABSENT-MINDED." Ibid., 519.

MARYA TOLSTAYA GAVE BIRTH TO HIS DAUGHTER. There is no information in the literature on what became of either the illegitimate baby or the Viscount Victor-Hector de Kleen. Masha came to live with Tolstoy at Yasnaya Polyana with her two legitimate daughters in the summer of 1864, as Tolstoy told A. A. Tolstaya in a letter of January 18–23, 1865 (Christian, *Tolstoy's Letters*, 1:192). Perhaps both the baby and the father died—considering the consumption, which was probably authentic in the case of de Kleen.

"MY DEAR, DEAR THOUSAND-TIMES." Ibid., 1:181.

page 143:

HE WANTED TO ADOPT. "WILL NOT PASS." Ibid.

"PITY, TENDERNESS, AND LOVE." "SHAME AND SELF-ABASEMENT." "IF I WERE NOT." *War and Peace*, trans. Maude, 663.

"PASSING IN HIS OWN SOFTENED." Ibid., 664.

page 144:

"VERY NOBLE." "BUT I AM UNABLE." Ibid., 661.

"NARROW AND BURDENSOME AND USELESS." Ibid., 857.

BE KILLED, NOT BY THE ENEMY. Ibid., 858.

"HORDE OF SLAVES." See Tolstoy's plan for reform of the Russian army in Troyat, *Tolstoy*, 118, and the entry for November 25, 1854 in *The Private Diary of Leo Tolstoy 1853–1857*, trans. Maude, 107. In the text the meaning of this passage has been deliberately blurred to get past the censorship. Prince Andrey thinks he will be killed the next day, not even by a Frenchman "but by one of our own men," and, he adds, "by a soldier discharging a musket close to my ear as one of them did yesterday," so that the shooting can be taken as accidental. *War and Peace*, trans. Maude, 858.

"AND TAKE ME BY THE HEAD." *War and Peace*, trans. Maude, 859. I have inserted "the." The passage reads "by head and heels."

"SWUNG BY THEIR LEGS." Entry of June 29, 1855, *The Private Diary of Leo Tolstoy 1853–1857*, trans. Maude, 127.

"POWERFUL IMPRESSION THAT I." Undated diary entry in Leon, *Tolstoy*, 95.

"IT IS DREADFUL NOW." Letter to Sergey Nikolayevich Tolstoy, fall 1860 (Maude, *Life of Tolstoy*, 1:199).

"WISHING FOR HIS DEATH." *War and Peace*, trans. Maude, 799.

page 145:

"NEEDLESSLY, IT WOULD HAVE." Letter to Sergey Nikolayevich Tolstoy, fall 1860 (Maude, *Life of Tolstoy*, 1:199).

"CALLING YOU ALL NIGHT." *War and Peace*, trans. Maude, 799.

"LOVED AND RESPECTED." Letter to Sergey Nikolayevich Tolstoy, fall 1860 (Maude, *Life of Tolstoy*, 1:199).

THESE CHARACTERS HE LOVED. In a letter to A. A. Tolstaya, January 18–23, 1865, Tolstoy said he wanted her to love "these children" of his for "I love them very much." Christian, *Tolstoy's Letters*, 1:192.

"ALL'S WELL THAT ENDS WELL." Christian, *Tolstoy's "War and Peace,"* 6.

"SUICIDE FROM SHAME." Entry of November 2–3, 1853, *The Private Diary of Leo Tolstoy 1853–1857*, trans. Maude, 38.

"ECSTATIC PITY AND LOVE." *War and Peace*, trans. Maude, 908.

TOLSTOY HAD FELT "TORN." In a diary entry on October 13, 1860, Tolstoy declared that Nikolay's death "has torn me terribly from life." Maude, *Life of Tolstoy*, 1:200.

page 146:

"NEARER" TO HIS "OWN DEATH." NOT "PAINFUL, BUT IMPORTANT." Letter to A. A. Tolstaya, March 6, 1874 (Christian, *Tolstoy's Letters*, 1:268). Tolstoy said this after the death of his sixth child, but he had learned it, he said, "at the loss of a dearly loved brother."

The Crimean War and the War of 1812

HEARING ABOUT SUCH A SPECTATOR. In a letter of November 11, 1812, M. A. Volkova told V. I. Lanskaya: "Prince Viazemsky had the temerity to take part in the Battle of Borodino as an ordinary spectator." It is also thought that Tolstoy knew something of Viazemsky's recollections of 1812, although they were not published until 1869. Christian, *Tolstoy's "War and Peace,"* 80.

HE VOLUNTEERED TO GO. In a letter to Auntie Tatyana Ergolskaya, September 4, 1855, Tolstoy tells her he arrived at Sevastopol on August 27, the very day it was heavily attacked and finally taken by the French and English, "so that I was present at the action and even took part in it as a volunteer." Sevastopol surrendered that day, and Tolstoy wept when he saw the town "in flames and the French flags on our bastions." Christian, *Tolstoy's Letters*, 1:52.

"HE MOVES AROUND." Ibid., 1:52n. Glebov is speaking of Tolstoy's participation as a volunteer on August 27.

FIGHTING THERE IS "FRIGHTFULLY HOT." "AROUND WHICH TENS." "AS CALMLY AS IF." *War and Peace*, trans. Maude, 883–85.

page 147:

"RUSSIA MUST FALL." Entry of November 25, 1854, *The Private Diary of Leo Tolstoy 1853–1857*, trans. Maude, 106.

"THE COSSACKS WANT TO." Ibid., 107.

"WITH US." "STUPID DRILL FOR." Ibid.

ABOLISHED "SHAMEFUL CORPORAL PUNISHMENT." Mazour, *The First Russian Revolution 1825*, 58.

"LOOSE AND EXTREMELY CORRUPTED." Ibid., 59.

324 LASHES TO A MAN. Zetlin, *The Decembrists*, 55.

page 148:

"TERRIBLE SLAUGHTER." "MORAL STRENGTH OF THE RUSSIAN." Entry of November 2, 1854, *The Private Diary of Leo Tolstoy 1853–1857*, trans. Maude, 104–5.

"PASSIONATE LOVE FOR THE." Ibid., 105.

"NAPOLEON INVADED RUSSIA." Raeff, *The Decembrist Movement*, 32.

"FIRST WHEN WE GAVE NAPOLEON." This is a quotation from the first chapter of "The Decembrists." Christian, *Tolstoy's "War and Peace,"* 3.

"FRIEND OF BACCHUS." "DISASTROUS CAMPAIGNS." "WITH A POIGNARD." Zetlin, *The Decembrists*, 23.

page 149:

POGGIO'S WIFE AND FIVE CHILDREN. Monas, *The Third Section*, 74–75.

POGGIO NEVER LEFT VOLKONSKY. He died in Russia at Volkonsky's estate "Voronki." Zetlin, *The Decembrists*, 348.

"MY DAUGHTER WHOM I HAVE." "AIMLESS LIE." *War and Peace*, trans. Maude, 1034.

TOLSTOY FIRST HEARD THE STORY. He reports hearing it in his diary on October 29, 1857 (Christian, *Tolstoy's Diaries*, 1:143, 362 n. 107, 369 n. 6). Tolstoy probably read V. A. Perovsky's memoirs of 1812.

WHOM SHE HAD KNOWN WELL. Apparently A. A. Tolstaya had been in love with Perovsky, but Christian's note is ambiguous. It reads: "Alexandra Tolstaya told the story of how V. A. Perovsky (a son of Count Razumovsky with whom she had been in love) was taken prisoner," etc., which could just as easily mean that she had been in love with Count Razumovsky as with his son Perovsky. Ibid., 1:362 n. 107.

"NO PLOT, NO SECRET SOCIETY." Such was the decision in an official history of the Third Section prepared for Alexander II in 1876. At the time, Ivan Petrovich Liprandi, the chief police spy on Petrashevsky, presented the Petrashevtsy to Nicholas's investigating committee as an "all-embracing plan of an over-all movement for change and destruction." Monas, *The Third Section*, 256, 259.

page 150:

"TO FILL OUT THE THIN RANKS." Ibid., 284.

TWENTY-ONE OF THEM. "HIS IMPERIAL MAJESTY." Lincoln, *Nicholas I*, 310.

"DISMAY, HORROR, AND CONFLICT." *War and Peace*, trans. Maude, 1070.

"FIVE CRUCIFIXIONS," AS HERZEN. Mazour, *The First Russian Revolution 1825*, 271.

"STOUT WHITE NECK AND CHEST." Entry of March 25 / April 6, 1857, *The Private Diary of Leo Tolstoy 1853–1857*, trans. Maude, 207.

"NOT WITH MY REASON." Quote from Tolstoy's *How I Came to Believe*, in Birukoff, *Leo Tolstoy*, 1:235.

A CATACLYSMIC REJECTION. After the execution, Tolstoy wrote in his diary: "What is certain is that henceforward I shall never serve any government. . . . The only ideal is anarchy." Leon, *Tolstoy*, 79–80.

EUROPE TO "DELIGHTFUL YASNAYA." Entry of August 8, 1857, *The Private Diary of Leo Tolstoy 1853–1857*, trans. Maude, 237.

pages 150–51:

"ZORIN" WHO WAS "BEING BEATEN." Ibid.

page 151:

"RUSSIA DISGUSTS ME." Ibid.

"HIS FAITH IN THE RIGHT ORDERING." *War and Peace*, trans. Maude, 1072.

ESTABLISHED AN ARTEL. The wealthiest Decembrists, such as Trubetskoy and Volkonsky, gave 2,000 or 3,000 rubles a year, and poorer Decembrists, such as Nikita Muraviev, gave 200 to 300 rubles. In this way the poorest and the destitute received at least 500 rubles. Zetlin, *The Decembrists*, 299.

LASHWOUNDS OF HIS "POOR COMRADES." Ibid., 333–36.

LUNIN DIED ON DECEMBER 3. Ibid., 337.

"ONE CAN FIND HAPPINESS." Ibid., 336.

pages 151–52:

"BARE, RAW, AND."

"NOT WITH HIS INTELLECT." "MAN IS CREATED." "SO THERE IS NO." *War and Peace*, trans. Maude, 1176.

page 152:

"DON'T FRET, FRIEND." Ibid., 1073.

"NEVER DECLINE A PRISON." Ibid., 1075.

"AS IF EVER READY TO EMBRACE." Ibid., 1077.

"THE GREAT THING IS TO LIVE." Ibid., 1075.

"Lay me down like." Ibid., 1076.

Russian words for "Christian." Aylmer Maude notes that the words "are very similar, and Karataev's pronunciation identified them." Ibid., 1078n.

"He baked, cooked, sewed." Ibid., 1077.

"with a new beauty." Ibid., 1076.

page 153:

"I took Tanya, beat her up." Christian, Tolstoy's "War and Peace," 84.

"a stone tied with a rope." Tikhon Polner, Tolstoy and His Wife, trans. Nicholas Wreden (New York: Norton, 1945), 141. This is a quote of Tolstoy in 1882.

"strong, handsome, and fertile." War and Peace, trans. Maude, 1281.

"would not have approved." Ibid., 1307.

pages 153–54:

"seemliness, happiness." Ibid.

page 154:

"because I cannot and." Tolstoy, "Drafts for an Introduction to War and Peace." Ibid., 1365.

Voyna i Mir

"Voyna i Mir." I have taken the Latin alphabet transcription "Voyna i Mir" from Isaiah Berlin, The Hedgehog and The Fox (London: Weidenfelt & Nicolson, 1954), 6n.

in March 1867. Tolstoy first used the title "Voyna i Mir" in the text of his agreement for printing the work as a whole, in which "1805" is crossed out and "Voyna i Mir" substituted by Tolstoy. Christian, Tolstoy's "War and Peace," 6.

"war" means "military actions." Ibid., 130.

mir, the Russian word. For the scene in which Natasha takes communion and prays for peace, Maude makes the following note: "The Russian word mir has two meanings. Sometimes—and especially in the Church service—it means peace, concord, and union. Natasha takes it as meaning the universe, the world, the commune, the village assembly, and so on." War and Peace, trans. Maude, 733n. Obviously the word has many more than two meanings.

page 155:

what is "good" or "moral." "That which unites." Leo Tolstoy, What Is Art and Essays on Art, trans. Aylmer Maude (London: Oxford University Press, 1942), 55n. The note is Tolstoy's.

"POSSIBILITY OF THE BROTHERHOOD." *War and Peace*, trans. Maude, 385.

"PIERRE, AND THAT YOUNG." Ibid., 462–63.

"COMPASSION, LOVE OF OUR." Ibid., 908, 1022, 1023.

"THE CONSTANT CHARM." *The Private Diary of Leo Tolstoy 1853–1857*, trans. Maude, 119.

"UNCONSCIOUSLY HAPPY SMILE." "A COMMON AND AS IT." "WHOLE ATTENTION WAS." *War and Peace*, trans. Maude, 885, 886.

"TO BE A SOLDIER." "TO ENTER COMMUNAL." Ibid., 940.

page 156:

"YES, ONE MUST HARNESS." Ibid., 941.

"IN PEACE [*MIR*], LET US." "IN COMMUNITY [*MIR*]." Maude translates Natasha's extension of the priest's words, "As one community, without distinction of class. . . ." I believe he has lost a parallel between the priest's words and Natasha's that must have been identical at the start, so I have made the translation of her prayer "In community, without distinction. . . ." Ibid., 733.

"HARMONIOUS TRIUMPHANT STRENGTH." Ibid., 1171.

"THE GREAT THING IS TO LIVE." Ibid., 1075.

"THE DEVELOPMENT OF HUMANITY." This conception of history was a fundamental belief of the Stankevich circle. Tolstoy had read both a biography of Nikolay Stankevich and his correspondence, and he must have heard much of him from Turgenev who, along with Mikhail Bakunin, had been a member of the circle. Tolstoy told A. A. Tolstaya, after his readings on Stankevich, "I've never loved anyone as I love that man, whom I've never met. What purity! What tenderness!" Edward J. Brown, *Stankevich and His Moscow Circle 1830–1840* (Stanford, Calif.: Stanford University Press, 1966), 5, 14.

"MILLIONS OF MILES AWAY." Letter to Prince Vladimir Petrovich Meschersky (Christian, *Tolstoy's Letters*, 1:237–38).

ART "DIRECTS ALL HUMAN." Letter to Prince Vladimir Petrovich Meschersky (Christian, *Tolstoy's Letters*, 1:237).

page 159:

"AN OVERCROWDED SIBERIA." Letter to N. N. Strakhov, June 1–5(?), 1881 (ibid., 2:351).

DID WEEP TO SEE SEVASTOPOL BURNING. Tolstoy wrote his Aunt Tatyana Ergolskaya on September 4, 1855: "I wept when I saw the town in flames and the French flag on our bastions." Ibid., 1:52.

page 160:

"WHICH MOVED THE MAN." Tolstoy, *What Is Art?* 121.

Index

The four major authors are referred to by initials—TM, RLS, EFG, LT—when distinguishing members of their families by relationship.